I0817720

Afro Texans

SERIES EDITORS: WILL GUZMÁN, KIMBERLY D. HILL, AND WILLIAM T. HOSTON

Also in the series:

Emmett J. Scott: Power Broker of the Tuskegee Machine
by Maceo C. Dailey Jr.; edited by Will Guzmán and David H. Jackson Jr.

Images in the River

The Life and Work of Waring Cuney

CYNTHIA DAVIS
AND VERNER D. MITCHELL

TEXAS TECH UNIVERSITY PRESS

This book is typeset in Adobe Jenson Pro. The paper used in this book meets the minimum requirements of ANSI/NISO Z39.48-1992 (R1997). ♾

Designed by Hannah Gaskamp
Cover design by Hannah Gaskamp

Library of Congress Cataloging-in-Publication Data

Names: Davis, Cynthia, 1950– author. | Mitchell, Verner D., 1957– author. Title: Images in the River: The Life and Work of Waring Cuney / Cynthia Davis and Verner D. Mitchell. Description: Lubbock, Texas: Texas Tech University Press, 2024. | Series: Afro-Texans | Includes bibliographical references and index. | Summary: "A family history and detailed biographical monograph of Harlem Renaissance poet and World War II veteran Waring Cuney, including 100 of his selected poems"—Provided by publisher.
Identifiers: LCCN 2023037125 | ISBN 978-1-68283-197-7 (cloth)
Subjects: LCSH: Cuney, William Waring, 1906–1976. | Cuney, William Waring, 1906–1976—Family. | African American poets—Texas—Biography. | World War, 1939–1945—Veterans—United States—Biography.
Classification: LCC PS3553.U466 Z63 2024 | DDC 813/.54 [B]—dc23/eng/20231114
LC record available at https://lccn.loc.gov/2023037125

Printed in the United States of America
24 25 26 27 28 29 30 31 32 / 9 8 7 6 5 4 3 2 1

Texas Tech University Press
Box 41037
Lubbock, Texas 79409-1037 USA
800.832.4042
ttup@ttu.edu
www.ttupress.org

TO THE MEMORY OF WILLIAM WARING CUNEY

And for our fathers,
The Late Russell Davis, US Marine Corps
The Late W. J. Mitchell Sr., US Army

Contents

Illustrations

Acknowledgments

WE ARE GRATEFUL TO MANY SPECIAL PEOPLE WHO CONtributed to the publication of this book. Waring Cuney's maternal descendants Lowell Waring Baker III and Howard Waring French generously offered great tidbits of information on the Waring-Cuney family. Waring Cuney's paternal relative Robert Powell provided letters, documents, and family photographs and gave generously of his time in personal interviews. Adeline Norris's nephew, Roger Anderson, shared his unpublished Norris family memoir, family photographs, and Adeline's letters. Our "fairy godmother," the historian and legal specialist Susan Salus, enthusiastically contributed a photograph of Amelia Cuney and her high school yearbook as well as census records, early newspaper articles, and transcripts of Maud Cuney Hare's court cases. Our dear Perida A. Mitchell, genealogist extraordinaire, helped construct the Waring and Cuney family trees. Finally, photographer Daniel Glenn Morris helped restore many early photographs of the Waring-Cuney family.

We also thank our "academic families," especially Dr. DeRhonda McWaine, Dean of Liberal Arts, and Professor Barbara Brown, English chair, at San Jacinto College, as well as Dr. Terrence Tucker, English chair, at the University of Memphis. Without their support and encouragement through the years, we could not have traveled to the archives, libraries, and interviews that provided us with primary sources.

Academic writing and research can sometimes be a lonely process, especially over the two years during which the world was challenged by Covid. We are enormously indebted to friends and colleagues in African American Studies and Literature who kindly offered their time and attention to our project. We extend special thanks to the late Dr. John Wharton Lowe, who made invaluable suggestions on an early draft: his pioneering work on African American writers has provided the impetus for research and recovery of so many authors, including Waring Cuney. Dr. Henry Louis Gates, whose groundbreaking research on African American literary theory, culture, and history continues to inspire us, offered kind comments and cogent suggestions on placing our book with a publisher. Our colleagues at Howard University, Dr. Dana Williams and Professor Catherine Saunders, helped us to access material from the Moorland-Spingarn Research Center. Dr. Jervette Ward, now at the City College of New York, generously shared her encouragement as well as her academic networking and cyber skills. Dr. Sharon Lynette Jones at Ball State University has always been supportive of our work. Dr. Bob Coleman, editor of *Studies in American Culture* at the University of South Alabama, published an early version of the chapter on Waring Cuney in the military and offered critical editorial advice. We are also indebted to Dr. Loretta McBride at Southwest Tennessee Community College; Dr. LaToya Jefferson-James at LeMoyne-Owen College; Dr. Dolan Hubbard at Morgan State University; Dr. John Edgar Tidwell at the University of Kansas; and the poet Christina Davis, curator of Harvard's Woodberry Poetry Room.

Our colleagues and friends in Texas have been particularly helpful with and encouraging of this project. We first became interested in the Cuney family in Texas through Dr. Douglas Hales's groundbreaking book, *A Southern Family in White and Black: The Cuneys of Texas*. Dr. Hales kindly sat for several interviews and provided invaluable data and research suggestions. We thank historian Yvonne Frear of San Jacinto College who introduced us to the East Texas Historical Association (ETHA), and we thank the ETHA members for their helpful comments when we presented the chapter on Maud Cuney Hare at the annual conference. John Termini, owner of Galveston's Lakeview Cemetery, personally showed Cynthia the graves of Norris Wright Cuney, Adelina Cuney, and Maud Cuney Hare and provided invaluable information on the graves of Black Galvestonians. We also thank our friend, Michele Fantt Harris, Esq., for her support of all our projects and for her company as we searched Harmony Memorial Cemetery in Hyattsville, Maryland, for the graves of Waring Cuney and his parents.

The unsung heroes of academic research are, of course, librarians, and we were fortunate in working with some of the very best. In Texas, we received invaluable assistance from a number of individuals. Rosalind Clifford and Angela Colmenares of San Jacinto College Library helped us to acquire rare and out-of-print materials through Interlibrary Loan. At Texas Southern University, Joyce Thomas and Ruth Bledsoe facilitated access to unpublished pamphlets and rare books on Afro-Texans. At Rice University's Fondren Library, we thank Min Yu Siu and Heidi Vieira for assistance in obtaining the scrapbooks of Norris Wright Cuney. At Prairie View A&M University, Phyllis Earles and Lisa Stafford helped us research Maud Cuney Hare's employment at Prairie View. For access to unpublished documents on the Cuney family in Galveston, on the heavyweight boxer Jack Johnson, and on the early Juneteenth celebrations, we thank the Galveston and Texas History Center (GTHC) at the Rosenberg Library; archivists Kevin Kinney and Sean McConnell were particularly helpful.

Our research took us across the United States, and despite the complications due to Covid, we were warmly received by many wonderful librarians. We gratefully acknowledge Lisa C. Moore, editor of Redbone Press and librarian at the Amistad Research Center, Tulane University, who discovered an unpublished photograph of Waring Cuney in his Army uniform. We thank Paul Civitelli, Beinecke Rare Book and Manuscript Library, Yale University, for assistance with the letters of Waring Cuney and Carl Van Vechten and with Cuney's poems. Bridgett Kathryn Pride, of the Schomburg Center for Research in Black Culture, New York Public Library, was very helpful in locating Eugene Gordon's interview of Charles G. Burroughs. We were kindly received at Williams College, Chapin Library Special Collections, and we particularly thank librarians Wayne Hammond and Anne Peale; Lisa Conathan, head of Special Collections; and Nelly A. Lin-Schweitzer.

Much gratitude goes to the staff of Texas Tech University Press for their commitment to African American studies, manifested in the important Afro-Texans series, and for their consummate professionalism. Our sponsoring editor, Travis Snyder, believed in the project from the very beginning and provided unwavering enthusiasm, unstinting patience, and wise counsel. We also thank editor Christie Perlmutter for her superb copyediting assistance.

Finally, for their inspiration and many acts of kindness, we thank our families and friends, most especially our children and their descendants, Renee, Matthew, Dylan, Jack, Caroline, Sofia, Cecilia, Annabelle, Jared, and Courtney; and, as always, Robert and Veronica, to whom this book is offered with love.

Images in the River

PART I

Waring Cuney and His Family

Introduction

ALTHOUGH THE POET WILLIAM WARING CUNEY (1906–1976) was born and raised in Washington, DC, he never forgot his roots as a member of a proud Afro-Texan family from Galveston. His father had moved from Texas to Washington to attend college, and Waring grew up just a few blocks from Howard University, where three generations of his family studied. However, despite his privileged upbringing among the city's Black elite, Cuney embraced his family's passionate commitment to racial uplift and civil rights. In exploring the relationship between African Americans and their environment, he was thus able to transmute into two books of poetry a broad cross section of African American life; his poems and songs canvass the lives of jazz musicians, athletes, domestic and railway workers, women and children, blues singers, prisoners, sharecroppers, and soldiers. His acutely perceptive poems about Black women's subjectivity reflect the strong and resilient women in his family, while his celebration of the victory of heavyweight boxing champion Jack Johnson against Jim Jeffries was undoubtedly inspired by his father's stories about his famous Galveston neighbor.

Most scholars would place Cuney adjacent to his friend Langston Hughes in the literary canon, and his poetry is often compared to Hughes's work in terms of style and subject. Yet Cuney was most explicit about the influence on his poetry of Paul Laurence Dunbar and of his fellow Washingtonians and close friends, Georgia Douglas Johnson and Sterling Brown. However, no one has hitherto examined the substantial body of Cuney's unpublished work, some of which is clearly in dialogue with the work of other Harlem Renaissance poets, including Helene Johnson and Claude McKay.

Cuney was particularly close to Helene Johnson (both born in the summer of 1906) whom he met, along with her cousin Dorothy

West, in Boston in the late 1920s. In his "Boston" period Cuney, like Johnson, skillfully mines age-old themes of loss, loneliness, and unrequited love. Consider Cuney's "Tell Irene Hello" and Johnson's well-regarded sonnet "Remember Not"; both poems capture intense romantic feelings, but Cuney's blues-inflected lyric is more economical and ironic, and probably more accessible for contemporary readers. Similarly, Johnson's "Love in Midsummer" and Cuney's "October Winds," both specifically set in Boston and written around the same time, draw upon the sensuousness of the seasons to celebrate young love; it is tempting to speculate that the poems may even allude to a romantic spark between the two, or, at the very least, to their time together in the city.

In addition to Cuney's connections to Helene Johnson, there are also interesting parallels between Claude McKay's celebrated sonnet "If We Must Die" and Cuney's powerful four-lined protest, "American Negro Labor." Cuney's lines surveying "three centuries of cruel offenses" and "the constant blows of Nordic prejudice" recall McKay's exhortation to "deal one deathblow" in retaliation for "their thousand blows." While McKay ends with the protagonist in a defensive posture ("dying but fighting back"), Cuney goes on the offensive with an ominous warning that anticipates the militancy of the poets of the Black Arts Movement: "My senses have dulled from much beating but think not that I sleep."

In evaluating Cuney's influence on contemporary poets, one is struck by his connections to Yusef Komunyakaa, the Pulitzer Prize–winning poet and Vietnam War veteran. Komunyakaa, in fact, is Cuney's most prominent literary descendant. Cuney was a pianist, singer, and songwriter, and the two artists shared an abiding interest in jazz and the blues; this is perhaps best seen in Cuney's poems "Bessie Smith" and "Charles Parker, 1920–1955" and in Komunyakaa's *Testimony, A Tribute to Charlie Parker: With New and Selected Jazz Poems* (2013). However, as we detail in chapter 5, the war verse of the two poets manifests an even stronger connection. Both were highly decorated US Army veterans: Komunyakaa received a Bronze Star for service during the Vietnam War and Cuney three Bronze Stars for combat during World War II. Cuney's martial poems display a wide range in form and vision and pay homage to combatants, survivors, family members, widows, orphans, and many others affected by war. His work provides for Komunyakaa and other African American war poets a model of writing as a vehicle for coping and repair. We have included several of his war poems, many written while he served in the South Pacific.

In addition to his literary peers, a major influence on Cuney's work was his illustrious family, and their story provides a lens through which to examine his oeuvre. The family saga thus not only illuminates the professional and artistic achievements of Cuney's maternal and paternal forebears but also corrects some of the errors and erasures that abound in African American history. While our major goal is to introduce the poetry of Waring Cuney, a concomitant purpose is to recover the social, political, artistic, and cultural contributions of the Cuney and Waring families. In this book, we argue that Cuney's poetry is shaped by his progenitors' sometimes tragic, but always life-affirming, experiences, and that he consciously seeks to celebrate their legacy in his music and poetry.

Despite the fact that no books or monographs have been written on Waring Cuney, his work is critically acclaimed nationally and internationally. In Leiden, Netherlands, his poem "Charles Parker," a paean to the jazz saxophonist, adorns a building as part of the city's *Dicht op de Muur* (Wall Poems project). An avowed Italophile who for many years wavered between careers in opera and literature, Cuney studied voice in Rome; the Marxist composer Giacomo Manzoni set his poem "Grave" to music. Upon publication, his poetry was quickly translated into Spanish, Yiddish, Italian, German, and Dutch. In the early thirties, he and Langston Hughes edited *Four Lincoln University Poets*; selections from the volume appeared in French, Dutch, and German venues. Cuney formed lifelong friendships with Rosey Pool, the Dutch anthologist and civil rights activist, and with her compatriot, Paul Breman, a translator and editor based in London. It was Breman who eventually published Cuney's two books, *Puzzles* (1960) and *Storefront Church* (1973). Arthur Spingarn, reviewing *Puzzles* in *The Crisis* magazine, praised Cuney's "brilliant" writing, while the African American scholar Arthur P. Davis lauded Cuney's "short, meticulously carved poetic vignettes [and] effective use of the blues form."[1]

The Cuneys of Galveston, although not widely known today, are an accomplished and peripatetic Afro-Texan family whose members include Waring Cuney's great-uncle, the charismatic Republican politician Norris Wright Cuney (1846–1898), and his cousin Maud Cuney Hare (1874–1936), a writer, concert pianist, and ethnomusicologist who was once engaged to W. E. B. Du Bois. William Waring Cuney's maternal line, after whom he was named, was equally eminent: the Waring family produced officers in the Revolutionary and Civil Wars as well as diplomats, physicians, lawyers, teachers, and administrators. The journeys of these families, as they claimed their space in a threatening and unpredictable American landscape, took them across many rivers and through domiciles in Texas, Virginia, Maryland, Ohio, Louisiana, Illinois, Pennsylvania, Massachusetts, Washington, DC, and New York. Their lived experiences, a microcosm of African American history, include bondage, the domestic slave trade, manumission, interracial relationships, racial passing, Civil War service, Reconstruction, Jim Crow, political leadership, the Labor Movement, the 1900 Galveston Hurricane, the Harlem Renaissance, service in both World Wars, the Civil Rights struggle, and the Black Arts Movement. Zelig-like, the Cuneys and Warings have been present at the major moments of African American history. Their lives thus not only epitomize Black agency in the nineteenth, twentieth, and twenty-first centuries but also testify to the fraught intersection of race, place, and mobility in America.

In fact, while researching this volume, we realized how very fraught the family's experiences were, and how much Afro-Texan history and culture has already been erased. One need look no further than the so-called Houston Mutiny at Camp Logan on August 23, 1917. The Cuney family, some of whom were still living in Galveston, would have been devastated to learn of the repercussions of members of the 3rd Battalion of the all-Black 24th Infantry Regiment at Camp Logan marching downtown to protest the city's harsh Jim Crow laws and the beating of a soldier by police officers. Despite the poor visibility of the dark, rainy night, and the absence of credible witnesses, a group of soldiers was summarily arrested and court-martialed; the Department of Defense is currently reviewing a clemency petition for all those convicted. After World War I, the 7,000-acre military base was dismantled and the site of Camp Logan is now completely obliterated; only a small marker, obscurely located on the easternmost edge of Memorial Park, commemorates the soldiers of Camp Logan.

Similarly, although the recent centennial of the Tulsa Massacre has generated a resurgence of interest, it was just a few years ago, while researching the event in the city's public library, that we found all newspaper articles about the massacre had been roughly ripped out of the bound volumes. When queried, the librarians claimed to have no knowledge of when or why this defacement had occurred.

Although less dramatic than the events in Houston and Tulsa, erasure also occurs when researchers accept and publish negative and discriminatory comments on African Americans without considering the credibility of their sources. For instance, the source for many accounts of the Cuney family in Galveston is the unpublished master's thesis by historian Virginia Neal Hinze (Rice University, 1965). In her ostensibly sympathetic account of Norris Wright Cuney's political career, to which both Waring Cuney and his twin brother contributed, Hinze undercuts his reputation with unsubstantiated claims that he was involved in gambling and prostitution in Galveston. She cites scurrilous letters from one of Cuney's avowed enemies, although deeper research in Texas State Archives would have clarified the political motivation for these comments. To reinforce her argument, Hinze cites Norris Wright Cuney's apparent lack of employment in Galveston between 1867 and 1870, based on his absence from the Galveston city directories. However, before 1870, African Americans were not included in the city directory; for example, the Sculls, another prominent African American family, are also absent from the directories, although their businesses are well documented elsewhere.

Hinze also fails to mention that when Cuney first arrived in Galveston, he worked as a nurse in the 1867 cholera epidemic; such an omission is baffling, considering that Maud Cuney Hare cites this fact in her biography of her father. Hinze does not mention Cuney's leadership in the Colored Men's Conventions that were held in major American cities immediately after the Civil War, nor acknowledge his relationship with his mentor, the African American senator George T. Ruby, who served as the Deputy Collector of Customs in Galveston in 1869, a position that Cuney would later hold. Finally, she does not mention Cuney's participation in the Texas chapter of the interracial Union League, of which Ruby was elected president in 1868, or that by 1873 Cuney himself was president of the Convention of Colored Citizens, a fact that certainly suggests his standing in the community during the preceding four years.[2]

Hinze does yet another disservice to the Cuney family in her description of the family matriarch, Adeline Stuart—Norris Wright's mother and Waring Cuney's great-grandmother. Adeline Stuart, who maintained a thirty-year relationship with Philip Cuny, the father of her six children, is described by Hinze as an "extremely clever . . . shrewd . . . artful" woman who initiated a "protracted liaison" with Philip Cuny and "manipulated" him into manumitting her and their children.[3] Again, Hinze ignores the fact that in Maud Cuney Hare's book, her grandmother Adeline is depicted as an intelligent, cultivated, resilient, and energetic woman who ensured that all of her children were educated.

Such a reshaping of the Cuney family narrative to feature the petty criminals and sexual adventuresses that abound in stereotyped accounts of Black life sets a dangerous precedent for future researchers of African American history. In fact, Hinze's work, consciously or unconsciously, reflects the typology of the seven racial stereotypes as delineated by Sterling Brown in *The Negro in American Fiction* (1937), including The Contented Slave, The Wretched Freedman, The Comic Negro, The Brute Negro, and The Tragic Mulatto. The ways in which these false tropes have legitimized racial discrimination and supported white supremacy are highlighted by Henry Louis Gates in his brilliant account of the depredations of Reconstruction, *Stony the Road* (2019). Despite the fact that Hinze's monograph on Cuney is an unpublished master's thesis, its ready availability online and the fact that few competing accounts exist have made it an important source for other researchers. Thus, a number of unfounded claims are repeated in internet articles and even in well-respected popular histories such as McComb's *Galveston* (1986). Our book thus hopes to address these baffling and erroneous assumptions and to establish Waring Cuney and his family as exemplars of Afro-Texan cultural achievement.

Images in the River is thus intended as both a compilation and a critical review of Waring Cuney's poetry and a corrective reclamation of his family's unique history. The book is directed at the general reader and the scholar of African American history, culture, and literature. To this end, we strive for a direct and jargon-free style; however, we do rely almost exclusively on primary sources and public records. These include unpublished archival papers; family interviews and letters; scrapbooks; yearbooks; obituaries; minutes of religious and fraternal organizations; contemporary newspaper articles; census data; military, social security, and Freedman's Bank records; ships' manifests; business directories; court documents; death certificates; and cemetery directories. Archival sources include Yale's Beinecke Library, which holds 175 pages of unpublished correspondence between Cuney and Langston Hughes; Williams College, which owns the papers of Waring Cuney's Dutch publisher and editor Paul Breman and of his friend, the poet Sterling Brown; the University of Massachusetts, which holds the letters of Maud Cuney Hare and W. E. B. Du Bois; Bennett College, the repository of the scrapbooks of Norris Wright Cuney; Howard University's Moorland-Spingarn Research Center, which holds papers pertaining to the Waring and French families; and Tulane's Amistad Research Center, which owns some of Cuney's unpublished typescripts and photographs.

Cuney's work has appeared in most major collections of African American literature, including those published by Oxford University Press (1976, 1995) and Viking (1994), and in the anthologies by Patton and Honey (2001) and Wintz (2020). Various websites reprint his poems, albeit sometimes with inaccurate information. In fact, due to the dearth of critical and biographical information about Waring Cuney, factual errors abound. A particularly egregious mistake on a website identifies a photograph of great-uncle Norris Wright Cuney as the poet, while Smethurst, in *The New Red Negro* (Oxford University Press, 1999), claims that Cuney never published a book. Conversely, several sources incorrectly state that his poem "Chain Gang Chant" was the title of his first book of poetry.

Waring Cuney wrote during the *soi-disant* Harlem Renaissance, although he would have agreed with his friend and fellow poet Sterling Brown that the label is an inaccurate description of African American writing of the period. Like Sterling Brown, but unlike their mutual friend Langston Hughes, Cuney spent very little time in Harlem during the 1920s and 1930s. Nevertheless, he published in all the major Harlem Renaissance journals and anthologies alongside the luminaries of the period, many of whom were good friends, including Hughes, Brown, Dorothy West, Helene Johnson, Claude McKay, Countee Cullen, Jean Toomer, Bruce Nugent, and Georgia Douglas Johnson.

Cuney's work has maintained its relevance since the Harlem Renaissance. In the late thirties he collaborated with blues guitarist Josh White on an album of protest and labor songs; the album was reissued and positively received in the nineteen-fifties. His poetry enjoyed a resurgence during the Civil Rights and Black Arts Movements, when his poem "No Images" was set to music by the African American women artists Nina Simone; Dorothy Rudd Moore, a composer and founder of the Society of Black Composers; and Ysaye Maria Barnwell, leader of the a cappella group, Sweet Honey in the Rock. More recently, the poem has been lauded as an example of ecowomanist ethics and is read by Betancourt (2016) as a way to engage "questions of environmental ethics through the lens of Black women's lived experiences of agency and struggle."[4]

The title of the book *Images in the River* is borrowed from Cuney's best-known poem, "No Images," written in 1926 when he was nineteen years old. In urging the subject of the poem to seek her reflection not in the dirty dishwater of the urban environment but in the clean water of a river, Cuney may well have been alluding to the actual rivers—including the Potomac, Sabine, Brazos, Allegheny, and Mississippi—crossed by his family in their peregrinations. We have selected the title of the book for its suggestion of the metaphorical rivers of injustice crossed throughout the history of the Black Atlantic. The river is, of course, an important trope in the art and spirituality of the Black Atlantic, not only in the Judeo-Christian imagery of American spirituals but also in Yoruba iconography, specifically in the water goddess Òsun, who evolved into the seductive River Mumma of Caribbean folklore. In fact, Betancourt maintains that "Cuney's dancing woman draws from the river with the power that Yoruban . . . tradition ascribes to the goddess Òsun."[5] The word "image" further suggests W. E. B. Du Bois's concept of "double-consciousness," which was demonstrated by members of the Cuney and Waring families as they negotiated racial and gendered conflicts in their pursuit of intellectual, artistic, and political achievement. Finally, the title alludes to major themes in Cuney's poetry: the celebration of the power of Black women; defiance of race and gender limitations; protest against an environment of discrimination and economic inequality; and the blues as voice and metaphor for the disenfranchised.

Cuney's literary reputation has undoubtedly been affected by his enigmatic and intensely private personal life and the fact that he left no heirs, children, or close friends to defend his literary legacy. Unlike Langston Hughes, Richard Wright, Countee Cullen, Arna Bontemps, and Dorothy West, Cuney did not work the literary circuit, publish a literary journal, or actively market and promote his work. Therefore, in the 1970s, when David Levering Lewis dismissed his verse, without further explanation, as "three parts Hughes and one part Cullen," no one protested.[6] To be sure, Sterling Brown had already claimed Cuney as an "authentic poetic voice of black America."[7] However, a serious blow to his reputation was the labeling of both Cuney and Gwendolyn Bennett as "second-echelon poets of the Harlem Renaissance" in an essay in Arna Bontemps's volume *The Harlem Renaissance Remembered*.[8] One wonders why Bontemps, a longtime friend of both writers, included this damaging assessment in his book. Both were multidimensional artists who combined literature with art (in Bennett's case) and music (in Cuney's), and this may have led to a diminution of their reputations. Gwendolyn Bennett's work has recently been recovered by Parascandola, among others, and this volume aims to do the same for Waring Cuney.

During World War II, Cuney served with distinction in the Pacific; he won combat medals and sent sheaves of poetry back to Langston Hughes in New York for safekeeping. Toward the end of the war, he was hospitalized in the Philippines and received a medical discharge; the exact diagnosis is vague, but we conjecture that he suffered from post-traumatic stress disorder (PTSD), and that even twenty years after the war, his wartime experiences affected his mental health. After the war, Cuney eschewed Harlem and settled in the Bronx, where he focused on a career as a songwriter and poet.

The book is divided into three parts: a six-chapter monograph on Waring Cuney and his family legacy; a collection of his poetry, some of which has never been published; and an appendix. Each chapter is introduced through one of Waring Cuney's poems. We include detailed genealogical charts of Cuney's paternal and maternal families in order to assist the reader in following this complex but fascinating family saga.

Part I: Waring Cuney and His Family

This section introduces Waring Cuney and argues for a consideration of his work in the context of African American culture and history, specifically in relation to the intersections of race and place. Throughout the six chapters, Cuney's poems are discussed in correspondence with his family history and life experiences.

Chapter 1 contextualizes Waring Cuney within his multiracial family history and reveals a number of closely guarded family secrets. The story begins with Cuney's paternal great-great-grandmother, Hester Neale Stuart (1800–1900?), a bondswoman belonging to the Neale family of Centerville and Alexandria, Virginia. Hester's daughter Adeline Stuart (1817–1900) was sold, at the age of seventeen, to the vicious slave trader John Armfield and transported to New Orleans on his domestic slaver the *Tribune*. Purchased by the Cuny family of Louisiana, Adeline became the lifelong partner of Colonel Philip Cuny (1807–1866), with whom she emigrated to Texas. Eventually, their three older sons, including Waring Cuney's grandfather John Nelson (usually referred to as Nelson), established themselves in Galveston. Norris Wright Cuney, the third child of Adeline Stuart and Philip Cuny, enjoyed an illustrious career in Texas politics, rising in the ranks of the Republican Party to become the most powerful African American politician in the country.

Chapter 2 examines the development of William Waring Cuney's poetry in the context of his cultural milieu, including his parents, his maternal family, his education and youth in Washington, DC, his friendships with writers Bruce Nugent, Sterling Brown, and Langston Hughes, and his participation in the literary salon of Georgia Douglas Johnson. Despite his privileged upbringing, Waring's poetry reflects his familiarity with less affluent sections of the city like the notorious

Seventh Street. Like Langston Hughes and Jean Toomer, Cuney was fascinated with the denizens of Seventh Street and wrote about them frequently.

Waring Cuney's second cousin, Maud Cuney Hare, was a major influence on the poet. Chapter 3 explores the life of Cuney Hare, the Boston concert pianist, writer, theatrical producer, and musicologist. After moving to Boston, Maud moved in the elite cultural circle of Josephine St. Pierre Ruffin, graduated from the New England Conservatory of Music, and became engaged to W. E. B. Du Bois. She returned to Texas to nurse her parents and taught music at both Prairie View State College and the Texas Deaf, Dumb, and Blind Institute for Colored Youth.

Chapter 4 delineates how, by the early nineteen thirties, every important Harlem Renaissance outlet featured Cuney's verse. Professionally, however, this was a difficult period for Cuney: employment opportunities were limited due to the Depression, and he was still undecided about whether to pursue a career in music or writing.

Chapter 5 documents that, following in the path of maternal grandfather Thomas J. Williamson, a Union soldier during the Civil War, Cuney served with distinction in the US Army during World War II. A member of the 857th Engineer Aviation Battalion, he rose from private to technical sergeant and spent two and a half years (February 1943 to August 1945) in the South Pacific. He composed war poetry in the early '40s, prior to enlisting, with pieces such as "Defense Factory Blues" and "Uncle Sam Says."

In 1960, as detailed in chapter 6, Cuney published *Puzzles*, a collection of his poetry. In his introduction, Paul Breman, the book's editor, argues Cuney's consideration as "one of America's major poets." The book features fifty-one poems, including "No Images," the lyric that gives this volume—*Images in the River*—its title. Although Cuney never married or had children, in the mid-1950s he began a lifelong relationship with Adeline Norris, to whom he dedicated his second book, *Storefront Church*.

Part II: 100 Selected Poems

This section includes one hundred of Cuney's best poems, most of which are prefaced with brief contextual notes.

One of the unique features of this volume is the combination of the subject's collected works, deep research in public documents, and the use of interviews and unpublished archives. Because so many African American writers did not have access to publicity in the mainstream press, including interviews, radio spots, and book tours, or recourse to major literary fellowships, patrons, and prizes, we rely on public sources in order to reconstruct the experiences, relationships, and events that shaped the writer's work. Today, as a broad base of readers seeks to understand and appreciate the nuances of the African American experience, a book about Waring Cuney's life and poetry and the accomplishments of the Cuney and Waring families is particularly relevant.

In the book, we discuss seven generations of the Cuney and Waring families. To help the reader keep track of so many names and relationships, we have included in an appendix two family trees: one of Waring Cuney's paternal relatives, the Cuneys, and one of his maternal relatives, the Warings.

Oh, my Lord
What a morning,
Oh, my Lord,
What a feeling,
When Jack Johnson
Turned Jim Jeffries'
Snow-white face
Up to the ceiling.
Yes, my Lord,
Fighting is wrong,
But what an uppercut.
Oh, my Lord,
What a morning,
Oh, my Lord
What a feeling,
When Jack Johnson
Turned Jim Jeffries'
Lily-white face
Up to the ceiling.
Oh, my Lord
Take care of Jack.
Keep him, Lord
As you made him,
Big, and strong, and black.

—"My Lord, What a Morning" (1962)

Chapter 1

The Cuney Family in Texas

HARLEM RENAISSANCE POET WILLIAM WARING CUNEY (1906–1976) penned his paean to world heavyweight boxing champion Arthur John ("Jack") Johnson fifty-two years after Johnson defeated Jim Jeffries on July 4, 1910. Cuney was not a star athlete like Johnson—at Armstrong Technical High School in Washington, DC, he had preferred debate, music, and the Military Cadet Corps to sports—but the two men shared Texas roots and a close neighborhood connection. Jack Johnson (1878–1946) grew up in Galveston's Twelfth Ward, a few blocks from Waring's grandfather, Nelson Cuney, his great-uncles, Joseph and Norris Wright, and the extended Cuney clan. Johnson and the Cuney cousins attended the same grammar school at which Joseph Cuney worked as a teacher and principal. As Johnson's boxing reputation grew, he would have figured prominently in the Galveston stories with which Waring's father regaled his twin sons in their home in Washington, DC. Although the devastating Hurricane of 1900 occurred before his birth, Waring knew that his paternal grandmother, his great-grandmother Adeline Stuart, and his uncle Richard all perished in the storm; he would also have heard of the heroic efforts of "Lil' Arthur," as Jack Johnson was known in the neighborhood, who worked tirelessly, saving people clinging to tree branches or trapped in the debris.[1] In the poem, which also alludes to Cuney family history, Johnson's victory thus celebrates not only his own skill, intelligence, courage, and determination, but also that of Waring Cuney's Afro-Texan forebears.

According to Galveston city directories and census reports, the Twelfth Ward in the East End was an integrated neighborhood; the city did not have a defined "colored" section, although a higher concentration of Black families lived in the Fifth Ward in the West End, probably because the very first Black Baptist church had been established in the West End in 1840, and the area was close to work in the bustling port and commercial district. More akin to Northern cities, Galveston was divided by class and economics rather than race, with poorer families, both white and Black, living in the shabby back alleys of affluent neighborhoods and in the industrial sections. In the 1870s, when the Cuneys first arrived in Galveston, they would have found Black families from Louisiana living next door to recent immigrants from Italy, Ireland, Finland, and Germany, since "most alleys [were] racially mixed."[2] The Johnsons had originally lived in the more commercial Fifth Ward, but through hard work and determination, they "managed to put enough money away to buy a plot of land . . . and build their own single-story home" at 808 Broadway, just a few blocks from the residences of the three Cuney brothers.[3] Significantly, the homes of the four African American families all fronted directly on main streets rather than in the alleys.

Growing up in Galveston's Twelfth Ward, Jack Johnson would have known and admired the three successful Cuney brothers, all of whom were civic, business, and political leaders. Joseph, the intellectual of the family, had graduated from Howard University Law School; a skillful writer and a civil rights activist, he barraged newspapers throughout Texas with letters of protest against Jim Crow policies. Nelson, Waring's grandfather, owned a painting and decorating firm, while the dynamic and irrepressible Norris Wright, nicknamed "the Sable Statesman" in the local media, ran a longshoreman's business for which Jack Johnson briefly worked; he also served as a city alderman and collector of customs, and led the Texas Republican Party.[4] The Cuney brothers would thus have provided "a constant reminder to neighbors like young Jack Johnson that a Black man need not limit his horizons."[5] In turn, Johnson's successful boxing career would epitomize for Waring Cuney the possibilities available to the African American community.

Both of Waring's parents were deeply interested in their respective histories: according to a young cousin of Waring's, the walls of his home on Florida Avenue were lined with old family photographs.[6] Waring's father shared with him the stories of the three Cuney brothers and how they all settled in the "Oleander City," as Galveston was dubbed by civic boosters in the 1870s.[7] After the Civil War, the deepwater port and railroad attracted important commercial entities. Joseph Cuney eventually opened his law office a few blocks from The Strand, the main business street, dubbed the "Wall Street of the Southwest" due to the many banks, cotton brokers, wholesalers, newspapers, and attorneys' offices all housed in modern, fireproof, cast-iron buildings. In addition to employment opportunities, the new schools and churches, the wide, clean streets, and the availability of fresh produce from local farms would have attracted newcomers like the Cuney brothers.[8]

The saga of the Cuney brothers begins in Virginia and Louisiana in the late eighteenth century and encompasses multiple generations whose lives were both enriched and entrammeled by their multiracial heritage. Waring Cuney's grandfather John Nelson was the oldest son of Philip Minor Cuny, a white plantation owner from Rapides Parish, Louisiana, and of Adeline Stuart, a bondswoman from Alexandria, Virginia.[9] The spelling of the family name changed after the birth of Philip and Adeline's children, and an "e" was added, possibly to distinguish between Philip's white and biracial offspring after Philip legitimized and manumitted them.[10] Philip Minor Cuny's Welsh grandmother Louise Cuny was an intrepid young woman who, with her little boy Richmond, immigrated to the United States around 1775. Her husband had been imprisoned by the British government for political reasons that may have involved his support of the American Revolution. According to Louisiana historian G. M. G. Stafford, Louise was instructed by her jailed husband to immigrate to New York, where he intended to join her. Stafford claims that Louise lived in New York for several years until her husband's death, at which point she and Richmond moved to New Orleans.[11] In a slightly different version of Louise's story, she first arrived in Virginia; after her husband's death, she married Caesar Archinard, a Swiss immigrant; after the Louisiana Purchase, the couple relocated to Louisiana and acquired property in Rapides Parish. In yet another version, Louise immigrated first to Martinique, where she had relatives, and then to New Orleans where she married Archinard.[12] In any case, Archinard became the proprietor of several sugar plantations in Rapides Parish and raised Richmond as his own son. Richmond eventually married Tabitha Wells, whose prominent family owned a neighboring plantation called Sugar Bend. Richmond and Tabitha lived close to Sugar Bend, on Clio Plantation, a gift from Archinard. There they produced six sons: Caesar John, Stephen Edmond, Samuel Cholett, Richard Roland, Benjamin, and finally Philip Minor, the youngest, born in 1807.[13]

The family was firmly committed to education: two of Philip's brothers became lawyers and one a physician.[14] In 1826, Philip enrolled as a freshman at Transylvania University in Lexington, Kentucky. Because the school had a strong medical curriculum, it seems likely that the family intended for him to become a doctor.[15] Although he did not pursue medicine, Philip Cuny's letters reveal an articulate, cultivated man with excellent penmanship who was fond of music and poetry and given to lyrical descriptions of nature.[16] Cuny's description of the fields of wild bluebonnets (lupines) that blanket East Texas in the spring is an early account of this annual tourist destination. Travelling near Georgetown, Texas, in April 1860, he writes: "my route lay over a gently undulating, beautiful and fertile prairie which was covered in every direction as far as the eye could reach with blue, variegated and white Lupines, filling the air with a most delicate perfume."[17] Cuny obviously enjoyed writing: his letters are filled with poetic description and sharp, sensory details. While Philip undoubtedly passed on his writing talent to several of his fifteen white and biracial children, we know for certain that his creative writing skills were inherited by his granddaughter, Maud Cuney Hare (the daughter of Norris Wright Cuney) and his great-grandson, the poet Waring Cuney.

According to Maud Cuney Hare, who wrote a carefully researched biography of her father, Grandfather Philip Cuny had intended to pursue a political career in Louisiana.[18] His family was affluent and well positioned, and in 1833 he married Carolina Scott, the daughter of a judge in Rapides Parish; she died ten months later, probably in childbirth, and the child did not survive.[19] The following year, the young widower's life changed dramatically when he met an attractive, accomplished seventeen-year-old bondswoman named Adeline Stuart (1817–1900) who had recently arrived at one of the Wells-Cuny-Archinard plantations, most probably Sugar Bend. According to Maud, who was clearly quoting Grandmother Adeline Stuart, Cuny was a handsome man: tall and blond with piercing blue eyes. Maud inherited his height and his piercing eyes, although she took her coloring from her grandmother. Adeline, according to Maud, was petite and shapely, with light brown skin, glossy black hair, dark eyes, and finely drawn features.[20]

Adeline Stuart was the daughter of Hester Neale, a bondswoman of Black, white, and Potomac Indian descent. Adeline's father may have been Aloysius Neale (d. 1817), of the prominent Neale family of Centreville and Alexandria, Virginia.[21] Hester possessed a relatively high status as a housekeeper for the Neale family and would have trained her daughter Adeline to excel in domestic etiquette and household management. Maud Cuney Hare claims a Virginia connection between the Neale and the Wells-Cuny-Archinards and suggests that Adeline's move to Rapides Parish as a bondswoman was a privately arranged transaction between the families. It is tempting to accept Maud's theory and to believe that when Adeline left Hester Neale in 1835, it was with the understanding that she had an opportunity, albeit within the depredations of bondage, to make her home with a "good" white family, possibly as housekeeper for the young widower, Philip Cuny. Maud does not indicate any bitterness or resentment on Adeline's part about her purchase by the Cuny family or describe any hardships that she experienced on her journey to Louisiana. She also takes pains to state that mother and daughter retained a close bond and remained in touch after Adeline's move to Louisiana, which suggests that Adeline's family connections were respected by her new owners. Mother and daughter did lose contact during the chaos of the Civil War, but after the war Adeline asked her son Joseph, who had just been demobilized from the Union Army and was living in Washington, DC, to locate his grandmother. Joseph found Hester Neale safely ensconced with relatives in Alexandria, Virginia; the family then remained in touch until Hester's death at the age of one hundred.[22]

In 1912, when Maud Cuney Hare was writing her father's biography, her grandparents had already passed, but she was still in contact with her father's octogenarian white cousins in Louisiana. Jane and Florida, daughters of Grandfather Philip's brother Benjamin, still lived on Sugar Bend Plantation. The sisters apparently described Adeline's arrival at Sugar Bend and her relationship with their uncle Philip; however, with the benevolent hindsight that colored so many memories of white Southerners after the Civil War, they implied that Adeline's purchase had been a humane private transactional arrangement between the two families, thus conveniently eliding the traumatic aspects of their slave-owning past. Unfortunately, Jane and Florida's account cannot be documented because all the records of the Wells-Cuney-Archinard properties and slave lists were housed in the Alexandria, Louisiana courthouse, and the courthouse was burned by retreating Union soldiers in 1863.[23]

What is clearly documented, however, in heartbreaking detail, is that Adeline Stuart's journey to Louisiana began with her purchase by

Isaac Franklin and John Armfield, the notorious maritime slave traders of Alexandria, Virginia. Notwithstanding her refined and protected upbringing by Hester Stuart in the Neale family, seventeen-year-old Adeline was put aboard the domestic slave ship, the *Tribune,* and disembarked in New Orleans on October 1, 1835.[24]

The heinous deeds of Franklin and Armfield are not well known today, thanks to a vigorous public relations blitz through which they scrubbed their slave-trading pasts and transformed themselves into philanthropic businessmen and educators; in fact, Armfield was a founder and trustee of Sewanee University. However, in the 1830s Armfield and Franklin were infamous among abolitionists for the slave factory they operated behind an elegant townhouse that still stands on Duke Street in Alexandria, Virginia. According to Calvin Schermerhorn, "The firm of Franklin and Armfield innovated in transportation and finance, and its business model helped to propel it to the front ranks of the US slave trade of the 1830s. . . . The firm developed a financial strategy dedicated to turning capital into captives in the Chesapeake and extending credit to buyers in the lower Mississippi Valley."[25] In developing their business, Franklin and Armfield took advantage of the decline of the tobacco economy in Maryland and Virginia and the concomitant demand for labor on cotton and sugar plantations in Louisiana and Mississippi. In addition, by becoming "the first domestic slave-trading company to purchase and operate its own slaver," Franklin and Armfield cut out the middlemen and greatly increased their profits.[26]

Although the importation of slaves had been illegal since 1808, Franklin and Armfield were able to manipulate a loophole since Congress "did not end domestic slave trading, effectively creating a federally protected internal market for human beings."[27] In fact, one of their colleagues in the domestic maritime slave trade had kidnapped Solomon Northup who, in his memoir *Twelve Years a Slave,* described his journey by sea to New Orleans from Washington, DC, where he had been drugged and captured.

In 1835, when Adeline boarded the *Tribune* for New Orleans, Franklin and Armfield were, according to New York abolitionist and judge William Jay, "trafficking between one thousand and twelve hundred enslaved people from the Chesapeake to the lower South every year."[28] Of course, the abolitionists knew exactly who they were and what they did: William Garrison's Boston anti-slavery newspaper *The Liberator* shared with its readers actual advertisements by Franklin and Armfield, including one horrific announcement that "we wish to purchase one hundred and fifty likely negroes . . . from twelve to twenty-five years of age. . . . We can always be found at our residence—West end of Duke Street."[29] However, being masters of public relations, Franklin and Armfield made a point to welcome Northern journalists and abolitionists to Duke Street, where they presented a façade of sanitary and humane accommodations, showed off carefully groomed and well-dressed slaves, and plied the Northerners with expensive liquor and cigars. For example, in July 1835, two months before Adeline's departure for New Orleans, the Connecticut lawyer and abolitionist Ethan Andrews visited Duke Street. A member of the American Union for the Relief and Improvement of the Colored Race (a more moderate organization than the American Anti-Slavery Society), Andrews was tasked with writing a report on the slave trade in Maryland, Virginia, and Washington, DC.[30] One of Armfield's clerks showed Andrews the kitchen, exercise yard, hospital (empty because the inmates were supposedly all healthy), and women's quarters. Afterwards Armfield, in good spirits because he had just closed on an important transaction, offered his guest refreshments. Unlike other visitors who, helped by the expensive alcohol, believed what they were shown, Andrews "was skeptical . . . and noticed signs of a hoax . . . among the enslaved women he spotted a few who seemed to have been weeping."[31]

Given the fact that Adeline was probably at the slave barracks at this time, one wonders if she was one of the distraught women observed by Andrews. Additionally, in a weirdly prescient and ironic reverse of the plot of Herman Melville's novella *Benito Cereno*, in which slaves take over the crew of a slave ship and stage an elaborate performance of normalcy for a visiting ship's captain, Andrews noticed a young man signaling him with his eyes in evident terror and distress. Knowing Melville's interest in slavery, it is tempting to speculate that he may have read Andrews's report about the Duke Street slave barracks and used it in his fiction twenty years later.

The *Tribune*, the slave ship on which Adeline Stuart sailed, had been commissioned by Franklin and Armfield from Hezekiah Child's shipyard near Haddam, Connecticut, in 1831.[32] Contrary to the idea that Northern businessmen were unaware of the depredations of slavery, Child knew that he was building a slave ship. The merchant brig, equipped with two square-rigged masts and two guns and crewed by eight men, was eighty feet long and twenty-three feet wide. A few passengers could be accommodated in staterooms, while the hold was divided into two large gender-segregated areas, with sleeping platforms that ran the length of the vessel.[33] The sea journey to New Orleans normally took four weeks; slaves then were either turned over to private owners who had prearranged the transaction and paid their passage, sold in the New Orleans market, or moved farther west for sale in Mississippi. According to Jane and Florida Cuny, Adeline belonged to the former category.

One of the most heinous aspects of Franklin and Armfield's slave business, which one can only hope did not affect the young and attractive Adeline Stuart, was the so-called fancy trade, "a euphemism . . . to describe young women peddled to customers as sex slaves."[34] This was a lucrative market: "the commoditized fantasies of racial and sexual domination were revealed in the prices paid" for these young women, which were "50 percent more than the prices for other women . . . and more than the prices for young men."[35] Often these vulnerable women, coded in slave advertisements as "seamstresses," were raped by the slavers themselves who then boasted of their conquests in vulgar letters to one another, mixing business and financial data with obscene jokes and comments.[36]

Ultimately, we have no way of determining whether Adeline was restrained at the Duke Street slave barracks or of knowing the circumstances of her four weeks on the *Tribune*. Had her journey really been prearranged between the Neale and Cuny families, as Maud Cuney Hare believes, she may have been safely sequestered in one of the staterooms; on the other hand, she may have been confined to the group hold and endured the narrow wooden sleeping shelves to which the other slaves were subjected. However, the fact that Adeline's connection to Philip Cuny began so quickly after her arrival at Sugar Bend just might indicate that special arrangements had protected her from the worst abuses of the slave trade. It does appear that she was intended from the beginning to serve as his housekeeper. The family probably never expected that Philip and Adeline would establish a liaison that produced eight children, coincided with his two marriages, and lasted until his death thirty years later. Waring Cuney, decades later, dedicated his last book of poems "To Adeline," and he may certainly have intended the book to honor Adeline Stuart. However, in an unusual coincidence, he himself was in a relationship of almost thirty years with another Adeline: Adeline Norris, a white nurse from Wisconsin. Although they never married, the dedication honors their longtime liaison, one that eerily parallels that of his great-grandparents.

Although there may have been earlier pregnancies, the first surviving son of Philip and Adeline, John Nelson (Waring Cuney's grandfather), was born in 1839 in Rapides Parish. Under different circumstances, Philip and Adeline would surely have remained in Louisiana where Philip intended to pursue a career in politics; his granddaughter Maud describes him as "an ardent politician."[37] Certainly, this passion for politics was inherited by his son with Adeline, Norris Wright. However, despite the prominence of his family, his political future in the state had been tainted by a dueling scandal six years earlier. In 1827, in an illegal, politically motivated group duel later known as the "Sandbar Fight," the established Wells and Cuny families battled other, more recent arrivals to Rapides Parish. Philip's older brother Samuel, as well as Norris Wright, the former sheriff of Rapides Parish, were killed. Jim Bowie, the future hero of the Alamo, was also involved.[38] The tragedy unquestionably made an impression on Philip, as he named his third son after Sheriff Norris Wright.

Philip was at school in Kentucky at the time, but the fallout from the duel may have precipitated his migration to Texas in 1837, along with Jim Bowie and several other Louisiana families. Author Douglass Hales points out that another reason Philip headed for Texas may have been that, as the youngest of six sons, he could not expect much of an inheritance from his parents.[39] It is also possible that Richmond and Tabitha, Philip's parents, hoped his move would end the connection with Adeline, which had already overreached the boundaries of a master-slave relationship. This was not to be: although Adeline had remained behind in Rapides Parish, she conceived Nelson when Philip returned for a visit. By 1840 she and Nelson were living with Cuny in Texas.

Through Stephen F. Austin, Philip Cuny had purchased part of the José Justo Liendo five-league land grant that Liendo had delegated Austin to sell in 1830.[40] Cuny's land was located on Iron Creek, a tributary of the Brazos River, between Bellville and Hempstead.[41] He called his 2,000-acre plantation of lush prairie grass, large oak trees, and rich, waxy soil "Sunnyside." We know that Adeline was living with Philip because the 1840 slave register for Sunnyside lists 22-year-old Adeline, although her name never appears in subsequent plantation documents. Interestingly, unlike the other babies at Sunnyside, one-year-old Nelson is never listed in the slave register. Nor do the names of Nelson's five siblings ever appear as slaves, which suggests that Cuny had always intended to manumit Adeline and their children. There is, however, a 34-year-old man on the plantation named James Stuart, who could be Adeline's brother.[42] It was rare for slaves to be listed with last names, and quite a coincidence that there would be two people on Sunnyside with the same surname.

Notwithstanding his amorous relationship with Adeline, two years after arriving in Texas, Philip Cuny married for the second time. Eliza Ware was a young white widow of property; she brought with her to the marriage 1,200 head of cattle, a number of slaves, sixteen mules, and $23,000.[43] It was Eliza's money that enabled Philip to expand his business and professional life, and it was shortly after their marriage that Cuny built a "Greek Revival home with large frontal colonnades."[44] There he established Adeline and Nelson alongside Eliza and his white children. The household was a busy one. Eliza gave Philip two sons in quick succession, John Powell (1842–1843), who died within a year, and Philip Minor Jr. (1843). The gap between Nelson's birth in 1839 and that of Adeline's next son Joseph in 1845 may be attributed to Cuny's "honeymoon" period with Eliza. The same year that Adeline gave birth to Joseph, Eliza delivered Mary Tabitha, named after Philip's mother. The next year, Adeline's third son Norris Wright was born, named for the murdered sheriff of Rapides Parish. The birth of Eliza's last child, Eliza Louise, coincided with her death in childbirth in 1849. Adeline undoubtedly then played an essential role in caring for Philip's three motherless children, in addition to her own three sons.

There is a gap of five years between Norris Wright and Adeline's next child, Henry Ernest. While this may have been due to miscarriages or child mortality, there seems to be a pattern here because, almost immediately after the death of Eliza Ware, Cuny courted and married his third wife, Adaline Spurlock. The coincidentally named Adaline, twenty years younger than Philip, was another wealthy white woman who brought her own slaves and property to the marriage.[45] The Spurlocks had also emigrated to Texas from Rapides Parish, Louisiana, and owned a nearby plantation on the Brazos River; the two families would have known each other well for years, which may explain why Cuny remarried so quickly. While Eliza Ware may have been initially unaware of her husband's relationship with Adeline Stuart, her successor certainly knew that Philip and Adeline had been together for more than ten years. And while Eliza seems to have accepted the presence of Adeline Stuart and her biracial children, Adaline Spurlock made immediate changes to the household.

Once safely wed to Spurlock, Cuny reestablished his intimacy with Adeline Stuart. In 1851 he was a proud father twice: he welcomed Henry Ernest, his fourth son with Adeline Stuart, and Miner Philip, his first with Adaline Spurlock. Two years later, Adeline Stuart's daughter, Laura, was born in 1853, followed by Adaline Spurlock's son Dixon in 1854. Adeline Stuart's last child, daughter Virginia (Jennie), arrived in 1855. According to Maud Cuney Hare, the children of Adeline and Philip, all of whom except Laura inherited Adeline's Mediterranean coloring, were particularly attractive. They were all slender and of middle height. Norris Wright was the darkest child and had his father's piercing and sparkling dark eyes. Joseph had his father's blue eyes, and Laura, with blonde hair and blue eyes, looked most like the Cuny side of the family.

Philip and Adeline appear to have chosen their children's names with care. Nelson's name suggests the naval hero of Trafalgar and his father's British heritage, while Norris Wright was named after the sheriff of Rapides Parish, a close family friend who had been killed in the duel along with Philip's brother. Joseph calls to mind the biblical hero, cast into bondage, who led his people to freedom, a prophetic choice since Joseph would become a leader of Galveston's Black community. The positive relationship between Joseph and his father is reflected in the fact that Joseph always called his second son Philip, although he had been christened Charles Sumner, after the Massachusetts abolitionist. Finally, Virginia's name seems to reference Adeline's birthplace and her connection with her own mother, Hester Neale. The family's racial history was never obscured or hidden, and all six children were given accurate information about both parents' dates and places of birth, as shown in the consistent census records for Nelson, Joseph, Norris Wright, Henry Ernest, Virginia (Jennie), and Laura.

Despite his constant travels for business and politics on a wide circuit that included Houston, Galveston, San Antonio, Austin, and Louisiana, Cuny was clearly a family man who enjoyed domestic life. His letters express contentment with the harmonious, well-appointed household that Adeline Stuart supervised and to which he always eagerly returned. In a letter to Adaline Spurlock, he quotes the sentimental line "there's no place like home," from John Howard Payne's 1823 ballad "Home Sweet Home," and closes with: "I think hourly with anxious solicitude of my peaceful and quiet home and its dear inmates."[46] Of course, it was Cuny's many bondsmen and women who enabled him to cultivate the life of a bon vivant and to enjoy elegant surroundings and gourmet meals. Thanks to the Sunnyside kitchen staff, he could vie with his friend and neighbor, Col. Leonard Groce, who was famous for meals prepared by his own enslaved New Orleans chef. Guests at Sunnyside would have enjoyed elaborate meals that included whole roast pigs; local venison and game; bass, catfish, and alligator from the Brazos River; and a well-stocked wine cellar.[47] In contrast, when away from home, Cuny deplored the unsanitary conditions, monotonous, poorly prepared meals, and the "shocking bad taste" he encountered at the homes of acquaintances or lodging houses.[48]

In addition to his slaves, it was his wives to whom Cuny owed this enviable lifestyle. Although on paper one of the richest men in Texas, his assets were always heavily mortgaged; it was thus Eliza's and Adaline Spurlock's money that provided the elegant appointments at Sunnyside, just as it was Adeline Stuart's firm hand on the domestic tiller that ensured the smooth management of his unconventional household. According to Maud Cuney Hare, Adeline enjoyed great respect in the household; she was "an especially active and industrious little woman who kept everyone about her busy."[49]

Adeline also ensured a comfortable and happy life for her children, all of whom were literate, intelligent, polite, and well-spoken. She and Philip held their children to strict standards of manners and decorum, and the Cuney brothers comported themselves as gentlemen. It would appear that Philip did not raise his sons in subordinate conditions and always intended that they would take their places as free men. Adeline's quiet older sons Nelson and Joseph, to whom she was very close, assiduously assisted their mother with household chores. Nelson in particular was skilled in carpentry, construction, and mechanics; he served as "a handyman around the house," which prepared him for his successful painting business in Galveston.[50] Joseph took care of his mother's correspondence and probably helped with household accounts. Norris Wright, however, had Philip's outgoing and gregarious personality, which would eventually lead him to follow his father's career in Texas politics. He was musically talented and had been taught to play the bass violin by "Henry the Fiddler," who was probably the same 22-year-old Henry listed in the Sunnyside slave register in 1855. Unlike his more compliant older brothers, Norris Wright resented and avoided duties associated with bondage and routinely "shirked" his domestic chores.[51] When not playing music, he escaped the household and roamed the woods and creeks of Sunnyside's 2,000 acres. Maud Cuney Hare does not mention the childhood of Henry Ernest so we know little about him; however, it appears that Philip was less involved with his upbringing, which may have contributed to ambivalence about his direction and identity and to his less than illustrious professional career.

The success of both the Cuney brothers and their half-siblings suggests that Philip was a supportive and affectionate father to his fifteen children. Although he did not correspond with Adeline, his letters to his wives never fail to mention their children. He was apparently proud of both his white and his biracial sons and included them on business and political trips. In the summer of 1852, Eliza's ten-year-old son Philip accompanied his father on a visit to their relatives in Louisiana. The next summer, Adaline Spurlock's sons Miner and Dixon traveled with Philip to his farm near Georgetown, Texas, where they swam in the San Gabriel River. Philip frequently took the talented Norris

Wright along on trips, where his son would play his fiddle and "furnish pleasure to admiring crowds."[52] At a time that offered few cultural amusements, bands of itinerant Black musicians, consisting of violins, guitars, woodwinds, and bass, were popular features of rural life, and Philip Cuny seems to have been proud of Norris Wright's ability. His musical talent would be passed on to his daughter, Maud, and to his great-nephews from Washington, DC, Waring and his twin brother, Norris Wright Cuney III.

Sunnyside, the mansion in which the family lived, no longer exists, but one can extrapolate its design and materials from that of the nearby Liendo Mansion, which was constructed in 1853 by the Groce family on part of the same José Justo Liendo grant.[53] Both the Groce and Cuny homes were, of course, built by slave artisans and laborers. Lumber for the house's frame would have been shipped from Houston in oxcarts. Bricks for the wine cellar, the kitchen, and the fifteen slave dwellings on Sunnyside Plantation would have been handmade from the red clay on the banks of the Brazos River.[54] The brick foundation was probably stuccoed with white plaster and the brick chimneys and front columns plastered in lime. The outer walls would have been drop-leaf siding, painted white, possibly with contrasting dark green shutters and blinds. In the Liendo house, today privately owned and used as an event venue, a broad hallway runs the length of the building, flanked by the dining room and reception areas. Spacious, high-ceilinged bedrooms occupy the second story. Floors and ceilings are tongue-and-groove yellow pine, and the interior walls are smoothly plastered. Ceilings in the reception rooms are plastered and adorned with painted friezes of flowers and plants. Visitors to the plantation homes on the Brazos River would have enjoyed views from the columned verandas of glossy hedges, gentle hills, dense thickets, and lush grassland of variegated greens that recalled the English countryside.

Thanks to his slaves and to the rich, waxy soil of the Brazos Valley, Cuny prospered in Texas. He established a diversified agricultural business "in the heart of the cotton and melon belt" amidst "prairies full of grazing herds of buffalo, through which roamed wandering Indian tribes."[55] The Brazos River, then free of steamers and commercial traffic, provided plentiful fish. Although he began planting cotton, by 1850 Cuny had pivoted to dairy farming and vegetables: in 1860 he produced 5,000 pounds of butter plus sweet potatoes and corn.[56] Many of his business trips with his sons involved escorting wagonloads of produce throughout East Texas.

In addition to managing his plantation, Cuny fulfilled his political aspirations by joining the Democratic Party and winning election to the Texas House of Representatives in 1843. Following statehood, he won election to the Texas Senate and also joined the Texas Militia, from whence he received his rank of brigadier general, although he is usually given the title of colonel.[57] As a wealthy, educated, cultured, and articulate man, he was well suited for his political career. His particular interests—which would be duplicated by his son Norris Wright in his own political career, albeit in the Republican Party—included education, finance, and infrastructure. He served as Chair of the Claims and Accounts Committee and on the committees for Public Lands, Education, and Internal Improvements; he also sponsored legislation to build a turnpike between Houston and Austin and was instrumental in establishing Bellville as the county seat and building the court house there.[58] Norris Wright would have been well aware of his father's political activities; seeing his father on the stump for his various elections certainly gave him a taste of the political life he would later embrace.

According to the 1860 census, Cuny was one of the 263 Texans who held more than $100,000 in real estate and who essentially controlled the state. In addition to land, he was one of forty-four individuals who owned more than one hundred slaves. He was also one of the more educated of the group: only twelve out of 263 boasted formal higher education. However, among these twelve, degrees had been granted from such prestigious institutions as Yale, Harvard, Princeton, William and Mary, and the University of Edinburgh.

Cuny's own alma mater, Transylvania University, was also represented by John Herndon from Brazoria County.[59]

Despite his thirty-year relationship with Adeline Stuart, his evident affection for and generosity toward their children, his strong religious convictions, and his apparent regard for his bondsmen and women, Philip Cuny was still a slave owner, commercially and philosophically committed to the euphemistically named "peculiar institution." According to Hales, he probably "considered himself a benevolent master."[60] Given that such an expression is indubitably an oxymoron, the Texas Slave Schedule and Cuny's own records show that he kept the same slaves for life and grouped them as families, designating husbands, wives, sons, and daughters. He also provided fifteen separate brick slave cabins, which would indicate the existence of a relatively stable and dignified family life on the plantation. When his second wife Eliza Ware died, Cuny purchased her slaves (who were also listed as families) from her executor, which ensured that they remained together on Sunnyside. In his letters home, Cuny frequently comments on the activities and health of the bondsmen with whom he traveled: he compliments their work and reports on their industry and skills. Never does he disparage or denigrate his bondsmen in his letters; rather he praises the skills of his foreman Sam and his cook Old Spot several times. At the same time, he clearly attributed his financial success to slavery and was optimistic enough about the institution to mortgage his slaves several times before the Civil War in order to purchase more land.

In his capacity as a Texas legislator, Cuny "supported keeping the laws established in the Constitution of 1836 pertaining to slavery. That document had legalized slavery, reversed Mexican laws against slave immigration, and forbidden the state to enforce slave emancipation."[61] In 1861, feeling that slavery was being threatened by Abraham Lincoln, Cuny voted to secede from the Union. On the other hand, perhaps with an eye to the manumission of his own family, he also voted for "an act allowing owners to free their own slaves if the owners so desired."[62] Texas thus allowed more individual autonomy than Georgia, which required an act of the State Legislature in order to free a bondsman or woman, regardless of the owner's wishes. His other votes related to slavery favored a ban on selling alcohol to slaves and one prohibiting slaves who had been in legal trouble in other states from entering Texas.

When Cuny freed Adeline and their six surviving children, manumission in Texas was unusual but not unheard of; on his trips to Galveston, where he negotiated loans from the prominent lawyers and brothers-in-law William Ballinger and Thomas Jack, he would have heard of several contemporaries who emancipated their slaves and left them money and property. For example, "in 1856 David Webster executed a will in which he emancipated his woman, Betsey, and gave her his entire estate."[63] Cuny often did business in the town of Webberville, near Austin, at the grist mill and cotton gin owned by John Webber. He would have known that Webber, a Vermonter who had founded the town and settled there, had manumitted his enslaved wife, Silvia Hector; however, the Webber family moved to Mexico during the Civil War.[64]

The manumission of Adeline and her children may have been precipitated by Philip's marriage to Adaline Spurlock in 1852. Despite the apparently harmonious twelve years in which Eliza Ware and Adeline Stuart shared the Cuny household, Adaline Spurlock was clearly less amenable than her predecessor to having all her husband's progeny, not to mention his longtime partner, living under the same roof. She may have insisted that her husband manumit her rival and establish her elsewhere, and shortly after his marriage, Cuny did exactly that.

Philip's newly enhanced income, courtesy of Spurlock, may also have enabled him to pursue his ambitious educational plans for his four sons. Eliza's son Philip (age ten) was sent to the preparatory Virginia Military Institute in Lexington, Virginia, with the expectation that he would complete an undergraduate degree on the adjacent campus of Washington & Lee, then called Washington College.[65] The fact that he chose a school in that state seems to support the idea of a Virginia connection, through which Adeline Stuart had been sent to Louisiana. He also sent sons Nelson (age fourteen) and Joseph (age nine) to the Wyle Street School, a boarding and preparatory institution for biracial youth in Pittsburgh, Pennsylvania.[66] Norris Wright followed his brothers to Pittsburgh a few years later. Cuny's intention was that all three sons would matriculate at Oberlin College. Cuny must have done careful research in order to locate the school that was run by George B. Vashon, an outspoken Black abolitionist, listed on the masthead of Garrison's anti-slavery newspaper as a Pittsburgh sales agent for *The Liberator*. Vashon was the first African American graduate of Oberlin College, and Cuny hoped that he would secure admission for his sons to that institution.[67]

The brothers apparently enjoyed their school days although, having been carefully reared in manners and deportment and taught to treat everyone with respect, they were shocked at the recalcitrant behavior of "a ring of bad boys at the school," one of whom attacked the venerable Mr. Vashon and "pulled his long black whiskers," of which he was inordinately proud.[68] Although much younger than his classmates, Norris Wright flew at Vashon's attackers, pummeling them until they fled the room. According to Maud Cuney, the brothers were quietly self-confident but had been taught by their parents to assert themselves when necessary; at school their "shy Texas manners and ways [and] frank friendliness" made them well-liked.[69] Though they all excelled in academics, the brothers were also athletic and loved the outdoors. They were popular with classmates but apparently preferred their own company and spent their free time "fishing, rowing and sailing in and about the beautiful pebble-bottomed Allegheny River."[70]

After the departure of his three sons, Philip made another major domestic change. He established Adeline Stuart and her three younger children in Houston while Adaline Spurlock remained at Sunnyside. In Houston, Philip pursued his business activities while his older brother Stephen, who had emigrated from Louisiana, remained at

Sunnyside as overseer. All the Cuny slaves remained on Sunnyside in their family groups. Some scholars suggest that the move was precipitated by the outbreak of an epidemic, possibly yellow fever, although it seems counterintuitive to leave the healthy countryside for the crowds and poor sanitation of Houston, particularly since his new wife remained at Sunnyside with their baby son, Miner. It is more likely that Cuny needed to be closer to his produce customers in Houston and to his bankers in Galveston.

The move may also have been a way to preserve peace among the women in his unconventional household. However, if Adaline Spurlock expected that the manumission of Adeline Stuart would eliminate the latter from her life, she was mistaken. When Cuny moved Adeline Stuart, along with Norris Wright and the baby Henry Ernest, to the Houston house, she was probably already pregnant with her fifth child and first daughter, Laura. Adaline Spurlock remained at Sunnyside with baby Miner, along with Eliza Ware's daughters, Mary Tabitha and Eliza Louise. Shortly thereafter, Philip's mother, Tabitha Wells Cuny, now twice widowed, moved to Houston from Louisiana; it is interesting that she chose to live in Houston with Adeline Stuart rather than with her legal daughter-in-law at Sunnyside. At this point, Tabitha and Adeline had known each other for more than twenty years; an amicable relationship between the two women is further suggested by the fact that Maud Cuney Hare stayed in touch with Tabitha's family at Sugar Bend, long after the death of her grandmother.

For the remaining ten years of his life, Philip would move back and forth between the households of the two women, located fifty miles apart. The new arrangement seemed to agree with him: in June 1853, he wrote to Adaline Spurlock that since arriving in Houston "my health has improved. I now feel quite well." However, lest she think of leaving Sunnyside and joining him, he added hastily: "Houston is very dull at present, no amusement of any kind in the place and the times are very hard." He conciliated her with the promise of an elegant frock, ordered from her dressmaker, that would arrive "by the return trip of the wagons" in time for a party she planned to attend. Spurlock seems to have enjoyed a busy social life among the planters' families of the Brazos River, while Cuny's business obligations and his mother always provided convenient excuses for his presence in Houston. In October 1853, he wrote to Spurlock, apparently in response to a demand that he return for a party at the home of their wealthy friend, Dr. Peebles: "Ma is complaining this morning of being unwell . . . and I must stay with her." He further bolstered his excuse with an obligation to "go to Pine Island to see Greer about hauling and cannot get back [to Sunnyside] in time . . . even if Ma was well."

The family relationships were complicated. Philip's life in Houston with Adeline Stuart, of which Adaline Spurlock was certainly aware, did not preclude his signing off to the latter as "your kind and loving husband and father." At the same time, he had two more children with Adeline Stuart, Laura Vivian (1853) and Virginia (1855). However, when at Sunnyside, Philip was not remiss in his attentions to Spurlock. Spurlock was twenty years younger than Adeline Stuart, and she gave birth to four more children, including Richard, born two years before Philip's untimely death in 1866. Despite the existence of Eliza Ware and Adaline Spurlock, Adeline Stuart, who survived Philip by forty years, always maintained her identity as his widow, and she is described in some public documents as his common-law wife.[71] The Cuney children certainly saw their parents' long relationship as a true marriage.

Unfortunately, the Civil War created a financial crisis for the family and disrupted Philip's plans for his children's education. In April 1861, Cuny wrote from Houston that "provisions are very high and rising—cotton, wool and hide cannot be sold for cash at scarcely any price and credit is out of the question."[72] His assets were heavily mortgaged, and he was unable to meet his obligations or pay his four sons' tuition at their schools in the East. As soon as war was declared, Joseph left school and joined the 63rd Pennsylvania Volunteers, where he fought in several battles in Virginia, close to Centreville, his mother's birthplace.[73] At the same time, his half-brother Philip left Virginia Military Institute and returned to Hempstead where he joined the 24th Texas Cavalry. Nelson also left school, although it is unclear what he did for the next few years. Norris Wright was urged by both his father and his older brothers to stay on at Vashon's school, but he too departed in 1863, when he was seventeen years old.[74]

After Philip Cuny's death in 1866, life changed drastically for Adeline and the three youngest children. She managed to educate Henry Ernest, Laura, and Jennie in the Freedman's Schools in Houston while she apparently worked as a housekeeper. Despite his vaunted reputation as one of the richest landowners in Texas, Cuny had died bankrupt, and it is unlikely that she received any help from Adaline Spurlock, who still owned her own property and assets. Nelson was the first to return to his mother in Texas; a skilled house painter, he would have found plentiful work in the state's building boom after the Civil War. He would have had to work his way back, and he did so via Mississippi, where he met and married his wife, Laura Glover.

After the war, Joseph, determined to fulfill his father's dream of a college education, settled in Washington, DC. He enrolled in Howard University, studied law, and worked for the federal government as a security guard. At one point he was employed with the Freedman's Bureau in Washington; he would certainly have been aware that the Galveston Bureau was considered one of the successes of Reconstruction, in part due to the energetic efforts of Maine journalist and former abolitionist George T. Ruby, who became a traveling agent for the entire region.[75] In 1870, Joseph sent for his younger siblings Henry Ernest and Virginia (Jennie). Henry soon found a good job with the US Patent Office, possibly through political connections of his father, and Jennie kept house for her brothers. Laura apparently chose to stay in Houston where she found work in one of the city's large retail emporiums. Laura, who was blonde and blue-eyed like her father, apparently passed as white in order to find employment.

It would seem that Philip Cuny had also planned to educate his daughters abroad in European finishing schools. Although he had died penniless, there may have been money earmarked for Laura's and Jennie's education. It is also possible that Joseph, out of respect for his father's wishes, financed his sister's education. Shortly after her arrival in Washington Jennie, along with Joseph's fiancée, Josephine Barber, departed for Mannheim, Germany, where both attended Madame Nichols's Institute for Young Ladies.[76] Both young women were trained and certified as teachers. By the time the ladies returned from Europe, Joseph had decided to return to Texas and, in 1872, the three relocated to Galveston. Joseph became a teacher at the East District Elementary School and was eventually promoted to principal, while his wife Josephine taught at the Barnes Institute, a school sponsored by the American Missionary Association.[77]

Joseph, Josephine, and Jennie were probably encouraged to move to Galveston by brother Norris Wright, who had already settled in the Oleander City. After leaving Vashon's school in Pittsburgh, Wright went to St. Louis where he found work on the *Grey Eagle*, a famous steamboat that plied the Mississippi River. It is possible that his older brother Nelson had preceded him and helped him to find work. Given his education, his rather slight physique, and the people with whom he associated, Wright would have worked as a steward. He was often in New Orleans, where he made friends with several politically influential individuals, including Col. James Lewis; P. B. S. Pinchback, the future governor of Louisiana and the grandfather of Waring's friend, the Harlem Renaissance writer Jean Toomer; and George T. Ruby. All three were prominent "race men" active in Reconstruction and the Republican Party.[78]

When Ruby took a job with the Galveston Freedman's Bureau in 1867, he undoubtedly encouraged Wright to join him. Ruby certainly mentored Wright in his political career.[79] It was he who arranged for Cuney's first political appointment as assistant to the sergeant-at-arms for the Twelfth Texas Legislature of 1870.[80] In fact, Wright "continued the leadership role, ideas, and agenda set in motion by Ruby and black Texans during Reconstruction."[81] Just as education, vocational training, suffrage, and public infrastructure were Ruby's concerns as a state senator, so they would become the pillars of Wright's political platform.[82]

By the early 1870s, all three Cuney brothers were living in Galveston. There were a number of reasons African American families like the Cuneys chose that city. Given their family's commitment to education, they would have known that schools were one of the first priorities of newly emancipated Galvestonians. Contrary to oft-repeated claims, African Americans did not wait for whites to set up schools after the Civil War. James Smallwood refutes the "revisionist" idea that "Negroes did not have the means to aid their own [educational] cause." He claims that "the educational movement was not imposed upon Negroes by over-zealous Northerners. Rather, blacks helped themselves in a major way."[83] Smallwood's claims are supported by eyewitness accounts of Black Galveston in several unpublished memoirs. Teacher Ralph Albert Scull (1860–1949) sat down every night and, before saying his prayers, wrote out his memories in an elegant cursive script. Scull denies that Galveston's very first schools for Black children were set up by the Freedman's Bureau and the American Missionary Society (AMS): on the contrary, "just after Emancipation there were a number of private [Black] teachers trying to instruct children. In the East End we had Miss Reedy who was a daughter of Rev. Reedy, then pastor of Reedy Chapel A.M.E. Church."[84] Reedy Chapel's commitment to education enabled it to pivot quickly and provide literacy classes immediately after Emancipation.

Later, when the Freedman's Bureau and the AMS did set up their schools, Scull notes that Galveston's prominent Black citizens, including Joseph Cuney, taught in and administered the institutions. Scull's claim of Black Galveston's commitment to education is corroborated by the unpublished journals of Sarah Barnes, a Connecticut schoolteacher who came to Texas with the AMS and set up the Barnes

School, where Josephine Barber Cuney taught for many years. Barnes recalls the warm welcome she received in the immaculately neat cottages of recently emancipated slaves and her surprise when they told her that their children were already in school.[85]

Another appeal of Galveston for the Cuney brothers would have been the many business opportunities. In addition to opening schools, Black Galvestonians started thriving businesses, such as the furniture store opened by Scull's father. In listing the employees of his father's furniture and construction businesses, he mentions the names of Black masons, carpenters, and painters. There was plenty of work for skilled artisans; carpenters and masons "just out of slavery" found ready employment in the postwar construction boom. He lists a number of African American craftsmen employed in his father's busy construction firm; in fact, one of the painters and decorators is none other than Nelson Cuney.[86] Scull also recalls the shouts of entrepreneurial "Negro peddlers," former slaves who, with no capital or financial backing, "improvise a living by selling homemade ice cream, vegetables, and charcoal."[87] Scull's memories are corroborated by Maud Cuney Hare in her book *Negro Musicians and Their Music* (1936): she interviewed members of her father's generation in Galveston who recalled the "street-cries of the hucksters and vendors who sell both raw and cooked food on the streets."[88] In addition to calls for watermelon, onions, and "chitlins," Cuney Hare's informants recalled songs by chimney sweeps and by vendors of rope and wood poles for clotheslines, all of which testify to the entrepreneurial spirit of the former bondsmen and women.

In Galveston's fluid racial atmosphere, both whites and Blacks patronized the thriving Black businesses in the East End, which included Aunt Rendy's, an attractive shop on 16th and L Streets that displayed "glass-covered cases with cakes and pies," as well as Thibodeaux's Restaurant and the Milk Dairy on 27th Street.[89] Similarly, Black customers were welcomed at the popular Triple Dip Ice Cream Parlor on the seawall.[90] Some businesses were more legitimate than others. Scull notes that "in the seventies saloons and gaming was a lucrative business."[91] He assiduously lists the names of six or seven proprietors of gambling venues. It is worth noting here that Norris Wright's name is never mentioned in this connection, and if Wright had been involved with illegal activities, as his detractors claimed, Scull would probably have mentioned this fact.

Yet another unique feature of Galveston was the encouragement of formal religious affiliation amongst bondsmen and women. Even before Emancipation, Texan "Methodists, Baptists, Catholics, Episcopalians, Presbyterians, and Disciples of Christ all accepted slave members . . . by 1860 Methodists claimed 7,451 bondsmen as members in Texas."[92] Not to be outdone, in 1840 Baptists in Galveston had welcomed slaves to the Colored Baptist Church in the West End. In 1855, a new site for the congregation, renamed the African Baptist Church, was purchased on L Street in the East End by the eminent white Galvestonian Gail Borden, of condensed milk fame.[93] The Cuney family's church, Reedy Chapel African Methodist Episcopal, founded in 1848, also began as a church for bondsmen and women. After the church was destroyed in a citywide fire in 1885, Nelson's construction company helped rebuild the current structure; the cornerstone, laid by the Prince Hall Masons, bears his brother Wright's name, and the church remains an elegant building on Broadway today. However, the various churches also reveal the definite class distinctions within the Black community, as represented by the Cuney and Johnson families. Given their education and family background, the Cuneys quickly took their places among Galveston's Black elite. They attended fashionable Reedy African Methodist Episcopal Chapel, while the Johnsons patronized one of the informal "store front" Methodist churches where Jack's father occasionally preached.[94]

Housing was another attraction for African American families. Galveston was laid out in a rather unique design: houses on main thoroughfares boasted deep lots with outbuildings facing alleys that ran parallel to the streets. During slavery, these alley houses were primarily occupied by slaves. However, a misconception promulgated by Ellen Beasley in her otherwise impressive volume, *The Alleys and Back Buildings of Galveston* (1996), and unfortunately repeated by other scholars including Hardwick (2002), is that after Emancipation, all African Americans lived in the alleys rather than on the main streets. This claim is contradicted not only by the addresses of the Cuney brothers' comfortable homes but also by those of less affluent families like the Johnsons, who lived on Broadway. Galvestonian educator Izola Collins sees the repetition of such inaccuracies as a way of making Black Galvestonians invisible, of writing them out of the city's history.[95]

Galveston also boasted many civic and social organizations. The Cuney family certainly would have participated in some of the city's twenty-one "Colored" social organizations including a Glee Club; two Black veterans' associations, the Grant's Rifles and the Lincoln Guards; the St. Elizabeth Society; the Daughters of Zion; and two fraternal organizations including Oleander Lodge and the Prince Hall Masons' Amity Lodge #4, of which Wright Cuney was the Grand Master. Church suppers, square dances, taffy-pulls, hayrides, and fish fries on West Beach were popular pastimes.[96] As in New Orleans, music was an important part of the community. According to Scull, "from the sixties Galveston had its brass and string bands. The Colored Cadet Band [was] the pride of Galveston for many years and was often employed at big white funerals and at street parades."[97] Of course, Juneteenth was a major event: after the first famous reading of the Emancipation Proclamation, festivities were organized every year by a Women's Committee (possibly the Daughters of Zion); these included a parade with floats, former soldiers in uniform, and beautiful young ladies costumed as the Goddess of Liberty and her Maids of Honor, as well as classical music selections, speeches, and the reading of the Emancipation Proclamation. The men, meanwhile, arranged an elaborate barbecue (free to people over fifty), and activities including a fiddlers' contest and boating excursions.[98]

In contrast to the Cuney family, Jack Johnson's parents represented the respectable poor: they were hardworking, religious, and ambitious for their nine children. Jack's father Henry Johnson, a disabled Civil War veteran who had been denied a military pension, was illiterate but encouraged his son to finish high school and become a preacher.[99] Johnson's mother Tina could read and greatly encouraged her son, who said in his autobiography, "too little credit has been given to my mother . . . [her] splendid influence and love was never forgotten by me."[100] Although the nine children enjoyed few luxuries, Johnson's parents ensured that they all attended at least five years of school. Both parents worked as janitors at the East End elementary school where Waring's father had been a student and where his great-uncle Joseph Cuney had been a teacher and principal. Despite his parents' urging Johnson did not, like the Cuney children, attend Central High, the African American secondary school that Wright Cuney had helped establish. Instead, Jack worked on the Galveston docks as a stevedore, where he would have learned that his employment had been made possible by Wright Cuney, who had broken the white monopoly on the docks and formed a union of African American stevedores and cotton jammers.[101]

In their contrasting educations, professional aspirations, and accomplishments, the Johnsons and the Cuneys thus illustrate the range, complexity, and variety of the Black experience in Galveston. Certainly, the city was a beacon of hope for both African Americans and foreign immigrants after the Civil War. Galveston undoubtedly appealed to African Americans because it was so different from other Texas cities. According to historian Andrew Muir, "it was less Anglo-Saxon than most places in Texas, less English-speaking, and less Evangelical Christian."[102] Walking along Market, the main commercial street, or through the bustling wharves, one could hear French, Spanish, Italian, and German, not to mention the occasional Irish brogue or West Indian patois. Izola Collins, whose great-grandfather Horace Scull, a former slave, built a raft and propelled his young family ten miles across Galveston Bay from Bolivar Peninsula to the city, remembers her grandfather's stories of the Galveston he knew as a young man and a contemporary of the Cuney family: "Galveston was a haven, an oasis from grief, and Black people of different nationalities walked the streets. Some . . . were free blacks who spoke Spanish, who had been freed years ago by the Mexican government. Some were dark-skinned people from India, with wavy long hair. . . . But most were abducted Africans."[103]

Finally, in addition to its advantages in education, employment, housing, and religion, Galveston was also "the garden spot of Texas . . . with her oleander-bordered streets and much-sounding sea."[104] As Maud Cuney Hare would write evocatively, the city's residents enjoyed the "deep white sand . . . breezes fresh from the Gulf . . . [and] the breakers of deep blue . . . [that] lashed and laved the glistening sands with that endless and fascinating sound of the sea for which an exiled native ever yearns."[105]

Once they decided on Galveston, the Cuney brothers wasted no time in establishing families. Nelson had married Laura Glover in Mississippi. Joseph soon married his fiancée Josephine Barber, and Wright married a young teacher and talented musician named Adelina Dowdie. Recreating the close bond they enjoyed at Vashon's school, the brothers settled their families within a few blocks of each other. Eventually Adeline Stuart moved from Houston to Nelson's home. The families all lived in the "Gingerbread" wooden houses typical of Galveston, with front verandas and large back gardens full of fruit trees: orange, plum, pomegranate, fig, and mulberry. Their children replicated the fathers' close connection: the eight Galveston cousins formed a tight bond, relying on each other for friendship and company. The family consisted of Nelson's children Richard, Norris Wright II (Waring Cuney's father), May, and Daisy; Joseph and Josephine's children Joseph Jr. (Nisi) and Charles Sumner (Philip); and Wright and Adelina's children Maud and Lloyd Garrison. The cousins all loved the beach and were often taken "surf bathing" by Uncle Wright.[106]

However, the tight family connection also enabled their parents to shield them from the depredations of racism, which still lurked beneath the city's vaunted tolerance and civility. Wright's daughter, Maud, recalled the night a white mob, angered by her father's creation of a Black stevedores' union on the Galveston docks, was rumored to be planning a march on their house. Although begged by her husband to take the children to Joseph's house for safety, Adelina kept vigil all night at a rear window.[107] Fortunately, the mob did not materialize; had they done so, Norris's friends, both Black and white, were ready for them.

In general, however, the Cuney cousins experienced a classic Victorian childhood: at Christmas the cousins enjoyed visits from Santa Claus, a candle-lit tree, and gifts of books. Education and culture were valued; the children, particularly Waring's father, memorized and acted out the works of Lord Byron and Shakespeare. All the cousins completed Central High; this imposing brick building, for which Wright had been a tireless advocate, was Galveston's first public Black high school. From Central, Waring's father would go on to Howard University, while Maud matriculated at the New England Conservatory of Music. The children grew up in a musical milieu, enjoying evenings at Wright's home where his wife Adelina, a beautiful soprano, sang opera arias and played the piano. Undoubtedly, Wright, who as a young man had been a virtuoso on the "bass fiddle," still played.[108] In addition to receiving culture, the children were instructed in moral behavior and self-control, and taught charity towards the less fortunate; at Easter, they helped Adelina strip her garden of flowers and transport them to the hospital.[109]

The fact that Adeline Stuart and three of her six children made their homes in Galveston after the Civil War seems to indicate an expectation that their relationship to Philip Cuny would be both advantageous and acknowledged, even if obliquely. Although he had died in 1866, Philip would have made many connections in the Texas House of Representatives, where he "left a competent if undistinguished legacy."[110] When Norris Wright arrived in Galveston in 1869, his half-brother Philip Cuny Jr., recently demobilized from the Confederate Army, was also starting his political career. In 1874, Philip Jr. was instrumental in creating Waller County out of Stephen Austin's original land grant.[111] The following year, Norris Wright ran for mayor of Galveston. Although he did not win the election, Cuney's family connections undoubtedly helped him; he subsequently forged a relationship with his white Democratic opponent, who praised him for "his excellent qualities as a public man."[112]

Norris Wright and Philip Jr. were not the only politicians in the family. Although his career was marred by scandal, Henry Ernest also drew on his father's connections to make a start in Washington, DC, politics; a posthumous article about his career, published in the *Houston Informer*, notes that Henry's "father and uncles were political leaders," a clear reference to Philip Cuny, and to the Cuny family in Louisiana. Henry, "a quiet but potent influence in politics" and a "confidante" of leaders of the national Republican Party, was described as a mentor to his older, more famous brother, Norris Wright.[113] In his history of the family, Carter Woodson acknowledges that Henry Ernest succeeded in politics for a few years before, as Woodson cryptically notes, he "passed from the scene"; this is a euphemism for the fact that Henry Ernest served a year in federal prison for embezzlement. Upon his release, he moved to New York where he became active in Harlem politics.[114]

The most famous member of the Cuney family was, however, Norris Wright. Waring's cousin, Maud Cuney Hare, would certainly have told Waring stories about Wright Cuney; she was passionately devoted to her "idolized father."[115] Fifteen years after Wright's death, perhaps at the urging of her lifelong friend and former fiancé, W. E. B. Du Bois, Maud drew on her father's scrapbooks and personal papers to write a meticulously researched, if hagiographic, book about him entitled *Norris Wright Cuney: Tribune of the Negro People*.[116] This volume would certainly have been read and discussed by Waring and his family.

Norris himself, although he emphatically identified as a "race man," frequently invoked his rights and privileges as a "gentleman" in an obvious claim to his paternal heritage. In 1875, he wrote a letter to the *Galveston News* defending himself against an accusation by the U.S. Marshals Service that he had not paid an excise tax and had assaulted a marshal: "I claim to have some knowledge of the civility that should subsist between gentlemen and I always endeavor to govern myself accordingly."[117] His proud and confident bearing, a legacy from both his parents, enabled him to enter any bastion of white privilege in Galveston, such as Toujeau's Café or the elegant Surf House, where he was received with the same courtesy he showed others. According to the *Galveston Tribune*, in an article written a few months after his death in 1898: "He was accepted not because he looked white or because he appeared Mexican, but rather because he was intelligent and courageous enough to fight for what he believed."[118] On one occasion, according to the *New York Tribune* (then the mouthpiece of the Republican Party), Cuney was staying at the Hoffman House hotel in New York when he happened to meet Leon Blum, one of Galveston's first millionaires; Blum "discovered Cuney, of whose presence in New York he was unaware and [came] over to greet him with a handshake and cordiality that denoted both respect and esteem."[119] As the leader of the Republican Party of Texas and the highest ranking African American public official in the South, Norris Wright's doings were always of interest to the readers of Horace Greeley's liberal newspaper.

Unfortunately, despite his "kindly nature, boundless heart, his desire always to be of service to the weak, his sense of justice . . . loyalty . . . and high ideals," Wright Cuney was roughly ejected from the Republican Party in 1898 by a racist faction called the Lily-Whites.[120] This betrayal probably hastened his premature death at fifty-two. Wright's funeral in 1898 was "the largest seen in Galveston in many a day . . . three thousand people attended the service, with another thousand waiting outside" Harmony Hall.[121] The San Antonio Guards (a Black militia regiment), a detail of mounted policemen, and a military band accompanied Cuney to Lakeview Cemetery, where he was laid beside his wife Adelina who had died two years earlier. The Prince Hall Masons were pallbearers; today, thanks to this lodge, a handsome memorial has been erected on his grave.

Although Jack Johnson was in Memphis when Wright was buried, his family would certainly have witnessed and described to him the funeral. Two years later, Jack was back in Galveston, and ironically it was in Harmony Hall, the handsome Victorian venue where Wright's funeral service had taken place, that Johnson and Jewish American boxer Joe Choyinski fought three rounds of an illegal match before the Texas Rangers stopped the fight.[122] In 1900, the Black community would still have been smarting from Wright's ignominious defeat by the Lily-White Republicans, and Wright's death may have led Johnson to consider abandoning boxing for politics; shortly after the fight with Choyinski, Johnson ran successfully for president of the Twelfth Ward Republican Club.[123]

Waring Cuney's poem about the boxer seems to draw parallels between his challenges and successes and those of the Cuney family in Texas. Written in 1962 at the beginning of the Black Arts Movement (BAM), "My Lord, What a Morning" was first published in Rosey Pool's anthology *Beyond the Blues*. In 1973, critic Bernard Bell praised the poem in *Black World* magazine, a major BAM venue. Bell cited Cuney's ironic use of the spiritual in the violent context of American racism; he also emphasized the importance that boxing held for Black men of Johnson's generation as a way to combat poverty and prejudice.[124] Jack Johnson was a symbol of African American resistance, one that would have resonated with the militant readers of *Black World*.

It is clear that Jack Johnson held a special significance for Waring Cuney. Despite the passage of time between Johnson's victory and the poem, the energy is palpable as Cuney exults in his "feeling . . . / When Jack Johnson / Turned Jim Jeffries' / Lily-white face / Up to the ceiling." The line is an unmistakable reference to the sabotage of Norris Wright Cuney's political career by the Lily-White faction of the Republican Party. Structuring his poem like the famous spiritual, Cuney also subverts Judeo-Christian tenets, acknowledging that "fighting is wrong," but imploring the Lord to make an exception and "take care of Jack . . . As you made him / Big, and strong and black." Paradoxically, Cuney positions religious faith alongside anger and protest aimed at racial discrimination.

This paradox was brought home in national marches and protests during the Civil Rights struggle and again in 2021 in the demonstrations against the murder of George Floyd; in both situations the clergy was actively engaged. Coincidentally, Floyd had a connection to both Jack Johnson and Norris Wright Cuney. Floyd grew up in Cuney Homes, the Houston public housing project named after Norris Wright Cuney. In the eulogy, Reverend Al Sharpton cited Wright Cuney and Jack Johnson, both of whom died, albeit indirectly, as a result of racism and discrimination.[125]

In his poem about Jack Johnson, Cuney could have deplored any of the racially motivated attacks on the athlete's personal life or described his violent death in a car crash after being denied restaurant service while driving to visit his family in Galveston. However, he chose to focus on Johnson's greatest triumph, thus linking his success, against heavy odds, to the successes of Waring's own family in Galveston, which were equally unprecedented. Like Jack Johnson, the Cuneys achieved much, but they also endured major blows and setbacks. Among the more painful were Norris Wright's callous ejection from the Republican Party and the deaths of several family members, a few years later, in the devastating Galveston Hurricane of 1900.

The poem may also reflect the fact that Waring Cuney himself had endured setbacks and bitter disappointments in his life. The untimely death of his father when he was only seventeen and on the cusp of his educational career certainly affected him deeply. His inability to establish a career in music, his first love, weighed heavily on him. He was crushed, as he shared with his friend Langston Hughes, when his application to Officer Candidate School was rejected, despite his required college credit and an outstanding military record.[126] Nevertheless, Cuney persisted, writing and publishing poetry in the final months of his life. As his poem about Jack Johnson suggests, this tenacious and talented family endured and triumphed.

Chapter 2

Waring Cuney in Washington, DC

Development of a Poet

He was our teacher
In machine-shop,
At Armstrong High School
A long time ago,
The kind of teacher kids like.

—"April Funeral," circa 1957 (previously unpublished)

WARING CUNEY'S HIGH SCHOOL EXPERIENCE PROFOUNDLY shaped his intellectual and creative development. Upon graduation, he matriculated in several colleges but never found the same connection and rapport with his instructors that he enjoyed at Armstrong Manual Training School. Waring, his twin brother Norris Wright III, and 109 others graduated in June 1923.[1] Washington schools were segregated, and of the high schools only Armstrong and its college preparatory sister school, M Street High School, admitted Black students. However, the District of Columbia was in the vanguard of African American education: in 1902 it had commissioned architect Waddy Butler Wood to design Armstrong's imposing Renaissance Revival building. Behind the school's sturdy brick walls and decorative metal doors, Waring and his classmates benefitted from a talented, dedicated faculty and found a refuge from the racism rampant in much of the nation's capital. Throughout his life, Waring kept in touch with his teachers and occasionally wrote poems about them; his fondness for his alma mater is apparent in his elegiac "April Funeral," written on the death of his former teacher, Mr. Clarence F. Keyes (1880–1957), a DC native and World War I Navy veteran. An enthusiastic member of Armstrong's military Cadet Corps, Waring would follow Mr. Keyes's example, enlisting in the US Army and serving in the South Pacific during World War II.

This chapter examines William Waring Cuney's life and the development of his poetry in the context of his family, his cultural milieu, his education, and his friends and neighbors, including childhood friend Ralph Clarke Wright, as well as his friendship with Langston Hughes and his participation in the literary salon of Georgia Douglas Johnson. The chapter also explores Cuney's maternal forebears, the Waring family, and their influence on his career in music and literature.

Waring and Wright would always think of their parents' residence at 503 Florida Avenue NW in Washington, DC, as home, but their Texas roots were close to the surface. Their father, Norris Wright II, lived with his parents, brother Richard, and sisters May and Daisy in Galveston until the age of twenty. Richard worked for their father in his painting and decorating business and eventually took a job with the Post Office, while Norris Wright II worked as a clerk with C. W. Preston Druggist & Chemist.[2] Preston was a prominent Galvestonian, and his drugstore on Market Street was one of city's largest. As an active Mason with an interest in education, he certainly knew the brothers' uncle, Norris Wright Cuney. A former Grand Master of the Prince Hall Masons, Wright Cuney was then a leader of the Texas Republican Party and, as Collector of Customs for the Port of Galveston, held the highest federal office of any African American in the country. A former city alderman, a member of the Water Board, and an advocate for the establishment of Central High School, Wright

Cuney worked assiduously for civic improvements and for the education of Galveston's students of color. With the rise of the Texas Lily-White movement in 1891 and an increase in racial tension, opportunities for Galveston's young people of color were limited, and it was undoubtedly through Wright's connections that his nephews obtained their jobs. However, the family expected the younger generation to pursue higher education. In the summer of 1891, Wright's daughter Maud left Galveston for Newport, Rhode Island, where she would vacation with friends before moving to Boston to attend the New England Conservatory of Music. A few years later, her brother Lloyd Garrison departed for Austin's Tillotson College, where he would prepare for the ministry of the Congregational Church. Norris Wright II, meanwhile, was saving money for his own educational experience.

In 1895, Norris Wright II took his earnings from Preston's drugstore and followed in the footsteps of his Uncle Joseph, moving to Washington, DC. Immediately after his service in the Civil War, and while still housed in "Union Barracks in Washington," Joseph had enrolled in the First Year Preparatory Course at Howard University. After completing the program, he enrolled in Howard's Law School and received his law degree in 1872.[3] Now, twenty years later, his nephew was matriculating at Howard University; perhaps influenced by his work in the pharmacy, he had decided to pursue a career in medicine. The Howard University Catalogue for 1895 shows that Norris Wright Cuney of Galveston, Texas, was a first-year student in Howard's Medical School. A testimony to the rigorous curriculum of the school was its high attrition rate: there were thirty-three freshmen, twenty-eight juniors, and only eleven seniors. Norris Wright, however, was well-prepared for college. Galveston's Central High School, whose principals included Dartmouth graduate Champion J. Waring and Wilberforce graduate John R. Gibson, offered a robust college preparatory track that included Latin, algebra, and rhetoric.[4]

For whatever reason, Norris Wright II did not complete his medical degree. Instead, he transferred to the law school, where he studied from 1900 to 1903, while working in the US Government Printing Office (GPO).[5] This proved to be a propitious decision. At the GPO, he rose through the ranks, ensured his family a comfortable living, and encouraged his sons and other relatives to follow the printing trade. From its inception shortly after the Civil War, under the leadership of Lincoln appointee John Defrees, the GPO demonstrated progressive employment practices, including the hiring of women employees.[6] Defrees, a journalist and ardent abolitionist from Tennessee, was committed to the advancement of African Americans. He once suggested that President Lincoln "send a message to Congress recommending the passage of a joint resolution proposing an amendment to the Constitution forever prohibiting slavery in the States and territories."[7] Lincoln drily assured him the plan was already under consideration.

Defrees's inclusive hiring practices provided a secure career path for many people of color and helped to establish Washington's Black middle class, and his values and precedents endured through the years. In 1911, in response to a complaint about Black masons employed on a building project, the supervisor at the time, Samuel B. Donnelly, firmly maintained the GPO's inclusive policies, stating: "there are 400 Negro employees in the Government Printing Office . . . [who] work in the various departments side-by-side with other employees. . . . I wish to declare with all emphasis that any employee of this department who tries to precipitate the devilish stricture of race prejudice will be immediately dismissed and will not again be employed."[8] Social and leisure activities at the GPO were still segregated, including a white bowling league and a Black baseball team, but employment was strictly inclusive. Thus, it would appear that Norris Wright II made a wise decision in moving to Washington, DC, and establishing himself in the GPO, since he also met his future bride, Madge Louise Williamson, in the city.

In his pioneering histories "The Waring Family" and "The Cuney Family"—which appeared, respectively, in the February and March 1948 issues of *Negro History Bulletin*—Carter G. Woodson traces the accomplishments and genealogy of Waring Cuney's forebears. Waring's mother Madge Williamson was an ardent family historian, and it was probably to her that Woodson turned for the photographs and anecdotes used in the articles. Madge Louise Williamson of Columbus, Ohio, like her future husband, had traveled East for schooling. After their parents' deaths, Madge, her sisters Maud Baker and Jeannette (Jennie) Williamson, and their younger brothers, moved to Washington. Madge's cousin Carolyn French noted in a 1981 letter, "One hundred years ago my great grandfather [William Waring III] took his sister's orphaned children from Ohio to Washington to educate them. One of them was Cousin Madge."[9] The Williamson sisters were intelligent and musical. Jennie attended Howard and took private music lessons. In June 1896, Madge completed the four-year academic course for the Colored Normal and High Schools. Her friend and classmate Edith Genevieve Wormley (who would later become Waring's relative by marriage) completed the scientific course of four years.[10] The following year Madge matriculated at Howard; as shown in the University Catalog for 1897, Madge Louise Williamson of Columbus, Ohio, was an undergraduate majoring in English. It is highly likely that Madge and Norris Wright met on the Howard campus.

Madge, like Norris Wright II, hailed from an enterprising and accomplished family with roots in Virginia. The Waring family began around 1750 with the birth of Scotsman William Waring; as a young man he immigrated to Essex County, Virginia, where he met bondswoman Arrica Vessels. With Vessels, whom he later manumitted, William had seven children, all born in Essex County, Virginia: David, Susan, Rosetta, William II, Maria, Henry, and Arthur. William II and his wife Lavenia Crutchfield were the parents of eleven, including William III—a minister, Union soldier, and Howard University trustee—and his younger sister Maria Louisa Waring, an Oberlin College graduate and schoolteacher.

Maria Louisa Waring was Waring Cuney's maternal grandmother. With her first husband, Noah Baker, whom she married in Columbus,

Ohio, in June 1867, Maria had three children: twin sons Schuyler (who died as an infant) and Lowell, and a daughter Maud. After Noah Baker's death she remarried in December 1874, this time to Thomas J. Williamson II, a Civil War veteran and carpenter originally from Madison, Tennessee, a rural settlement north of Nashville.[11] She had five children with Thomas. In 1885, the household included Lowell Waring (age 17), Maud Crutchfield (age 16), Jeannette Crutchfield (age 9), Madge Louise (age 7), Annie (age 6), Thomas III (age 4), and Walter Waring (age 2). The Williamsons resided in a multiracial neighborhood in Columbus at 258 East Gay Street, a few miles south of Ohio State University. There they provided a stable, middle-class upbringing for their children, who attended integrated neighborhood schools.

After high school the oldest child, Lowell, apprenticed with his father as a carpenter. By 1896 he was an instructor of carpentry at Wilberforce University in Ohio, where he lived with his wife, son, and daughter; in 1904, after passing a civil service exam, he began working as an architect and construction superintendent for the federal government.[12] His sister Annie died in childhood and their brother Thomas III worked in real estate in Detroit. Walter studied at Howard University and then moved to Chicago, where he married Ruby Lowry of Superior, Wisconsin, and had a son and daughter. After an accident resulted in the loss of two fingers on his right hand, the family spent a year in Brazil, from December 1916 to February 1917, where Walter received medical care. Back in Chicago, he worked as a civilian employee with the US Army and as a clerk for the US Post Office.[13] The three sisters, Maud, Jennie, and Madge, attended Howard University and became schoolteachers.

Following in the footsteps of her mother, Maud C. Baker was a pioneering teacher and administrator. Born in 1869 and educated in Columbus's public schools, she was among the first cohort of middle-class African American students to attend integrated schools. In 1882, the Columbus Board of Education ordered the city's public schools integrated, a full seventy-two years before the US Supreme

Court ruled segregated schools unconstitutional. However, presaging much of post–*Brown v. Board of Education* America, due to redlining and other acts of white resistance, de facto segregation continued. Maud received her baccalaureate from Howard University in 1888 and promptly began her career as a public schoolteacher.[14] That year the Columbus City Directory listed her as a teacher residing at 98 North Washington Avenue.[15] She taught initially at Columbus's Stevenson School and then transferred to Champion Junior High School. At Champion she worked first as a teacher and then as principal from 1910 to 1920. She then taught in Chicago and subsequently retired with a pension.[16] As principal, Maud Baker was one of the few Black women to lead an urban school in the North, a position virtually unheard of in the South.

Maud's younger half-sisters, Jennie and Madge, upon completion of their degrees at Howard, taught in the DC public schools. The 1940 US federal census shows that Madge and her daughter-in-law completed four years of college, while her twin sons, Norris Wright III and Waring, completed two. For the late nineteenth and early twentieth centuries this was a major accomplishment, for as late as 1940 less than 2 percent of Black women held college degrees. Jennie, like Maud, never married, but Madge was smitten by a dashing young Texan with a secure government job: Norris Wright Cuney II.

During their courtship Norris Wright II was a frequent visitor at the R Street NW home of Dr. William Conner, a physician, and Mrs. Conner, where Jennie and Madge were boarders. After a brief engagement, the couple married on August 21, 1905, in Washington. He was thirty-three and she was twenty-seven; the following year, on Sunday, May 6, they welcomed the twins, Norris Wright III and William Waring.[17] Shortly afterwards, the couple became homeowners. In 1907, secure in Norris Wright's salary as a foreman for the GPO and Madge's as a teacher, they purchased a $2,675 three-bedroom, 1,400-square-foot row house in LeDroit Park, a middle-class neighborhood a few blocks south of Howard University.[18] The three-story brick house, still located at 503 Florida Avenue NW, was built in 1900 and adorned with a bow window and a turret; it was conveniently situated six blocks southeast of Norris Wright's job at the GPO on North Capitol Street.

Waring and Wright Cuney were raised on Florida Avenue in a multigenerational household. After his wife's death in the Galveston Hurricane of 1900, Grandfather Nelson Cuney joined the family in Washington. He must have spoken often of his late wife, the devout and spiritual Laura Glover Cuney; many years later, Waring dedicated a group of religious poems to his paternal grandmother. Madge's sister, Jeanette (Jennie) C. Williamson, also lived with the family. It was Aunt Jennie who taught the brothers the piano and sparked their lifelong interest in music.[19] Some credit for musical talent must also be given to the Cuney family. The twins may have inherited their skills from Great-Uncle Norris Wright Cuney, who sang and played the bass fiddle. His daughter, Maud Cuney Hare of Boston, frequently passed through Washington en route to concerts at which she provided piano accompaniment for the Canadian baritone, William H. Richardson. Maud seems to have taken a particular interest in Waring, and she would encourage him to follow in her footsteps and enroll in the New England Conservatory of Music. Maud was especially close to her cousins by marriage, Madge and Jennie; the three women travelled in the same social circles and often vacationed together on Maryland's Chesapeake Bay.

Although Waring's parents, Madge and Norris Wright II, were not wealthy, they were active members of the exclusive, close-knit society of African American families along the East Coast from Boston to Newport, New York, and Washington, DC. In 1905, Madge and Wright's friends included the Wormleys, Murrays, and Terrells of Washington, as well as the Butler Wilsons, Dabneys, Hemmings, and Ruffins of Boston. They also socialized with Wright's Cuney cousins Charles Sumner and Lloyd Garrison who had relocated from Galveston. In 1903, Madge and Jennie, along with Maud Cuney Hare and her brother, Lloyd Garrison Cuney, attended the society wedding of Annie Smith and George Dabney of Boston. Annie was the daughter of the former Librarian to the House of Representatives and a classmate of Maud Cuney's at the New England Conservatory. Jennie Williamson played the "Wedding March." These intertwined families faithfully attended each other's baptisms, graduations, weddings, and funerals.

Madge and Norris Wright's next-door neighbors, the Wrights, were also young professionals and newlyweds. John Ralph and Gertrude Clarke Wright had married on July 1, 1905, a month before Madge and Wright, and like the Cuneys they had a young son.[20] John worked as a law clerk at the Department of Justice. Their son Ralph and the twins, who were born a year apart (April 18, 1907, and May 6, 1906), grew up together and became best friends. Ralph, an honors graduate of Dunbar High School, became a physician, and his wife, Carolyn, a schoolteacher.[21] John, Gertrude, Madge, Jennie, Wright II, and Wright III lived in the Florida Avenue homes the remainder of their lives.[22] After five years of marriage, Ralph and Carolyn had saved enough to purchase a two-bedroom house a block away at 514 T Street NW; however, he continued using 505 Florida Avenue as his doctor's office.[23] Waring also eventually moved away, although he returned to his parents' home periodically for extended stays.

During the early nineteenth century, Florida Avenue, then named Boundary Street, constituted the city's northern border. Boundary Street ran east to west and traversed LeDroit Park, "a beautiful little village" founded in 1873 as "an exclusively white suburb situated on the edge of the city."[24] Abutting LeDroit Park to the northeast was Howard Town, a Black residential community founded in 1870, adjacent to Howard University. As was typical of Black communities, Howard Town contained a mixture of working-class and higher-income families, many of whom were staff and faculty at Howard. The developers of LeDroit Park apparently had the residents of Howard Town in mind when they "encircled their sub-division with a combined cast-iron and wood fence, complete with imposing gates on all street entrances and a watchman who was 'to keep out intruders and undesirables.'"[25] As the city's population grew, its boundaries expanded; by 1890 Boundary Street was no longer the northern border and it was renamed Florida Avenue.

Between 1893 and 1894 two African American families managed to purchase homes in LeDroit Park. Unfortunately, the first residents, Missouri and Octavius A. Williams, a barber who worked at the Capitol, and their infant daughter Vivian, were greeted with violence. Years later, Mrs. Vivian Williams Pelham recalled her father telling her, "Just after we moved in and were having dinner one night someone fired a bullet through the window." She noted that her father "left the bullet in the wall for years so his grandchildren could see it."[26] At her passing in 1938, Mrs. Missouri B. Williams, a member of the Phillis Wheatley Society and grandmother of Maureen and Harryette, still resided in the family home at 338 U Street NW in LeDroit Park.[27]

Following the Williams in purchasing a house in LeDroit Park were Robert and Mary Church Terrell, a young couple beginning their married life and careers in the city. They had met at the legendary M Street School (later Dunbar High) where Mary Church, an Oberlin College graduate, taught Latin and Robert, a Harvard graduate and Howard University–trained lawyer, served as principal. They married shortly afterwards in 1891. In her autobiography, *A Colored Woman in a White World,* Terrell, or "Lady Mollie" as she was affectionately dubbed, described the challenges she encountered while seeking to purchase her first home. She had found the perfect six-room house on the border of Howard Town and LeDroit Park; because the house was adjacent to Howard Town, Terrell did not expect any objections. She was chagrined to hear from a decorated Civil War veteran about the infamous fence that the whites had built "to separate their bailiwick from Howard Town, so their colored neighbors could not walk through LeDroit Park on their way to the city. Every night the fence was kicked down by the colored people."[28] Nevertheless,

Terrell persisted and, with the help of the white proprietor of "an old, well-established real estate firm" she obtained the house.[29] Her friend induced a wealthy businessman, who was also sympathetic to the race and who employed a colored secretary, to purchase the house and resell it to the Terrells.

A few years later, Terrell wanted a larger home in the same neighborhood, but "was shown nothing but residences which had been discarded by discriminating people because they were old-fashioned and devoid of modern improvements."[30] Again, she encountered blatant prejudice before finally acquiring a house for which she was obliged to pay several thousand dollars more than the asking price. To her satisfaction, however, the house was on the same street as the former homes of Presidents Wilson and Hoover; in addition, more families of color were moving to the gracious homes in LeDroit Park. By 1907, when Norris Wright II and Madge purchased their home at 503 Florida Avenue, African Americans had established LeDroit Park as part of the city's U Street District, a commercial and residential neighborhood similar to Harlem in New York and Roxbury in Boston.

Although their homes in LeDroit Park were modern and well-appointed, the Cuneys and their friends, like their white counterparts, sought to avoid Washington's humid, sweltering summers. Storer College in Harpers Ferry, West Virginia, was a popular holiday destination for the city's African American elite. Founded by the Freedman's Bureau and the New England Freewill Baptists in 1867, the school was endowed by Maine philanthropist and patron of Bates College, John Storer, with the stipulation that it welcome all races. Storer Normal School became the center of a thriving African American summer colony. Boardinghouses and cottages, nestled among the picturesque hills, provided vacation lodgings, and Black families who wished to do so were encouraged to purchase lots from the college. For several years, Judge and Mary Church Terrell and their family enjoyed lectures and concerts on the "sweeping lawn . . . an ideal playground for children."[31] Maud Cuney Hare was a close friend of Mary Terrell and in August 1906, Maud's friends from Boston, including W. E. B. Du Bois, Monroe Trotter, and the charismatic preacher Reverdy Ransom of the Charles Street A.M.E. Church, led the Niagara Movement's first public meeting at Storer College.

Another popular destination for the Cuneys and their friends was Highland Beach, located on the Chesapeake Bay, five miles from Annapolis. Maj. Charles Remond Douglass, a Civil War veteran and son of Frederick Douglass, purchased the 40-acre tract in 1893; he began building a home for his father so that Frederick Douglass, "a free man, could look across the Bay to the Eastern shore where I was born a slave."[32] The Terrells, the Wormleys, poet Paul Dunbar and his wife Alice, and Anna Julia Cooper bought adjacent lots.[33] Sadly, Frederick Douglass died before the house was completed, but Harriet Tubman, Charles Chesnutt, Georgia Douglas Johnson, Paul Robeson, Mary McLeod Bethune, W. E. B. Du Bois, Emmett Scott, and Booker T. Washington all vacationed in the community.[34] Madge Williamson and her sister Jennie first vacationed there as young schoolteachers in August 1903.[35] Later, the Williamson sisters, along with Madge's twin sons and her cousin-in-law, Maud Cuney Hare, enjoyed the sandy beach and the waters of Chesapeake Bay.[36] Waring Cuney would have remembered the rustic but charming accommodations: the cottages boasted stunning views of the bay from expansive screened porches but had no gas, electricity, or running water. The vacationers swam and sailed in the bay and picked the "Queen Anne's lace, goldenrod, black-eyed Susans, and tiger lilies [that] fringed the dirt roads."[37] At night the adults played the gramophone and danced sedately while the children "captured fireflies [and] spied Harriet Tubman's Drinking Gourd that pointed the way to Douglass's North Star."[38]

Back in Washington, the Cuney twins, Norris Wright III and Waring, enjoyed the proximity of a devoted extended family. Their father's first cousins, Charles Sumner Cuney (a lawyer like his father Joseph) and Lloyd Garrison Cuney (a bindery operator for the Government Printing Office and the son of Texas politician Norris

Wright Cuney), lived a few blocks away at 1940 11th Street NW and 144 Seaton Place NW. In 1911, Charles married Cora Townsend of Hamilton, Ohio, but they divorced a few years later without having children. After Norris Wright II's early death, Charles mentored and counseled the twins and became a bit of a surrogate father. In 1917, Lloyd Garrison Cuney, Maud Cuney's younger brother, married Jacqueline A. Smith (née Gary), a young widow from Birmingham, Alabama. The twins spent considerable time at the couple's home since their mother and Jacqueline Cuney were quite close. Like Madge, Jacqueline was active in public education and civic affairs. She served as president of the Bloomingdale Civic Association, as vice president and secretary of the District of Columbia Public Schools Association, and as a board member of the Phillis Wheatley YWCA.[39] In March 1952, area newspapers announced a testimonial dinner honoring Mrs. Mary Church Terrell, Mrs. Minnie L. Wright, Dr. Paul Cooke, and Mrs. Jacqueline A. Cuney, who were lauded as "four Negro civic leaders"; the dinner was held at Howard University, "with more than 300 persons attending."[40] Earlier, Jacqueline Cuney had testified before a US Senate subcommittee and secured $10,000 in supplemental funding for Shaw Junior High, an all-Black school south of LeDroit Park.[41]

Among the Cuneys' LeDroit Park neighbors, the Wormleys, descendants of hotel magnate James Wormley, would play a paramount role in the family's history. In 1871, with the help of his wife Anna, James Wormley had opened an elegant five-story 150-room hotel on the corner of 15th and H Streets NW. Reportedly the first integrated hotel in Washington, it anchored a business empire that included a candy shop, a catering service, and extensive real estate.[42] Politician Wright Cuney would certainly have patronized the hotel on his many visits to Washington in connection with his leadership of the Texas Republican Party. The Wormleys were the parents of three sons and a daughter: William Henry, James Thompson, Garrett Smith, and Anna Matilda. After James Wormley's death in 1884, his son James Thompson Wormley, a pharmacist and graduate of Howard

University's Medical School, managed Wormley's Hotel until the family sold it in 1893.[43] Laura Amelia Wormley, Norris Wright III's wife and Waring Cuney's sister-in-law, was a great-granddaughter of James and Anna Wormley and a granddaughter of their third son, Garrett Smith Wormley. Garrett Smith, a school principal and Howard graduate, and his wife Amelia[44] were the parents of Garrett N. Wormley, who later married Laura Amelia's mother, Cora Nickens.

In this distinguished family, Laura Amelia's father, Garrett, was the unfortunate exception. Cora Nickens was the second of his three wives. Although married to Cora, Garrett was arrested in June 1909 and charged with propositioning a white woman. At the time, Garrett had established Cora, their seven-year-old son Julian, and two-year-old daughter Amelia at 1305 Hamlin Street NE, a newly developed, semirural area near Catholic University.[45] As reported in the Washington, DC, *Evening Star*: "Wormley sent a letter containing alleged obscene matters through the mails to the home address of [a] female clerk. The letter indicates that he had previously attempted to attract the attention of the clerk by a former epistle without success. The writer seeks to persuade the clerk to meet him at Dupont Circle or out Massachusetts avenue extended after 6 o'clock. He advises her to be heavily veiled and to take a coupe at the circle."[46] In his defense, Wormley, who could easily have passed as white, protested that he was as fair-skinned as the object of his affections and insisted that the affair was consensual. In fact, the designated trysting spot on Dupont Circle, the heart of affluent, segregated white Washington, speaks to Wormley's confidence at passing and to his defiance of racial boundaries. However, that his race would even be introduced into the case speaks to the fraught issue of passing and to the determination of white Washington to draw the color line.

With news of his arrest and conviction awash in the press, Garrett moved to Michigan and in January 1912 filed for divorce from Cora. Although he discontinued the action four months later, on May 4, and attempted a reconciliation, it was not successful.[47] Cora, who must have been heartbroken and humiliated, took the children from their home in the bucolic northeast section of the city and relocated to 1013 U Street NW, in the considerably less affluent, predominantly African American, U Street district. At the end of the year, tragedy struck. As reported in the *Washington Times*: "Cora Wormley, colored, was found dying in a second-floor front room at her home . . . early today, having swallowed carbolic acid. An ambulance was summoned but she was pronounced dead."[48] One can only hope that she was not found by Amelia and her little brother.

Meanwhile, Garrett was officially passing for white. On June 24, 1914, now age forty-two and working in Detroit as a cook, he took a third wife, Emily F. Russell, who was also able to pass. The marriage took place in Ann Arbor, and both were listed as white and never previously married.[49] Their son John Gearit Wormley was born in Ann Arbor on December 25, 1915.[50] By 1920, Emily and her son were living with her widowed father, John J. Russell, in Ann Arbor. The fluidity of racial parameters can be seen in the fact that Emily is now listed as married and Negro, but Garrett is not in the home.[51]

With their mother deceased and their father lost to the race and living in Michigan, Julian and Amelia were embraced by Garrett's siblings, who brought them to Philadelphia. Four-year-old Amelia lived with her aunt Edith Wormley Minton and her husband Dr. Henry McKee Minton, a physician and superintendent of Philadelphia's Mercy Hospital.[52] However, she returned to DC for middle school. In June 1922, she graduated from Garnet-Patterson's eighth grade and then entered Dunbar High.[53] While in Washington, she lived with her uncle Clarence Sumner Wormley, a dentist, and Clarence's aunt Martha W. Bell at 997 Florida Avenue NW, just a few blocks away from the 503 Florida Avenue home of the handsome and witty Cuney twins, Norris Wright III and Waring.[54]

Why Amelia Wormley returned to Washington is unclear, although the family probably decided she should attend Dunbar High, successor to the famous M Street School. Like its predecessor, Dunbar was renowned for its world-class faculty. During Amelia's four years at the school, Dr. Anna Julia Cooper taught Latin; Dr. Eva Dykes taught English; Mary Loraine Europe, the pianist and younger sister of bandleader James Reese Europe, served on the music faculty. The Harlem Renaissance playwright Mary P. Burrill, Angelina Weld Grimké's partner, taught English, as did Clarissa M. Scott.[55]

Clarissa Scott, like Waring Cuney, had Texas forebears and was a Harlem Renaissance poet. A Phi Beta Kappa graduate of Wellesley College, Clarissa was the daughter of Emmett Jay Scott, secretary to Booker T. Washington, and Eleanor Baker Scott. After Washington's death, Emmett Scott left Tuskegee and served as secretary treasurer of Howard University from 1919 to 1933.[56] Before joining Washington at Tuskegee in 1897, Scott, a Houston native, had worked as secretary to Waring's great-uncle Wright Cuney in Houston and Galveston.[57] Clarissa Scott left Dunbar High in 1926, upon her marriage to attorney Hubert T. Delany, and moved to New York City.[58] She appears in most critical assessments of the Harlem Renaissance as Clarissa Scott Delany. Her husband was a brother of the famous Delany sisters, Sadie and Bessie, and uncle of the writer Samuel R. Delany.

Clarissa Delany's student, Amelia Wormley, was a member of the Dunbar High School class of 1926. The class yearbook features Angelina Grimké's sonnet "To the Dunbar High School" and a photograph of each of the 182 graduating seniors.[59] Next to Amelia's senior portrait is the inscription,

> Amelia is quite fascinating, and coquettish 'tis true;
> If left all alone, she is solemn and blue.

As evidenced in the photograph, Amelia was a beautiful, albeit wistful, young woman. It is tempting to speculate that losing her parents at such a young age, and her mother to suicide, may have caused her to remain "solemn and blue." The inscription ends, noting that she plans to become a teacher and intends "To enter Miner Normal School."[60]

Meanwhile, like their neighbor Amelia Wormley, the Cuney twins were also thinking about their futures. Given the fact that both of their parents had attended Howard University, one might have expected the brothers to enroll in the academic Dunbar High School. However, perhaps because their father felt that printing was a good career choice and because the twins were musical, they were sent to Armstrong Manual Training School. The technical and vocational institution was named for Samuel Chapman Armstrong, a white general who led the 8th US Colored Troops during the Civil War. First opened in 1902, the school taught trades such as printing, bricklaying, carpentry, and blacksmithing. The prestigious African American institution boasted an excellent music department; famous alumni include Duke Ellington and Billy Eckstine. There, Waring studied voice and piano as well as English and physics, and he helped found the science club; brother Norris Wright III studied English and piano and, like his father, learned the printing trade.

Armstrong and Dunbar High were adjacent, each in an imposing brick building, on 1st and O Streets NW. There, the two student bodies famously congregated, visiting before and after school. The brothers found academic and social success at Armstrong. Charismatic and outgoing, Waring participated in the Science Club, the Memorial Committee, and the Junior ROTC.[61] In 1922, he was elected president of the senior class; the following year, on Tuesday night, June 19, the school held its twenty-second annual commencement exercises. Waring graduated at the top of the class and won a scholarship to Howard University.[62]

The celebration and festivities, though joyful, were attenuated by changes occurring in the Cuney household. Three months before graduation, tragedy struck. On Saturday, March 24, 1923, the twins' father, Norris Wright II, died; the funeral was held the following Tuesday at the Florida Avenue residence.[63] Madge Cuney insisted, however, that her sons continue with their college plans. That fall, Waring and Norris matriculated at Howard, Norris Wright III in the School of Music and Waring in the College of Liberal Arts. Waring concentrated in literature but also pursued his interests in science and studied with the pioneering biologist, Dr. Ernest Just, who described him as "a man of excellent character and fine spirit."[64] The family suffered an additional loss in November, with the death of the twins' paternal grandfather John Nelson Cuney, in Galveston, Texas. Eighty-four-year-old Nelson had been living in Washington with Norris Wright II and his family; however, after the February 1921 death of his youngest brother, Henry Ernest Cuney, in Washington, he returned to Texas.

The loss of their father must have proven especially difficult for the twins. It may have left them unfocused and unable to adjust to college; after two years, Waring lost his scholarship. With his widowed mother unable to finance two Howard tuitions, Waring transferred to Lincoln University, near Philadelphia, since one had "plenty of time there to read and write" and "the tuition was cheaper than at Howard."[65] Waring's brother also left Howard, but rather than transfer to another university, he began teaching printing, first at the Phelps Trade School and later at Armstrong.

Wright's decision to seek employment may also have been influenced by his desire to take a bride. He had fallen in love with and become inseparable from his beautiful young neighbor, Amelia Wormley. Upon learning of their engagement, Waring was elated but not surprised. Norris Wright III and Amelia married on Christmas Eve 1933 in Washington's 15th Street Presbyterian Church; he was twenty-seven and she was twenty-six. The church's pastor, Rev. Francis J. Grimké, officiated.[66] Waring wrote excitedly to a friend, "my brother [is] married." He added, "Washington is still a very pretty city, in fact it is more beautiful than ever. . . . But I never stay there very long."[67]

In the summer of 1925, on a visit to his mother and brother, Waring met Langston Hughes by chance on a Washington streetcar. Throughout the summer, Cuney and Hughes, along with Bruce

Nugent, an aspiring graphic artist, a graduate of Dunbar High School, and a school buddy of Waring's, formed an iconoclastic trio. Hughes wrote to Carl Van Vechten that he had met "a couple of interesting fellows about my own age—one a pianist and the other an artist."[68] The three amused themselves by "going downtown to the white theatres 'passing' for South Americans" and by annoying conservative African American Washington by "walking up Fourteenth Street barefooted on warm evenings for the express purpose of shocking the natives."[69] Although Cuney's and Hughes's bohemian behavior apparently stopped at this point, Nugent created further scandal by his flagrantly queer performance; after a visit to Washington, Jessie Fauset warned Hughes that association with Nugent could hurt his literary reputation.

The initial meeting would prove propitious for both men. Cuney sang the praises of Lincoln University, and in October 1925 he sent Hughes an application, noting, in an apparent reference to the racial makeup of the teachers, "Our faculty is *fair*." As Hughes would soon learn, this was an understatement: the school was rigidly segregated, the students all Black and the faculty, administrators, and trustees all white. Cuney further assured his friend of the accomplishments of the faculty, stating, "There are only three members who have not Phi Beta Kappa Keys."[70] Apparently convinced, Hughes matriculated the following February, joining a student body that in addition to Cuney included the future Supreme Court Justice Thurgood Marshall (class of 1930). Funded by his "secret benefactress," the poet and National Association for the Advancement of Colored People (NAACP) official Amy Spingarn, Hughes remained at Lincoln for three and a half years, graduating in June 1929.[71]

Despite their solidly middle-class upbringing, Cuney and Hughes spent much of their time on Washington's raucous Seventh Street, and it was here that Waring and Langston, like their friends, Jean Toomer and Sterling Brown, found inspiration for their urban poetry. Hughes lived with his cousins, who resided in elegant LeDroit Park. Waring had always enjoyed close and fulfilling relationships with his parents' friends and neighbors, but Hughes found LeDroit Park residents "unbearable and snobbish" and the denizens of Seventh Street "a sweet relief."[72] Similarly, despite his refined upbringing, Waring's poetry reveals his affinity to the rough, vibrant Seventh Street, described by Hughes as "the long, old, dirty street, where the ordinary Negroes . . . played the blues, ate watermelon . . . and fish sandwiches, shot pool, told tall tales, looked at the dome of the Capitol and laughed out loud."[73] Waring, however, did not romanticize the poverty and raffish atmosphere as did Hughes; rather he focused on the economic destitution and lack of opportunity for the neighborhood's residents. His first famous poem, "No Images," was probably inspired by scenes he had witnessed on Seventh Street. Similarly, his poem "Side Street" depicts the neighborhood's hopeless environment in the back alleys:

> Here where cupboards are empty
> And walls are bare
> And children go hungry
> With no clothes to wear —
> Life has a greedy heart too
> Broken to care.

Waring would continue to write on societal and governmental indifference to obstacles faced by the poor, in poems such as "Hard Time Blues" and "Nineteen-Twenty-Nine." In fact, protest against discrimination, institutionalized racism, and economic inequality would emerge as major themes in his poetry.

Like Hughes, Cuney created nuanced portraits of people he encountered in the bars, pool halls, and blues clubs of Seventh Street. The local character, Beasley Daniels, two years younger than Waring, was a personal favorite; poet Sterling Brown also memorialized Daniels in verse. In Brown's "Sporting Beasley," Daniels appears in a "Tophat / . . . A red carnation; Prince Albert coat . . . / and a cane"; he struts to the front of the Howard Theater where, to the laughter of the audience, he pulls out his "opera glasses," bows, and takes a seat in Row A.[74] In contrast to Brown's realistic rendering of a flamboyant figure, Cuney's "Lord Daniels" transports the audience to a world of Afrofuturism and the speculative:

I dreamed I saw Lord Daniels
Standing at 12th and G —
He twirled a satellite
In his big black hand
Where his cane used to be,
He wore a space suit
In place of his cut-a-way.
He looked up and down
He looked all around,
Then he said,
    Hey! Hey!
    Hey! Hey!

Every time he saw an ofay

Fit and nearly six feet tall, Daniels was born on December 27, 1908, to farmers Arthur and Fannie Daniels in Davis Station, South Carolina. He moved to Washington as a teen, before settling in the nineteen thirties with his younger brother Moses in Baltimore, Maryland.[75] Both poems acquaint us with a man who lived an ordinary life but who managed, if only for a moment, to replace insults and misery with splendor and dignity.

In addition to everyday people like Beasley Daniels, Cuney wrote on popular performers like blues singer Bessie Smith, jazz saxophonist Charlie Parker, and blues and ragtime pianist Ferdinand "Jelly Roll" Morton, most of whom he witnessed during their visits to Washington's Seventh Street. Like the poet Jean Toomer, he was able to imaginatively recreate and transmute their performances into poetry. For Toomer, "Seventh Street [was] a bastard of Prohibition and the War," breathing its "jazz songs and love, thrusting unconscious rhythms."[76] The lyrics and rhythms are not meant to be consumed and understood by those outside of the culture, as Cuney's "Jelly Roll and Lucky" makes clear, although people outside of the culture do indeed consume and may understand them. The poem opens to Jelly Roll Morton playing "Twelfth Street Rag," which tells the listener

soup
can't carry
in a
paper bag.

It ends with Charles Luckeyeth "Lucky" Roberts playing "Railroad Blues":

it
tells you
dimes
and nickels
add up
ones and twos.

Apparently, the poor, lacking funds to purchase a bowl of soup, try instead to purchase a bag. With the stanzas in dialogue, part two offers a solution, as saving dimes and nickels yields dollars. In this cryptic poem, Cuney uses the blues as voice and metaphor for the disenfranchised.

On a more erudite and serious side, Cuney, Langston Hughes, and Bruce Nugent, along with Waring's brother Wright, were favorites of poet Georgia Douglas Johnson, to whose Saturday night literary salon they received much-coveted invitations. One Saturday night, the list of attendees included Mollie Gibson-Brewer (a French teacher), Grant Lucas, Effie Lee Newsome, Bruce Nugent, Rebekah West, Wright Cuney, E. C. Williams, B. K. Bruce, Glen Carrington, Jessie Fauset, Adella Parks, Frank Horne, and Zora Neale Hurston.[77] Johnson provided a nurturing but intellectually and aesthetically challenging atmosphere in which African American artists honed their craft; there, as Hughes recalled, they would "eat [her] cake and drink her wine and talk poetry and books and plays."[78] Cuney would memorialize Johnson in his 1960 poem, "Skies Less Grey."

The meeting with Langston Hughes proved to be propitious for Cuney's literary career, and it marked the beginning of a lifelong friendship between the two men. By the end of the summer, he had persuaded Langston to join him at Lincoln University, where he was studying literature and singing in the Glee Club. Encouraged by Langston, whose first book of poems, *The Weary Blues*, would soon be published, Cuney swiftly found success. Hughes probably introduced him to cultural influencers like Walter White and James Weldon Johnson and to philanthropists like Amy Spingarn, all of whom encouraged his work. In 1926, "No Images," his poem addressing alienation, cultural hegemony, and the self-image of Black women, shared first prize in the *Opportunity* journal contest.

Waring Cuney and his family were part of Washington, DC's elite professional class who devoted their lives to racial uplift. Waring's poetry, however, reflects his familiarity with less affluent sections of the city like the notorious Seventh Street, an area of vaudeville theaters, pool halls, bars, and cheap hotels. He was thirteen during the anti-Black riots on Seventh Street in the infamous "Red Summer" of 1919, an event that left thirty dead and was sadly repeated at the same location fifty years later, in the race riots of 1968. Unlike his friend Langston Hughes, who chafed against the city's "brown bourgeoisie," Cuney forged lifelong bonds with its artistic and politically engaged families who lived in LeDroit Park and the U Street corridor.

Chapter 3

A Woman Ahead of Her Time

Maud Cuney Hare in Boston

LANCELOT,
If you could see the garden now

—"Elaine," 1935

IN APRIL 1935, THE JOURNAL *OPPORTUNITY* PUBLISHED Waring Cuney's poem "Elaine." A variation on Tennyson's lyrical ballad about the eponymous heroine's unrequited love for the faithless Lancelot, the poem is a stylistic departure for Cuney. The medieval setting and imagery are quite unlike the social criticism of "Café Chantant," a disapproving look at the hedonism of Harlem nightclubbers in the midst of the Great Depression, which had been published a few months earlier in *The Crisis*. Nor does the poem's diction resemble the jazz-inflected "Play a Blues for Louise" (1929), in which a woman boards a fast train to Chicago in order to forget her faithless lover. "Elaine" is actually more akin to Countee Cullen's Keatsian sonnets than to Cuney's vernacular, proletarian poems which are often compared to those of Langston Hughes. However, despite the archaic language and mythical subject, there are significant differences between Tennyson's original and Cuney's variation. In "Lancelot and

Elaine" (1859) Tennyson depicts a fragile woman who, unable to win Lancelot from the sensual and married Guinevere, drowns herself. Tennyson's Elaine is voiceless: "Then like a ghost she lifted up her face / But like a ghost without the power to speak." In contrast, Cuney's Elaine speaks firmly and forcefully, addressing her lover in peremptory capital letters: "LANCELOT"; in fact, she is not dead at all, and it is Lancelot who is "love's ghost." Taking agency in the relationship, Elaine says: "I shall greet you / With love upon my face." Then, subverting Victorian propriety, she offers an eroticized invitation to her "garden," assuring him, "I shall not be a bitter host." In fact, the rhyme of "ghost" and "host" clearly contrasts Elaine's strength and control with Lancelot's frailty.

Several clues indicate that Waring's second cousin, Maud Estelle Cuney Hare (1874–1936), is the inspiration for "Elaine," and the poem seemingly alludes to Maud's complex history and unique personality. Of all his family, Maud Cuney Hare had a major, sustained influence on Waring's life and work. He had been close to her since childhood: she was his father's first cousin and a frequent visitor to their home in Washington, DC. She shared musical interests and social connections with his mother Madge Williamson Cuney and his aunt Jennie Williamson. The three women attended the same weddings and parties and had vacationed together at Highland Beach, the Chesapeake Bay summer community developed by the sons of Frederick Douglass. Since Maud was of his parents' generation, Waring referred to her as his aunt in a letter to Langston Hughes,[1] and it was probably she who encouraged Waring to leave Lincoln University in 1926 and study at the New England Conservatory of Music. In Boston, she introduced him to the Saturday Evening Quill Club where he read his poems and met lifelong friends, including Eugene Gordon, Dorothy West, and Helene Johnson. She also invited him to live with her and her husband in their home in Jamaica Plain. This chapter, in tracing the talented Maud Cuney Hare from Galveston to Boston, seeks to provide a deeper understanding of Waring Cuney's family and life.

Waring certainly knew of Maud's affinity for Tennyson's work and her passionate connection to nature. Tennyson had been one of her father's favorite poets, and she included two of his poems, "Old Yew" and "The Oak," in *The Message of the Trees,* her anthology of nature poetry (1918). In the same volume, she included two poems by a Victorian painter-poet closely associated with Tennyson, Dante Gabriel Rossetti: "The Trees in the Garden" and "A Young Fir-wood." Not only did she create an entire anthology on poems about trees, but she constantly referenced the trees and flowers of Galveston in the biography she wrote about her father. Thus, the extended metaphor of the garden in "Elaine" may be seen as an allusion to Maud's love of nature.

Maud's names and her circumstances in 1935 also suggest connections to the poem. Her middle name, Estelle, which she emphasized whenever possible, aurally suggests the name "Elaine." Given her father's love of Tennyson, one of his most popular poems, "Maud," may even have inspired her first name. The famous first line of that eponymous poem, "Come into the garden, Maud," is an invitation given by a man to a woman; however, in "Elaine," Cuney reverses the sex of the host, thus giving agency to the female speaker. When he wrote the poem, Cuney knew that Maud Estelle was terminally ill, and in fact she would pass away within months. Perhaps he sought to celebrate, albeit in an oblique way that preserved her privacy, the accomplishments of his artistic mentor as well as her ability to challenge the social, cultural, legal, political, and aesthetic conventions of the day. In a poem about a modern and self-actualized woman, Cuney seems to acknowledge the ways in which Maud Estelle had maintained the Victorian conventions of decorum and respectability even while subverting them in order to blaze her own path as a "New Woman."

In thinking about the visual imagery of the poem, Cuney may also have made a visual connection between Maud's exotic, Pre-Raphaelite beauty and the popular illustrations of Tennyson's work by his friend, Dante Gabriel Rossetti. Although Tennyson's poems seem old-fashioned today in their reification of gendered Victorian values, his work is inextricably linked to—and, ironically, subverted by—the illustrators of his books, whose iconography then redefined conventional standards of beauty. The group of avant-garde painters associated with Tennyson's poems include Dante Gabriel Rossetti, William Holman Hunt, and John Everett Millais; dubbed the "Pre-Raphaelite Brotherhood" (PRB), they specialized in bold, colorful interpretations of mythical, medieval, and biblical subjects. Although Tennyson purportedly disliked their choice of models with androgynous features and long, untamed hair, his publisher correctly anticipated that the illustrations would sell books. For their models, the PRB often chose darker skinned women with curly hair, such as Jane Morris or the Jamaican model Fanny Easton. In privileging the exotic, they eschewed the Anglo-Saxon features, pink complexions, sleek hair, and preternaturally tiny hands and feet preferred by other Victorian artists. In both their lives and art, the PRB rejected conventional depictions of femininity that reinforced "the social order and . . . [presented] British attitudes to race and class in a seemingly rational guise."[2] Their favorite models were tall women with high cheekbones, full lips, irregular noses, strong jaws, and large hands and feet.

In fact, Jane Morris, whom Maud Estelle resembled, was an early supermodel whose ubiquitous image, inspired by PRB paintings and disseminated through commercial advertising, helped create the more inclusive definition of beauty that permeated popular culture and would have been familiar to Waring's generation. Morris had piercing eyes, "a columnar neck, thick lips, a heavy mantle of hair [and] well-defined jawline and brow."[3] Her appearance recalls W.E.B. Du Bois's description of Maud as "lithe, imperious and more than merely beautiful . . . [her] eye unflinching, [her] courage unfaltering."[4] Like Jane, an unconventional artist and model who lived life on her own terms, Maud was tall and slim, with a long neck, large hands, masses of dark curly hair, a strong nose, full lips, and deep-set eyes. Certainly, the young W. E. B. Du Bois was smitten when he met Maud in Boston in 1891. In fact, he proposed marriage to the "tall, imperious brunette with gold-bronze skin, brilliant eyes, and coils of black hair."[5] It thus seems plausible that, in composing a poem to celebrate Maud Estelle Cuney Hare's life, legacy, and contribution to African American art, Waring Cuney drew upon a constellation of visual and aesthetic associations from both literature and popular culture.

Although born in 1906, Waring's cultural references, like Maud's, were essentially Victorian; however, as someone who chafed against social constraints, he would have recognized the ways in which Maud subverted Victorian values; she very much epitomized the quintessential New Woman, linked in popular culture with financial and sexual independence, and visually associated, as was Proust's Albertine, with mobility. Maud Estelle was highly mobile and an inveterate traveler. From her first voyage from Galveston to Newport, Rhode Island, and Boston, via the Mallory Steamship Line and the railway, she traversed the United States several times, lived briefly in Puerto Rico, and visited Mexico, Cuba, and the Virgin Islands. For an African American woman one generation removed from bondage, mobility and the freedom of travel would have resonated in political and historical terms. As a professional pianist, writer, musicologist, teacher, historian, journalist, anthologist, businesswoman, playwright, and biographer, Maud displayed agency and determination in everything she did. Not only did she create a successful musical career under the most discouraging circumstances, but she fought and won a bitter divorce and child custody battle and established a community theater and arts center. Although she married twice, Maud's personal life was not particularly happy: she seems never to have achieved the transcendent passion suggested by Tennyson's romantic lines, though Cuney's poem intimates that she was capable of such love.

Sadly, within a year of the publication of "Elaine," Maud Estelle was dead at the age of sixty-one. In 1936, Waring was living with his family in Washington, but he would have known that, even though her husband William Hare survived her, Maud had arranged to be transported to Texas and buried with her parents. Today, in an unmarked grave in Galveston's Lakeview Cemetery, Maud reposes next to Adelina Cuney (1855–1895) and Norris Wright Cuney (1846–1898). Her mother's modest stone flanks her father's imposing obelisk, erected by the Galveston Prince Hall Masons to commemorate the founder and first Grand Master of the Texas Lodge. Two of Maud's uncles, Joseph Cuney (1845–1928) and John Nelson Cuney (1839–1923), are buried nearby.[6]

The graves of Maud and her parents are only four miles from their home on Avenue L in Galveston's East End. Maud describes her "particularly happy" youth in the family's "modest" gingerbread dwelling in the Twelfth Ward. There, doted upon by her handsome father and affectionate mother, she and her "seven cousins" played in a garden full of oleanders and orange trees, three blocks from the white sand and pounding surf of the Gulf.[7]

The Cuney family was exceptionally close-knit. Maud maintained a lifelong connection to her first cousin, Waring's father, Norris Wright II. He in turn was particularly close to Maud's father, Wright Cuney, for whom he had been named, and the two shared a love of music and literature. Norris Wright II lived with his parents, Nelson and Laura, and his siblings, Richard, May, and Daisy, just a few blocks from Maud's house. Uncle Joseph also resided nearby with his wife Josephine Barber and his two sons, Joseph Junior (nicknamed Nisi) and Charles Sumner (called Philip). In addition to the Cuney relatives, Maud's maternal grandmother, Maria Dowdie, lived with Maud's family when she was not employed as a private nurse.[8]

Maud's biography of her father is the most important source of Cuney family history and is exceptionally reliable; many of the details she includes on the family and on her father's political career are easily corroborated from other sources. However, the family kept some dramatic secrets, and Maud did not betray them in her book. In the first place, she only mentions seven cousins and two uncles, but in reality, the family consisted of eleven first cousins, two aunts, and three uncles, not to mention an even closer relative who lived a few blocks from Maud's home on Avenue L. The absence of Uncle Henry Ernest is understandable since he left Texas in 1874 and lived in Washington, DC, and New York, but Aunts Laura and Virginia lived in Houston, thirty miles away. Four of her cousins are also missing from Maud's book: Virginia's two children Nellie and Cornelius McGee, Laura's daughter, May Carroll, and Nelson's daughter May Cuney. The latter omission is particularly puzzling since May and Maud, both born in 1874, would have grown up together. Maud does mention her grandmother, Adeline Stuart, but omits the fact that while Adeline lived with Virginia, she often visited her sons in Galveston. However, Maud had a very specific reason for eliding her relatives from the family narrative: her cousins May, Nellie, and Cornelius and her Aunts Virginia and Laura were all passing for white.

As Afro-Texans, the Cuneys certainly encountered challenges. After the Civil War, Maud's Aunt Virginia (Jennie) was sent to an aristocratic finishing school in Germany, along with her future sister-in-law Josephine Barber. The family may have expected that she would pass as white, marry, and remain in Europe, a situation that was not uncommon among African American women who studied abroad. For example, Maud's friend Mary Church Terrell, who, like Jennie, studied abroad, cites several acquaintances who made this choice.[9] However, after a year, Jennie returned with Josephine, who immediately married her fiancé, Joseph Cuney. Joseph and Josephine moved to Galveston, where both became teachers; Jennie probably made her home with them. She had the same qualifications as Josephine and could have taught in the Galveston schools had she wished to do so.

Josephine was fortunate to have met a man who matched her educational and cultural background and with whom she shared common values and a commitment to racial uplift. Jennie, on the other hand, struggled to find a partner and a place in life. Her olive skin, petite features, and dark, straight hair enabled her to pass as Hispanic or Mediterranean, particularly in multicultural Houston. She had enjoyed a privileged childhood with a wealthy white father and a superior education, but the family's financial decline after Philip Cuny's death in 1866 left her in jeopardy. Since she rejected a teaching career, marriage was her only option and yet, given that only 2 percent of Afro-Texans shared her educational level, it was difficult for her to find a partner.

Eventually, however, she met a light-skinned barber from Alabama named Alexander McGee. In 1874, the year of Maud's birth, Jennie married Alexander in Galveston.[10] Although Alex's education did not match his wife's, he had a steady income, and the couple made their home in Houston. Their daughter, Nellie B. McGee, was born on August 26, 1874, and their son, Cornelius Noble McGee, four years later on March 16, 1878. Jennie's mother, Adeline, also lived with the family.[11] Sadly, in 1882, when Nellie was eight and her brother four, Alexander abandoned the family and threw their lives into disarray.

Historian Carter G. Woodson asserts that Maud's aunts Laura and Jennie were the first in the family to pass: Woodson claims that they "crossed over to the white race" while young women living in Houston in the 1880s.[12] It was likely Laura, who had inherited her father's blonde hair and blue eyes and who had been passing for at least five years, who convinced Jennie to do so as well. After Alexander left her, Jennie reinvented herself as a "widow" although, as she well knew, her husband was still alive. Alexander had settled in Belton, Texas, sixty miles north of Austin, married a biracial woman twenty years younger than himself, and fathered three additional children: a son, Alex Jr., and daughters Margaret and Christine.[13] Apparently unwilling to move to Galveston where her three brothers would certainly have helped her, Jennie turned to her sister Laura, two years older and her best friend, for emotional support. The Houston City Directory for 1882 shows Laura residing at 60 Emanuel Street, on the corner of Preston. Jennie lived a few blocks away at 144 Washington, between 10th and Preston.[14] The designation of "widow" would have lent Jennie an aura of respectability, especially with the implication that her deceased husband was white. Furthermore, both women would have benefitted from their association with the white Cunys: their father had been a state legislator and a well-known member of the Houston business community, and their stepmother and stepsiblings lived only sixty miles away, on Sunnyside, the family planation.

That both Laura and Jennie passed successfully is evidenced in the Houston City Directory, where neither of their names was prefaced with a "c"—the label that marked the city's "colored" residents. Thus, both women passed in plain sight simply by playing on assumptions and taking advantage of "the odd quirks in how race was lived in the post–Reconstruction South."[15] In the absence of any firm physical criteria to determine race, sometimes only "code-shifting" sufficed; in addition to the "respectable" label of widow, Laura and Virginia relied on "dress, social standing, and community reputation" to establish a white identity.[16] By so doing, both sisters found employment in Houston's large haberdashery stores, jobs that would have been denied them due to race. Although Laura and Jennie managed successfully to live and work in Houston, their decision must have isolated them from the family. They probably kept in touch through Adeline Stuart, who traveled between her "white" children in Houston and her "Black" family in Galveston. Eventually Laura married and moved to Chicago where her daughter, May Carroll, was born and also listed as white.[17]

The sisters may have been helped in their journey of passing by an intimate friend and political supporter of their brother Wright Cuney who racially had already reinvented himself in San Antonio, Texas. William Ellis, born to enslaved, mixed-race parents near Victoria, changed his identity simply by speaking Spanish and converting his name to Guillermo Eliseo; with his deep olive skin, straight black hair, and imposing demeanor, he passed easily for a member of the "Tejano commercial elite, linked to well-placed family members across Mexico and Cuba."[18] In the San Antonio directory, there was no "c" next to his name, even though two sisters lived near him and identified as Black.[19] In many ways a classic African American trickster figure who moved easily, and often carelessly, across the color line, Ellis took advantage of the fact that in the fraught years after Reconstruction, no one would dare to challenge him because accusing someone of having Negro blood could have legal implications; thus Southeast Texas, with its large Hispanic population, enabled many African Americans like Ellis and the Cuney sisters to cross the color bar. Ellis would remain a close friend of the Cuney family; in addition to looking out for Laura and Jennie, he was one of the few guests at Maud's first wedding in 1898.

After Laura left Houston for Chicago, brother Joseph, who long had a soft spot for Jennie, convinced her to move to Galveston where she worked in a cotton mill that only employed whites. Her mother Adeline Stuart then moved in with Nelson and his family. For a brief period, Jennie's fortunes improved. On February 4, 1896, her daughter Nellie married a man named Louis Gamble in Pennsylvania.[20] Jennie and her seventeen-year-old son, Cornelius, then joined the newlyweds in Pittsburgh. But their happiness was short-lived: in March 1898, Jennie's beloved brother Wright Cuney died in San Antonio of tuberculosis. At the end of the year, Jennie herself took ill; after fifteen days, suffering from a defective heart valve possibly caused by childhood rheumatic fever, she died on Christmas Eve, 1898, at age forty-three. She was buried two days later, in Pittsburgh's Home Wood Cemetery.[21] On Jennie's death certificate, Nellie, who had been raised by her grandmother and undoubtedly knew her history, stated unequivocally that her mother was the daughter of P. Cuney and Adeline Cuney, thus granting her grandmother the status of a legal wife. She identifies Jennie as Mulatto, her biracial identity finally restored. Although the Cuney family received some advantages from passing, the decision proved not only painful and tragic, but deadly. For example, had Adeline Stuart remained in Houston with her daughters Laura and Jennie, she would have survived the devastating Hurricane of 1900 that claimed her life.[22] Considering Wright's and Jennie's deaths, the Galveston Hurricane, and painful events in Maud's personal life, 1898–1900 was a particularly distressing time for the family.

Perhaps learning from her mother's experience, Nellie McGee chose not to endeavor to pass as white. She and Louis welcomed their daughter Mildred on September 18, 1896; they went on to enjoy a fifty-year marriage in Pittsburgh. By contrast, Nellie's brother Cornelius passed as white and lived an unhappy life. He was married briefly to a white woman from West Virginia before moving to Chicago, working as a butcher, and dying alone in 1945.

The contrasting passing narratives of Maud's cousins Nellie and Cornelius McGee parallel those of another set of cousins, the daughters of Nelson Cuney, and the sisters of Waring's father, May and Daisy. A few years after Jennie's and Wright's deaths and the Galveston Hurricane in which she lost her mother, brother, and grandmother, May, undoubtedly traumatized by family tragedy, moved to Chicago and passed into the white world.[23] Her sister Daisy, by comparison, moved to Washington, DC, where her brother Norris Wright II and her uncle Henry Ernest were living. Daisy worked as a seamstress and continued her education. In 1909, she married Frank Alexander Byron, a 1908 graduate of Howard University Law School. Byron enjoyed an impressive career: as clerk of the US House of Representatives Naval Affairs Committee in 1921, Byron "occupied the highest place of any man of color on Capitol Hill."[24] The couple subsequently moved to Chicago's Washington Park, the community of choice for many of Black Chicago's cultural and professional elites, although it is doubtful that she and her sister May acknowledged their relationship. At her death in 1951, Daisy Cuney Byron was survived by a daughter, Sarah Byron Hickman, and two grandchildren. Her funeral, a grand celebration of her life, was held at her home church, St. Edmund's Episcopal, still extant and "one of the oldest and most renowned and active predominantly Black Episcopalian congregations in Chicago."[25] Of all the Cuney relatives, it is Daisy Cuney's descendants who are still alive and well, in Colorado and Illinois. May Cuney has left no trace, and it has not been possible to locate any of her descendants. Significantly, Waring and Wright III remained in contact with their aunt Daisy and their cousin Sarah.[26]

With its roots in survival and resistance to slavery, racial passing has occurred throughout American history and remains an important element not only in Cuney family history but also in African American writing. Rafia Zafar observes, "Over two centuries of systematic interracial rape and concubinage had produced thousands of light-, if not white-, skinned Americans of African descent; countless slaves took advantage of their phenotypical similarities to their owners and made tracks for the North."[27] Among the runaways were the married couple William and Ellen Craft, with whose Boston descendants Maud would establish a lifelong friendship.

Ellen, like Maud's aunts and uncles, was the daughter of a white planter and an enslaved mother. In their 1860 memoir *Running a Thousand Miles for Freedom*, the Crafts recount their daring escape from slavery in Macon, Georgia, to freedom in Philadelphia. Realizing that it is only as a white man that she can travel freely, Ellen disguises herself as a white gentleman traveling with his slave, William. From Macon, they take a train to Savannah, then steamships to South Carolina and North Carolina, and trains to Virginia, Washington, DC, and Maryland. In Baltimore, "the last slave port," they feel "more anxious than ever, because we knew not what that last dark night would bring forth."[28] Finally, after many close calls, they reached Philadelphia, and freedom. Ellen could, of course, have more easily passed as a white woman, but she would have then appeared as a white woman traveling with her Black male slave. Given society's extreme anxiety at the prospect of a white female/Black male "mixture," William and Ellen would never have considered this option. However, for nineteenth-century readers, the Crafts' drama of disguise and deception would have provided both a moral justification for passing and a strategy for doing so. But as the Crafts make clear, their plan is only a means to freedom; once safely in the North, they reclaim their race and devote themselves to racial uplift. From Philadelphia,

Ellen moved to Boston, and then, to escape bounty hunters operating under the Fugitive Slave Law of 1850, to England. After the Civil War, William and Ellen and their five children returned to the US and, with the help of Boston abolitionists, started a school for African Americans in Georgia.[29] Their grandson, Henry Kempton Craft, who graduated from Harvard with a bachelor of science degree in engineering in 1907, married Bessie Trotter; she and her sister Maud Trotter were lifelong friends of Maud Cuney.

Freedmen and women continued to pass after Emancipation; in fact, with increased mobility and the opportunity to reinvent oneself completely in large Northern and Western cities, passing occurred in even higher numbers. Journalist Roi Ottley estimated that by the 1940s there were five million "white Negroes" in the United States, and at least forty thousand passed annually.[30] In an article published in *The Messenger* in 1925, Maud's and Waring's friend Eugene Gordon pointed out that in cities like Boston with large immigrant populations, racial reinvention was not difficult: "Suffice it to say that there are hundreds of 'Portuguese' who were once just plain Jack Johnsons and Mary Browns. . . . There are scores of 'Armenians' and 'Greeks' and a few 'Italians' who came to [Boston] from Shoe Button, Mississippi [or] Hop Toad, Georgia."[31] According to Gordon, "it is a simple matter to become 'white' where so many whites, were they in Georgia . . . would without question be classed as colored."[32]

A number of Harlem Renaissance writers explored the fluidity of racial identity. For example, race in early twentieth-century Los Angeles is examined in "Three Dogs and a Rabbit" by Anita Scott Coleman.[33] In the story, published in *The Crisis* in 1926, a beautiful young slave travels westward to California, marries her master's son, raises a family, and lives as white. As an elderly woman, she impulsively hides an innocent Black man pursued by the police and subsequently reveals her race to an amazed community to whom she has always been "white." The tragic lengths to which a New York family goes to protect its "white" identity is explored in Dorothy West's tale of infanticide, the quietly horrifying "Mammy," which appeared in *Opportunity* in 1940. The family's terrible decision must be considered in light of the fact that the severely curtailed prospects and the rise of Jim Crow violence motivated many to pass, such as the protagonist of James Weldon Johnson's classic novel, *The Autobiography of an Ex-Colored Man* (1912). Perhaps the literary account that best parallels the Cuney narrative is Nella Larsen's 1929 novel *Passing*, in which two childhood friends, Clare and Irene, choose different racial identities and attempt to reconnect in Harlem, with tragic results. Clare has lived in Europe as white, while Irene has embraced her African American identity and is happily married to a Harlem physician and civil rights leader. The fictional women's experience is remarkably similar to that of several pairs of Cuney siblings and cousins who are separated by the color line.

May Cuney, her Aunt Laura, and Laura's daughter May Carroll disappeared into the white world, although for others, like Jennie Cuney and Ellen and William Craft, passing was temporary. But for those who crossed the color line permanently, passing was inevitably sad and tragic. James Weldon Johnson's ex-colored man would agree: "I cannot repress the thought that, after all, I have chosen the lesser part, that I have sold my birthright for a mess of pottage."[34] Maud herself would come to know exactly how painful selling her birthright would be.

In her biography of her father, Maud is extremely careful to keep the family's secrets of passing: in 1917, while giving a series of concerts in Chicago, Maud notes a visit with her cousin Daisy Cuney Byron but makes no mention of her cousin May Cuney or her Aunt Laura or Laura's daughter May Carroll, all of whom were also living in the city. It is unlikely that she ever spoke of her relatives who passed as white. However, Daisy would have been aware of her sister, her aunt, and her cousin in Chicago, and it was probably she who passed on the information to historian Carter Woodson when he wrote an article about the family in 1948.

Maud had several opportunities to assess the social implications of passing. On a visit to a New York hotel with her father, they are mistaken for Hispanic. Actually, according to Maud, they are also mistaken for newlyweds, but that is a different discussion. When she immediately declares her race, she is met with protests of disbelief and must endure insulting comments and "hazy ideas concerning the results of race admixture—texture of hair and shade of complexion, which led to a serious discussion of the Negro problem."[35] Maud notes that Wright praised her courage in the face of such blatant prejudice: "He abhorred above all things the supposedly easier way of 'passing for white,' and instilled in my young brother and me a hatred and contempt for the cowardly method which is upheld by many who can successfully disown their Negro blood."[36] Waring's many poems on Black pride and his strident protests against Jim Crow suggest that he shared his great-uncle's sentiments.

Maud was also close to her mother, Adelina Dowdie Cuney, whom she described as "religious without being pious . . . her Christianity was one of sunshine and cheerfulness."[37] Adelina, Maud, and Lloyd Garrison, along with other members of Galveston's Black elite, attended Reedy Chapel, the historic African Methodist Episcopal (A.M.E.) church located within walking distance on Broadway and 20th Street. Yet, despite the appearance of a secure, idyllic family life, a major family secret lay hidden beneath the surface, one even more dramatic than the decision of various family members to pass as white. In 1873, two years after his marriage to Adelina Dowdie, Wright Cuney was elected to chair the Men's Colored Convention in Brenham, Texas. It is probably then that he met a young woman from Brenham named Alice Brown. The two began a relationship, and he established Alice in Galveston, just a few blocks from his family home on L Street. On June 20, 1875, Alice gave birth to their son Charles. Just as his own father had done, in establishing two families at Sunnyside Plantation, so Norris Wright maintained simultaneous relationships with both Adelina and Alice. Maud had been born in February 1874, and his son Lloyd Garrison was born in 1880. Meanwhile Norris Wright's brothers, Nelson and Joseph, were welcoming their own children. Joseph's family included Joseph Jr. (1876) and Charles Sumner (1878), while Nelson's family included Richard (1868), Norris Wright II (1871), May (1874), and Daisy (1879). Alice meanwhile had married a man named Burroughs, who possibly hailed from Jamaica, and who agreed to give Charles his surname. In any case, she and Charles continued to live in Galveston, and Charles attended Galveston's Central Colored School along with his half-siblings and cousins. Given that Joseph Cuney was the principal of the school, the paternity of Charles Burroughs was certainly an open secret. In addition, Charles looked exactly like his father and resembled him more closely than his half-brother, Lloyd Garrison.

At a time when only 6 percent of Americans graduated from high school, the Cuney cousins all completed primary education. In 1887, the *Galveston Daily News* reported on the "Semi-Annual Examination and Promotion" at the Central Colored School: Maud was successfully promoted to seventh grade and Charles Burroughs to sixth. Charles then joined his siblings and cousins at Central High, Galveston's first Black high school, located a few blocks from Maud's home on L Street. The *Galveston Daily News* of June 2, 1890, presented a glowing account of the high school's first commencement exercises, attended by both white and Black Galvestonians. In his opening remarks, Principal J. R. Gibson praised Wright Cuney's advocacy, stating that "in 1885 when the two [elementary] schools . . . were full to overflowing, when there was no place for our higher grades, nothing to do except to quit the public schools with a mere smattering of sixth grade work . . . the honorable gentleman who is now the collector of the port of Galveston came to the front and succeeded in inducing the board of education to establish a central school for colored youth."[38]

Maud, a junior in 1890 and an officer in the Literary Society that sponsored the program, was already demonstrating her musical and writing skills. Her prize-winning essay, "The Importance of a High School Education," was described as "well-written, sensible and practical. The writer took a conservative view of . . . higher education, yet showed its absolute necessity to the well-being of society."[39] Of the six musical numbers, Maud's rousing piano solo, "Fanfare Militaire" by Dutch composer Joseph Ascher, "was of a really high order of merit, showing an ability to interpret and execute classical music with accuracy and expression."[40] Unfortunately, Charles Burroughs did not follow Maud and graduate during the third commencement; unlike his half-siblings and cousins, he had left school at age fourteen and spent the next two years working as a porter for a Galveston shoe merchant, Louis Schlesinger.

One wonders how Charles felt as he saw all his relatives begin their academic careers. Maud would leave Galveston to study music at Boston's New England Conservatory, while her brother Lloyd Garrison matriculated at Tillotson College in Austin. Nelson's older son Richard graduated from high school and had passed the Texas Bar before his untimely death in the Galveston Hurricane.[41] Richard's brother Norris Wright II (Waring's father) first matriculated in Howard University's Medical School, and later he enrolled in the Law School. Their sister Daisy also matriculated at Howard; she had left for school shortly before the Hurricane of 1900, which probably saved her life. Joseph sent his sons Joseph Jr. and Charles Sumner to high school in Boston. They boarded with a family in Saugus, a predominantly white, working-class suburb north of the city, but unfortunately Joseph Jr. died of typhoid fever at the age of seventeen.[42] His brother Charles Sumner went on to Wilberforce University in Ohio and Howard Law School and established a successful law career in Washington. After two years, however, Charles had apparently saved enough money to matriculate in Wilberforce University; it is unclear whether his father helped him. There he studied with a young W. E. B. Du Bois, as well as with Rev. Edward A. Clarke, and Major Charles Young, with whom he would later serve in the Spanish–American War. Interestingly, both Maud and Charles were interested in music and drama; they would later join forces in the production of plays in Boston.

The Cuneys would have carefully researched various colleges

in order to find the right fit for Maud. They particularly liked the seventy-five-page prospectus of Boston's New England Conservatory of Music. Elegantly illustrated with engravings, the catalogue touted the school's Judeo-Christian values, its professionalism, and its emphasis on the career placement of graduates in music, teaching, missionary work, and even the construction and repair of pianos. The curriculum included a complete liberal arts education in addition to "a thorough musical training."[43] The presence of famous abolitionists Julia Ward Howe and Richard Dana on the Executive Board would have implied a warm reception for African American students. In fact, twenty years earlier the conservatory had welcomed two African Americans, Rachel Washington and Nellie Brown Mitchell, both of whom had established fine careers in Boston as musicians and teachers.[44] The imposing building was located on Franklin Square, in Boston's then-elegant South End, and was easily accessible via streetcar to cultural attractions such as the Old Boston Music Hall, Harvard University, and the Public Library. Finally, since Maud was only seventeen, the hygienic, well-supervised dormitory for five hundred women would have been an important consideration. Her parents must have been relieved to read in the prospectus that, due to the meticulous sanitation, healthy water supply, and on-call resident physician, the school had never lost a single student.[45] These advantages, coupled with Wright's Boston connections through the Prince Hall Masons and the Republican Party, certainly factored into the selection of the conservatory for Maud's education.

Maud was an immediate success at school. However, she was soon to be embroiled in the very racial unpleasantness her parents had sought to avoid. In October of her freshman year, some students from the South complained about the presence in the dormitory of Maud and Florida Desverney, an African American woman from Savannah. Florida's background was very similar to Maud's. Her father, Anthony Desverney, was a Civil War veteran and prosperous cotton broker; his daughter had been raised in an elegant home, surrounded by "aristocratic graces, traditions, and manners."[46] Like Wright Cuney, Desverney chose the conservatory in the expectation that his daughter would be welcomed in this bastion of culture and the abolitionist tradition. But in response to the complaints by the Southern students, the Executive Committee wrote to the Cuneys and the Desverneys that "we find ourselves confronted with a problem . . . which seriously affects the interests of the Conservatory . . . [and] for which there seems no adequate solution save in the disposition of parents of colored students to provide them homes outside the Conservatory."[47] As justification, the administrators added: "we have a large number of pupils who are affected by race prejudices, and the Home must be conducted so as to insure the comfort and satisfaction of the largest number possible, otherwise . . . the success of the Institution, which is entirely dependent upon its patronage, is imperiled."[48]

Wright fired back in his inimitable style immediately: "I notice with extreme reluctance the bewildering fact that glorious Massachusetts, with her long line of immortal heroes—William L. Garrison, Wendell Phillips, Chas. Sumner, John A. Andrews, John Boyle O'Reilly— . . . [can support] a dying prejudice which your great State has done so much towards rendering nauseous in the eyes of enlightened humanity."[49] He cited the values described in the school's catalogue, pointing out, "I believed that your principles were fixed in the foundations of humanity, justice and honor, and not subject to the control of a few misguided girls or parents."[50] Wright immediately contacted his friends in Boston's Colored National League, an early civil rights organization sponsored by the Charles Street A.M.E. Church and helmed by Edwin Garrison Walker, the son of abolitionist David Walker. The league promptly threatened to sue. Even Maud's new friends at Harvard got involved: Du Bois recalled that "when the New England Conservatory of Music tried to 'jim-crow' her in the dormitory, we students rushed to her defense and we won."[51] At this point, the administration quickly reversed its position. The African American newspaper *Boston Courant*, in an amusingly contemporary turn of phrase, stated that, after learning all the details, the school administrators "got woke up" and refused the Southerners' petition.[52]

Maud had been approached by the administration even before the letter was sent to her parents; she was apparently given a choice to leave or remain because, even before responding to the telegram her father sent her, she had already announced her decision to stay in the dormitory. When Richard Dana, a member of the conservatory's Executive Committee, subsequently lost the election for mayor of Cambridge, rumors circulated that African Americans blamed him for the debacle and refused to vote for him. However, Dana maintained that he was the victim of political propaganda and claimed that many people of color voted for him after he explained the situation to their satisfaction. According to Dana, Wright Cuney had misinterpreted the letter from the school; in fact, his daughter had been *given a choice* of remaining in the dormitory or boarding elsewhere "as many of the white students do." Without naming either Maud or Florida in the article, Dana claimed that one student chose to remain and the other wished to leave; however, the conservatory thought it best that both students remain in the dormitory, which they did. Dana blamed Wright Cuney for "inflaming the situation" by writing to his Boston friends, which resulted in the unfortunate "misunderstanding."[53]

Years later, Du Bois recalled that Maud was extremely popular in Boston: "She was a princess [who] reigned in colored Boston, with me among the hosts of young men bowing before her throne."[54] Another of Maud's close friends was Annie Hare. When Maud met Annie and her brother William Parker Hare, they were living with their parents in a large Victorian house on a leafy street in Jamaica Plain. Like her mother, Annie spent her time in volunteer activities, but William Parker was employed with the Post Office. His two uncles, James and Parker Bailey, listed the family home as their legal address, although they commuted to Washington, DC, where they taught at the famous M Street High School. Undoubtedly because of the pooled resources, the family could afford not only a large and comfortable home but also summer holidays in Newport, Rhode Island, Saratoga, New York, and Cottage City on Martha's Vineyard, all of which were noted in the "Social News." Like so many of Maud's friends, the family was musical: according to "Social News," Parker never missed a concert or a cantata, and William played the banjo.

Maud spent four happy years in Boston, surrounded by friends, performing at charity concerts and local churches, and building her resume with an eye to a future musical career. Unfortunately, her mother's fragile health had begun to deteriorate: "She had suffered for years from tuberculosis, but enjoying yearly travel and the tenderest care, she was always cheerful and active."[55] In 1894, Maud left all her friends and prospects in Boston and returned to Texas. Thinking that a drier climate than that of Galveston would be beneficial, she and her mother moved to San Antonio. Although Wright had remained in Galveston, his old friend, William ("Guillermo") Ellis, looked after the family. Hoping that Adelina might benefit from Mexico's even drier climate, Ellis proposed that he escort Maud, Adelina, and Lloyd to Monterrey, where they stayed at the elegant Hotel Iturbe and patronized the mineral springs of Saltillo and Topo Chico; Adelina particularly loved "the wonderful gardens in the foot-hills of the Sierra Madre mountains."[56]

In August 1895, Adelina felt well enough to accompany Maud to Austin to the annual convention of the Colored Teachers State Association of Texas (CTSAT). Created in 1884, CTSAT's mission was to establish a Black institution of higher learning in Texas. Prairie View College, for which Wright Cuney had lobbied strenuously, was the result. However, the school had been established on the vocationally oriented Tuskegee model; by the 1890s the CTSAT wanted a broader education for African American students in Texas, and they successfully petitioned the state legislature to convert the curriculum to a full-fledged liberal arts university. When Maud attended the conference, it was an important venue for Black educators to network, job hunt, and enhance professional development. There she connected with her friend, Cora Smith, the secretary of CTSAT and the Texas correspondent for *The Woman's Era*.

In the fall of 1895, Maud accepted a job in Austin as Director of Music at the Texas Deaf, Dumb, and Blind Institute for Colored Youth, an institution for which her father had been a strong advocate. Established in 1887 in "a beautiful and healthful location" on one hundred acres of farmland northwest of Austin, the school's twenty-eight buildings included a hospital, woodworking shop, dining hall, dormitory, chapel, laundry, power plant, dairy, and blacksmith's shop.[57] The institution was organized along the line of Tuskegee, and the students were encouraged to learn trades and achieve independence. During Maud's tenure she maintained extremely high standards for her students, and she gave them the full benefit of her own excellent education at the New England Conservatory. Sadly, there is absolutely no trace of the historic institution today. The buildings were all demolished in 1965 after the school merged with the Texas School for the Deaf; the open fields off Bull Creek Road now serve as an informal, leash-free dog park.[58]

Maud's brother Lloyd had enrolled at nearby Tillotson College where he planned to study for the ministry. Adelina's health continued to worsen, so Maud and Adelina rented a cottage close to City-County Hospital, which had opened in 1884 as the first public hospital in Texas. Adelina's physician was Dr. J. Frank McKinley, a Meharry Medical School graduate from Tennessee who was on staff at the Texas Eye, Ear & Throat Charity Hospital.

Unfortunately, Adelina Cuney passed away in October 1895; she was only thirty-nine years old. Maud recalled that her father was "utterly crushed and heart-broken" and "all of the final arrangements for our sad return to Galveston were necessarily completed by me."[59] After the funeral and interment in Lake View Cemetery, Maud dealt with her grief exactly as she would after future tragedies: she returned to the Institute and threw herself into her work. The school's end-of-year report noted that "the music pupils, under the instruction of Miss Maud E. Cuney, have made satisfactory progress" although the "overcrowded conditions [have] interfered materially with [their] work." The rigorous curriculum included Maud's classes in Piano, Advanced Point Writing and Harmony, and Chorus; she also offered enrichment lectures on "Breathing and Respiration," "The Orchestra and Instruments," "Bach, Handel, and Scarlatti," "Ludwig von Beethoven," and "Chopin."[60] At the end of the school year, Maud returned to Boston and Newport for the summer where her friends, including Georgina Glover and Annie Hare, consoled her with "a hearty welcome."[61]

The following year the German pianist Emil Ludwig visited Maud in Austin. Ludwig, along with Tchaikovsky, had studied with the pianist and composer Anton Rubinstein, and he was well versed in the business of music. In Austin he gave Maud private lessons and proposed that they give a dual piano concert at the Austin Opera House; however, when they learned the audience would be segregated, they cancelled and rebooked at Maud's school, which was an integrated venue.[62] Patrons flocked to the rural location, and the Austin papers gave the concert excellent reviews. Wright Cuney attended the concert, and Maud was happy to see that he seemed "tired but less depressed."[63] Also present at the concert was undoubtedly Dr. John Frank McKinley, who had maintained a connection with Maud since the death of her mother. A slender, handsome man twenty years her senior, McKinley probably provided support and consolation to the grieving young woman. Like Maud's father, McKinley was the intelligent and ambitious son of a white father and enslaved mother. Wright may have encouraged the match, seeing in McKinley a man who matched his daughter's education and background and one who could, on paper, provide a comfortable and secure life.

Wright Cuney's health, meanwhile, had failed: years of insomnia and heavy smoking, his crushing political defeat at the hands of the racist Lily-White faction of the Texas Republican Party, and heartbreak at the death of his beloved wife three years earlier exacerbated a longstanding lung condition and he became gravely ill. His brothers,

Joseph and Nelson, his mother Adeline, and his son Lloyd were all with him in San Antonio when he died on March 3, 1898, in his daughter's arms. Once again, Maud was obliged to put aside her grief: despite her wish for "quiet ceremonies," she helped plan the elaborate funeral that began with a wake at St. Paul A.M.E. church in San Antonio. A private train, donated by the Southern Pacific and Santa Fe Railroads, bore the cortege to Galveston, attended by the San Antonio Guards, a Black militia regiment. Three thousand people, Black and white, attended the memorial service at Harmony Hall. One thousand mourners at Reedy Chapel listened to a funeral service that combined elements from Masonic ritual and A.M.E. liturgy. Cuney's old friend, William ("Guillermo") Ellis, was listed as one of the honorary pall bearers. Ellis had relocated to New York where he was now passing on multiple levels as a Wall Street millionaire.[64] Wright was laid to rest among the tall trees and elegant shrubbery of what the Galveston papers described as "beautiful Lakeview Cemetery."[65]

In late September 1898, Maud abruptly married her mother's former physician, Dr. J. F. McKinley. The wedding, coming six months after Wright's death while Maud was still in mourning, must have shocked the family. Although her beloved grandmother Adeline, her Uncles Nelson and Joseph, and several cousins lived in Galveston, and although she and McKinley must have had mutual friends in Austin, Maud and her future husband traveled across the country to marry in New York City. None of the family except Lloyd attended. One wonders whether the family objected to the twenty-year age difference or whether there were other reasons to suspect McKinley's intentions toward Maud. It is quite possible that he thought Maud would inherit a substantial amount of money from Wright's estate. The family may even have guessed that McKinley was already dissatisfied with his medical career in Austin's Black community and had decided to relocate to Chicago, leave the race, and establish a more lucrative white practice. To do this, he would need a gracious, cultured, and equally "white" wife at his side. Certainly, Uncle Joseph, a canny and experienced man of the world, would have had reservations about both McKinley and the haste in which the wedding had been arranged. By way of incentives, McKinley must have offered to provide a home for Lloyd and probably also suggested that Maud could restart her musical career in a large city like Chicago.

The couple married at the elegant Manhattan townhouse of Maud's godfather, Thomas B. Francis, where she had often stayed while en route from Boston to Galveston. Francis was an old friend of Wright's and of journalist T. Thomas Fortune; he was active in Republican politics and in the vestry of the fashionable St. Philip's Episcopal Church on nearby 25th Street. The pastor of St. Philip's, Rev. Hutchens Chew Bishop, performed the ceremony.[66] Many years later, Maud's cousin Waring Cuney would interview Bishop's son, the Rev. Shelton Bishop, as part of a Works Progress Administration (WPA) series on Black New York; one wonders if he made the connection between Maud and the senior Rev. Bishop. Maud's bridesmaids were her two dear friends from Boston, Georgine Glover and Annie Hare. Brother Lloyd and the ubiquitous William ("Guillermo") Ellis stood up for the groom.

It may well have been Ellis, perhaps feeling responsible for the future of Wright's family, who urged Maud to marry McKinley and who offered to pay for the New York wedding. He had already proven himself a trusted friend during Adelina's illness when he hosted the family in Mexico. Now, in his new identity as a wealthy Cuban Wall Street broker, Ellis was described in the press as sporting "a long brown overcoat of costly texture . . . [a] thick white silk handkerchief around his neck. . . [and] fingers sparkl[ing] with many diamonds."[67] Despite being involved in a sex scandal with a glamorous white grifter from Atlanta, Ellis had solidified his new persona and was in the process of buying up municipal water works with money lent to him by the widow of the Hotchkiss arms company.[68] As a successful manipulator of the color line, Ellis may also have encouraged McKinley to pursue the idea of passing in Chicago. Having known Wright Cuney for years, however, he would probably have warned McKinley against making his plans known to Maud.

The marriage seems to have soured quickly. According to the *Colored American* of October 1, 1898, Dr. McKinley claimed to own "a lovely home in a cottage at 59th and Butler Streets in Chicago, where the happy pair will reside."[69] McKinley had indeed established himself in Chicago before proposing to Maud; however, the house on Butler Street was probably a complete fiction, because when the couple arrived in Chicago, they lived at Du Chesne Hotel. Two years later, they were living at Cottage Grove and 32nd Street, nowhere near Butler and 59th. Well before Maud's arrival, McKinley had been boarding with a white woman named Caroline Ennis, with whom he probably was having an affair, and whom he eventually married. Ennis was self-sufficient financially and was the manager of a large hotel.

When the couple arrived in Chicago, Maud was immediately discouraged from entertaining her Black friends; she recalled that "few colored persons who called on the McKinleys made a second visit." She was even forbidden to recognize her friends on the street. McKinley then dropped his bombshell: in order to expand his medical practice and make more money, they would henceforth pass as white. "He told me," she testified, "that he would rather practice among whites and starve than live in plenty and treat Colored persons."[70] An immediate difficulty would have been Lloyd who, unlike his sister and brother-in-law, could not pass as white. Maud must have worried about her husband's intentions toward her brother, while remembering her father's admonitions that passing was a cowardly and despicable act.

Maud was not, however, the demure and tractable spouse that McKinley, twenty years her senior, had anticipated. She immediately defied her husband's edicts. First, she decided to volunteer, not at an affluent white church where she might have met people and attracted new patients for her husband, but at the Institutional African Methodist Episcopal Church and Settlement House on Dearborn Street. Newly opened by the charismatic minister Reverdy Ransom to serve poor Black families, the Institutional Church epitomized the tenets of the Social Gospel that Maud had learned from her parents. At the settlement house, Maud taught piano to children and probably engaged in fundraising concerts, as she had done in Boston. Yet another bone of contention would have been Maud's membership in the African American St. John's Literary Club, led by the well-known Black journalist and novelist Katherine Tillman. McKinley must have been infuriated at the article in the *Chicago Daily News* that proclaimed Maud, along with poet Paul Laurence Dunbar, as the "star[s] of the annual summer meeting of the colored people's club."[71] However, the last straw would have come shortly after the birth of their daughter in 1900. When McKinley registered Vera Adelia, named for both Maud's mother Adelina and her grandmother Adeline, he listed her race as "American-Spanish."[72] This must have been insupportable to Maud and shortly thereafter, the couple separated. McKinley, apparently tired of conflict and eager to solidify his relationship with Caroline Ennis who, he boasted, had an income of $250 a month and savings of $25,000, promised Maud custody of Vera if she agreed to a divorce.

Given the fact that Galveston was still reeling from the deadly Hurricane of 1900, Maud, Vera, and Lloyd could not have returned to Texas; instead, they moved to Washington, DC. Maud's Uncle Nelson, mourning the death of his mother Adeline, his wife, and his oldest son in the hurricane, had joined his daughter Daisy and his younger son, Norris Wright II, in DC. A number of Maud's musical friends from Boston also lived in the city, including Parker Bailey, the uncle of Annie and William Hare. Bailey taught at the famous M Street High School. Through Annie Smith, a friend from the New England Conservatory and Boston's Charles Street Circle, Maud met sisters Madge and Jeannette Williamson. Jeannette was also a pianist, and Madge would soon marry Norris Wright II. He was a foreman at the US Government Printing Office, where Lloyd was soon hired. Maud had obtained a clerical position with the US Land Office, but she also began performing publicly in hopes of reestablishing her musical career. In April 1903, she "gave a small musicale" at her home.[73] She accompanied the noted tenor and family friend Sidney Woodward; another good friend from Boston, Clarence White, played the violin. Parker Bailey attended the concert and may have alerted his nephew William Hare that the beautiful Maud Cuney was now separated from her husband. The following month she performed at a Service of Sacred Song at Lincoln Temple, the Congregationalist church founded by Mary Church Terrell and her friends that merged with the larger Lincoln Memorial Congregational church in which Lloyd Cuney would become very involved in the vestry.

Maud and Vera were happy in Washington. Contemporary accounts describe Vera as "a child of rare sweetness and attractiveness."[74] Maud's friend, Mary Church Terrell, often "used to see this accomplished young woman and her little daughter, who was both fair and pretty." Maud apparently confided in Terrell, who depicted McKinley as a callous man, willing to sacrifice his beautiful family in order to pass as white and enjoy "his large and growing practice." She added: "I could not help wondering how the husband and father could have summoned the strength to tear himself away from them and bid them good-bye."[75] Maud enjoyed an active social life in the city. She was among the six hundred fashionable guests at Annie Smith's wedding; other guests included Judge and Mrs. Mary Church Terrell; the Canadian baritone William H. Richardson, with whom Maud would share a musical partnership; violinist Joseph Douglass, the grandson of Frederick Douglass; and Madge and Jeannette Williamson.[76]

Maud was restive doing clerical work in segregated Washington and may have wanted more involvement in music. In 1903, she resigned her position with the government and returned to Texas where she taught music at Prairie View College, another institution for which her father had been a champion. Meanwhile, McKinley had changed his mind about releasing Maud, had divorced her on the grounds of abandonment, and had sued for and received custody of little Vera. Although Maud immediately contested the decision, as a single mother she was considered less capable of providing for her child and the courts ruled against her. Reluctantly, she brought Vera back to Chicago where McKinley was now living with his white wife.

The need to establish a more financially secure home for Vera may have motivated Maud to reconnect with the Hare family. Annie was now married, and William, now thirty-one years old, had a secure job at the Post Office. Although the marriage appears never to have been based on a passionate relationship, William presumably urged Maud to consider the stable home he could provide for her and Vera and the financial help he could offer with legal fees. When the school year at Prairie View ended in June 1904, Maud moved to Boston where she found an apartment and began teaching music. She and William must have come to an understanding fairly quickly because in August 1904, exactly a month after her divorce from McKinley was finalized, Maud and William married in Boston. On the marriage certificate Maud is identified as a divorced colored teacher, age thirty. She lived at 21 Westcott Street in Dorchester; after the wedding she moved three miles to William's home at 108 Sheridan Street in Jamaica Plain. Mary Bailey, now widowed, would live with her son and daughter-in-law and in 1910, they would purchase a brand new three-bedroom home at 43 Sheridan Street where they would spend the rest of their lives. In 1926, Waring Cuney, likely at Maud's urging, moved to Boston and lived with her and William in their Jamaica Plain home.[77] By 1928 he had saved enough to rent an apartment two miles away at 12 Gannett Street, in Dorchester.

Once married to William, Maud hired two prominent African American lawyers in Chicago and sued for custody of her daughter. McKinley now demanded that Vera live with him and his new wife, Caroline. However, Maud argued that McKinley had taught Vera to believe that she was white and to hate and disrespect African Americans. Eventually, after a humiliating exposure of her private life, avidly reported in the Black press, Maud achieved an unprecedented victory and was awarded full custody of eight-year-old Vera, except for summer vacations that would be spent with her father. But tragically, on September 1, 1908, just before she was due to rejoin her mother, little Vera died suddenly in Chicago, of appendicitis.[78] Maud received the news by telegram; she was devastated but turned a stoic face to the world. Her Boston friends surrounded her with affection but "dared not affront this suffering soul with offers of either help or sympathy."[79]

After this devastating blow, Cuney threw herself into a rich professional life in music and literature. Throughout the previous ten years, her tragedies had multiplied relentlessly and yet, as Du Bois recalled, "she was in her extremity of need and ecstasy of pain so magnificently self-sufficient, alert, determined . . . she asked [for] only what she had earned . . . no dole, no charity, no gift."[80] A year after Vera's death, she quietly reestablished her musical career with a private Christmas concert in Washington in honor of her brother Lloyd.[81] In October 1910, she made her first public appearance in a chamber concert at Lincoln Temple Church, along with her close friend, violinist Clarence Cameron White, and Mary L. Europe, the younger sister of bandleader James Reese Europe.[82] Lloyd, whose affiliation with Lincoln Temple had probably enabled him to arrange the chamber concert there, undoubtedly encouraged his sister's musical career, as did Waring's parents, Madge Williamson and Norris Wright II, and Madge's sister, Jennie Williamson.

By 1913, Maud had begun a twenty-year partnership with the Canadian baritone, William H. Richardson. Richardson was born in Nova Scotia to a family of English, Dutch, and African descent and moved to Cambridge, Massachusetts, as a child. There he received excellent vocal training that prepared him to be a soloist at several white and Black churches. He was the only Black singer for the Boston Philharmonic Society and by 1910 was "one of the leading black baritones on the East Coast."[83] Cuney and Richardson began by booking concerts at African American churches throughout the country, but they eventually developed a costumed lecture series that became so popular that "two booking agencies, the Eastern-Empire

Lyceum Bureau and Biggs and Company, had to arrange concerts a year or more in advance."[84] Much in demand, they crisscrossed the entire country, performing in Oklahoma City in 1920 and going on to California. On the East Coast, they "performed at such institutions as the Brooklyn Academy of Music, Syracuse University, and the Harvard Musical Association."[85] Their work was widely praised in both the Black and the mainstream press. In November 1916, the *Boston Globe* announced their program at Ford Hall, a venue across the street from the Massachusetts State House; their program was a blend of classical pieces and spirituals arranged by their friend, Boston composer Harry Burleigh. In 1924, Washington's *Evening Star* placed them "among the leading colored artists in music in the country." For this program, they performed, in costume, several French Creole and Arabian songs transcribed by Maud, as well as folk songs from Cuba, Argentina, and Mexico.[86]

As popular as Maud's musical performances were, "the most tangible gift she bequeathed to future generations was her intellectual musings on the history of African American music . . . like Zora Neale Hurston, Cuney-Hare was very interested in the African roots of blacks in the New World."[87] Her interests were thus completely in tune with the Harlem Renaissance, and although a generation older than most of the artists, she made an essential contribution to the period. When she was young, her father has sung her the chants and ditties of the roustabouts on the Mississippi and the stevedores in New Orleans and Galveston. As an adult, she traveled constantly, collecting folk songs and interviewing performers in Mexico, Cuba, the Virgin Islands, Puerto Rico, Haiti, Louisiana, and the Cape Verdean community in Provincetown, Massachusetts. She was as interested in the visual manifestations of dance as the aural, and "traced African bodily aesthetics in the tango of Argentina, the habanera of Cuba, and the bamboula of Louisiana."[88] Throughout her life, Maud published her research, not only in *The Crisis,* where she was the musical editor, but also in such mainstream venues as *Musical Quarterly, The*

Christian Science Monitor, Musical Observer, and *Musical America.* She also contributed a monthly music column for *The Crisis.* As Tera Hunter points out, her life's work culminated in her last book, *Negro Musicians and their Music,* on which she worked up to her death and which was published posthumously.

In addition to music, Maud was extremely interested in the theater. As a pianist, she would have been long familiar with Rimsky-Korsakov's 1868 symphony, *Antar.* The romantic story involves the sixth-century Arab poet-warrior Antarah ibn Shaddad and his love for the Queen of Palmyra, Gul-Nazar. In the 1920s Maud began researching Antarah as well as the seventh-century African mulatto musician Mabed ibn Ouhab; she wrote articles on both artists for *The Crisis.* In 1924, she drew on her research and wrote a four-act play entitled *Antar of Araby,* with incidental music by Amanda Aldridge, the youngest daughter of African American Shakespearean actor Ira Aldridge, and by violinist and composer Clarence Cameron White. Maud particularly liked White's "use of black rhythms and folk themes in his compositions."[89] Staged in 1925, the production was a Who's Who of Black Artistic Boston and shows how well-connected Maud was in the arts community. The multiracial cast featured students from Boston University and Emerson College. The sculptor Meta Warrick Fuller directed the production. Costumes were designed by the young artist Lois Mailou Jones, then a student at Boston Normal School. In addition to the students, the actors included members of Boston's Little Theatre Movement, including journalist Eugene Gordon, Maud's brother Charles Burroughs, and historian Benjamin Quarles. Baritone William Richardson sang a selection of Arabian folk songs, collected by Maud Cuney Hare. The *Boston Globe* gave the production a glowing review.[90] Waring Cuney, who was living in Boston during this period, would certainly have met Charles Burroughs, his father's Galveston neighbor and first cousin.

The Boston years were among Waring's most productive. At Maud's urging, he joined the Saturday Evening Quill Club and penned several of his most acclaimed pieces. On Saturday, May 14, 1927, the Quill Club held "a semi-formal reception" in honor of its four members who won prizes, the previous Saturday in New York City, during the 3rd Annual *Opportunity* Awards Dinner: club president Eugene Gordon and Dorothy West in the short story, and Helene Johnson and Waring Cuney in poetry. Gertrude McBrown, chair of the Quill Club's entertainment committee, noted that "The studio piano was used through the courtesy of Mrs. Maude [*sic*] Cuney-Hare, director of the Allied Arts Center," who also gave an "impromptu address."[91]

In 1926, encouraged by the reception of *Antar of Araby*, Maud founded the Allied Arts Center, an interracial venue that she hoped would encourage African American children in the arts. She wrote optimistically to W. E. B. Du Bois: "I want to establish a music centre . . . that will embrace an experimental children's Little Theatre. . . . I have not a penny to start my venture, but I am making plans just the same."[92] By the following year, still without a penny, she had secured a venue on Huntington Avenue, across from the New England Conservatory and a block from Symphony Hall. What she had done was to convince the whites-only South End Music School to admit Black students. She then offered to join the board. Meanwhile, "impressed by [her] success in opening up the music school, the Black League of Women for Community Service offered to help" and secured the location.[93] Shortly thereafter, she mounted a successful production of *The Bonds of Interest* by the Spanish dramatist Jacinto Benavente y Martínez. On February 26, 1927, she wrote again to Du Bois, extolling the production and the enthusiastic reception by an audience that included "several Harvard professors." She asked him to serve on an Executive Board, adding the names of several other luminaries who had agreed to serve, including Richard Dana whom she had apparently forgiven for having asked her to leave the New England Conservatory dormitory so many years before.

When Maud Estelle Cuney Hare died in 1936 after a painful and debilitating illness, W. E. B. Du Bois called her "the bravest woman I have ever known."[94] Although she never stopped demanding the civil rights of African Americans, Maud Cuney celebrated and acknowledged her complex heritage. When, in 1930, she built her dream home, a beach cottage on Boston's South Shore, she named it "Sunnyside" after her grandfather's plantation on the Brazos River. She had asked to be buried with her beloved parents in Galveston's Lakeview Cemetery where the scent of jasmine blends with the salty air of the Gulf and the sound of the surf is still faintly audible. Throughout her years in Boston, Maud would have remembered the twenty-acre Lakeview Cemetery as a verdant showplace; it was planted with oaks, palms, and pines, adorned with lush shrubbery, and surrounded by a sturdy brick-and-mortar wall. Despite the many tragedies and disappointments in Maud's life, it is somehow reassuring that her final resting place retains vestiges of her elegance and beauty.

Chapter 4

Waring Cuney and the Harlem Renaissance

And dish water gives back no images.
—WARING CUNEY, JUNE 1926

It was Harlem's Golden Age, that of the twenties.[1]
—LANGSTON HUGHES, 1966

HARLEM RENAISSANCE JOURNALIST EUGENE GORDON, reflecting on the movement's poets, lauded only six for producing credible work: Countee Cullen, Helene Johnson, Langston Hughes, Arna Bontemps, Sterling Brown, and Waring Cuney.[2] Although recent recovery efforts have directed well-deserved attention toward Harlem Renaissance writers, little notice has been taken of the talented William Waring Cuney, whose work bested the competition in the famous *Opportunity* literary contest of 1926. Although he is little known today, Cuney's poetry appeared in every one of the important journals and anthologies of the period. This chapter traces Waring Cuney through the 1920s and '30s to illuminate a key period of his life; in analyzing his poetry in conjunction with that of his contemporaries and his family background, we argue for the centrality of his poetic contribution, both to the Harlem Renaissance and to American letters.

In 1935, the editor of *Challenge* magazine declared, "Poetry making is his second love. Singing is his first." So wrote the Harlem Renaissance novelist Dorothy West about her friend Waring Cuney. Although one might quibble with the order, all who knew him agreed that poetry and singing were his twin loves. "On with the Dirge" and "Play a Blues for Louise," focused on women and penned during his halcyon Renaissance years, are among the dozens of poems that capture Cuney's love of music. Both poems, as is typical of the blues, concern love, tribulation, and sadness. When "On with the Dirge" appeared in April 1929, readers believed it was occasioned by the recent, sudden death of the beloved Broadway star, Florence Mills, at age thirty-one. While in Europe in 1927, appearing in *Blackbirds* and singing her trademark song, "I'm a Little Blackbird Looking for a Bluebird," Mills became ill and had to return to the US. She died shortly afterwards of appendicitis, in November 1927. Cuney's poem appears to announce her passing:

Play, O jazz band!
The dance-girl is dead.
(If any one asks for her
Tell him softly
That she has gone).

Marrying music and poetry, the jazz band plays, at the behest of the speaker, to honor the deceased dance-girl. Notice however that the parenthetical clause, softly revealing her passing, is an inversion or contradiction of the poem's opening. Together the lines powerfully capture the speaker's conflicting emotions and sadness brought on by the young woman's death.

While composing the poem Cuney, then in his first semester at Lincoln University, wrote to Langston Hughes for advice on the title.[3] This, however, was two years prior to Mills's demise. "On with the

Dirge" celebrates the talent and energy of the performing arts, epitomized by Mills. It was eerily prescient because even though composed in November 1925, two years before her untimely death, it perfectly described the loss felt by all.

Cuney's speaker again summons a jazz band in "Play a Blues for Louise."

> O jazz band,
> Play a blues for Louise tonight —
> Play a moanin' sobbin' song
> For a good gal
> Whose man done her wrong.
> O play a blues for Louise tonight.

Through rhyme and repetition, the poem communicates its central feeling of sadness. The "moanin' sobbin'" onomatopoeia, for instance, deftly captures both the band's playing and simultaneously Louise's distress. The blues, however, is ultimately a music of triumph, and Louise, having endured heartache and pain, is now "Chicago boun'." The band salutes her, as she leaves town on a "fast, fast train." Poems such as "On with the Dirge," "Play a Blues," and the prize-winning "No Images" display an intense sensitivity to Black women's plight and validate Cuney's well-earned recognition as a male feminist.

Waring Cuney's life as a public artist began at the height of the Renaissance when he was a student at Lincoln University in Pennsylvania. In October 1925, he thanked his Lincoln classmate, Langston Hughes, for giving him a "start [with] *Opportunity*."[4] The premier Harlem Renaissance journal published Cuney's first and best-known poem, "No Images," in June 1926. A few months later it appeared in the *Paris Times*[5]; it then appeared, recalled Hughes, "in the first German anthology of American-Negro poetry, *Afrika Singt*, published [in] Vienna and Leipzig."[6] It was soon reprinted in publications across Europe, and translated into Spanish, Yiddish, Italian, Dutch, and Czech. In fact, 1926 was a banner year for Cuney in which he saw several of his poems published in important Harlem Renaissance venues.

The subject of "No Images" is a poor Black girl who stands alone amidst dirty dishes in a low-end café or a slum apartment, unaware of her natural beauty and her proud African history. The topic seems an unusual one for a young man raised in a family that celebrated African American achievement and encouraged his talents and ambitions. While Cuney would have seen his mother and her friends doing the dishes in their modern, well-appointed kitchens in LeDroit Park and would have noticed the uniformed maids serving tea in the drawing rooms of neighbors like Dr. Ionia Whipper, Judge and Mrs. Terrell, and Georgia Douglas Johnson, none of these individuals would have projected the bleak prospects of the girl in the poem.

It is more likely that Waring saw the model for his poem on Seventh Street, a neighborhood several blocks from respectable U Street and LeDroit Park. The title of Langston Hughes's second collection of poetry, *Fine Clothes to the Jew* (1927), was inspired by the many pawn shops on Seventh Street. This title proved to be an unfortunate choice and offended many readers; nevertheless, Rampersad maintained that the Seventh Street poems formed Hughes's "greatest collection of verse [and] marked the height of his creativity."[7] Although poems like "Po' Boy Blues" reflect the general disillusionment of the poor in urban spaces after the Great Migration, several poems, including "Beale Street Love" and "Gal's Cry for a Dying Lover" specifically give voice to vulnerable young Black women who are victimized by poverty, lack of education, and predatory men. The protagonist of "No Images" is thus a sister to the women in Hughes's Seventh Street poems.

There is no question that Waring Cuney, along with Hughes, Bruce Nugent, Sterling Brown, and Jean Toomer, drew poetic inspiration from forays into this seedier side of Washington, DC, exploring the blind alleys, dead-end lanes, and tenements that were located only blocks from the White House. Goat Alley, one of the most notorious addresses, had inspired the eponymous play (1921) by white playwright, Ernest Culbertson. Rife with awkward, embarrassing, and stereotyped dialect, the play purportedly depicted Black life in Washington through the travails of a young woman named Lucy Belle. In reaction to such cultural appropriation, African American poets were already offering more authentic perspectives. In contrast to Culbertson's crude portrayals of African Americans, Jean Toomer's prose poems "Seventh Street" and "Theatre" in *Cane* (1923) asserted the dignity of Black life as seen in the store front churches, the "shanties . . . theaters, drug stores . . . cabarets . . . [and] the pool rooms and restaurants and near-beer saloons."[8]

While it may have been in one of these locales that Cuney spotted the girl in the poem, he must also have realized that the authenticity and vitality that he and his middle-class poet friends found on Seventh Street would have had a very different effect on a poor young woman without protection or advantages. His poem thus empathetically sees her perspective on her environment, suggesting that the toxic milieu of Seventh Street, an evolution of the depredations of slavery, has deprived the protagonist of her confidence and separated her from her heritage. Arna Bontemps could well have been speaking of Cuney when he said that Toomer, in writing about the authenticity of Seventh Street, understood that "civilization, by imposing on us a number of meaningless bourgeois values, denies to the human soul the only thing which makes us human, the ability to empathize with one another."[9] Thus Cuney's compassionate rendering of this character in his first published poem shows how willing he was to critique race and class in America and to challenge the attitudes of the "brown bourgeoisie."

The same year, Cuney's poem "The Death Bed" appeared in the avant-garde but short-lived *Fire!!*, edited by Wallace Thurman; here his co-contributors included Zora Neale Hurston, Langston Hughes, Helene Johnson, and his high school buddy from Washington, Bruce Nugent. The poem depicts, as the title suggests, a tense deathbed scene, one that recalls Emily Dickinson in its clash between the religious and the secular. The dying man is more confused and troubled by his praying relatives, gathered around his bed, than by his imminent demise: "There is no need of prayer, / He said, / No need at all." The shocked relatives heed his request and move to a room across the hall. Relieved, he attempts to sing, until he notices that some continue praying:

> And all the time it worried him
> That they were in there praying
> And all the time he wondered
> What it was they could be saying.

The chasm between Cuney's dying man and his relatives creates dissonance and even humor. Here prayer functions as a vise troubling the man's final moments rather than as a spiritual balm easing him to the afterlife. The graphic realism of the poem may well have been inspired by recent family deaths. His great-uncle Henry Ernest had died in 1921 while visiting the latter's brother, Cuney's grandfather, in Washington, DC. Grandfather John Nelson Cuney passed away two years later, after surviving not only a childhood in slavery but the terrible Galveston Hurricane of 1900 in which he had lost his wife and a son. However, the most traumatic death for Cuney would have been that of his father in 1923 at the relatively young age of fifty-one.

In 1926, Countee Cullen included Cuney's "Grave" in his guest-edited issue of *Palms,* Idella Purnell's Modernist journal from Guadalajara, Mexico, to which D. H. Lawrence and Witter Bynner also contributed. "Grave" consists of a series of lyrical, fragmentary images and addresses sorrow, the natural world, and death. It was later set to music by the Italian composer Giacomo Manzoni. In 1927, Cullen again included Cuney, this time in his anthology *Caroling Dusk,* along with Paul Laurence Dunbar, W. E. B. Du Bois, and Sterling Brown.

Religion played an important role in Cuney's verse throughout his career, but it is especially evident in his later poetry, including his final collection, *Storefront Church* (1973). Consider the brief, aphoristic "Prayer":

When I was a boy
The old-folks used to say,
If you never
Prayed for your enemy,
You never learned to pray.

This poem, though pithy, speaks volumes about the importance of prayer in the African American community. Where those outside of the cultural tradition might find praying for one's enemies strange, Cuney's "old-folks" are firmly inside the tradition. They appreciate the example set on Calvary, as Christ, even while being crucified, cried out, "Father, forgive them; for they know not what they do."[10] "Prayer," then, helps us to understand the family's horror, as their dying relative proclaims, "There is no need of prayer." Cuney's deftly drawn "The Death Bed" invites readings through the lens of theology and psychology, as well as literature.

On May 4, 1926, Charles S. Johnson, the editor of the journal *Opportunity* and organizer of the second literary competition, wrote to inform Cuney about the results of the contest.[11] He had won one-half of the first and second poetry prizes for "No Images," described by Clement Wood as "an exquisite, successful piece." William Rose Benét, another of the judges, found in it "a true poignance and wistful beauty," although he preferred Gwendolyn Bennett's "Hatred," which he characterized as "almost flawless."[12] Cuney shared the award and the eighty-five-dollar prize with Fisk University student Lucy Ariel Williams, who, like Waring, was a poet and pianist. With his poem, he triumphed over Claude McKay, Wallace Thurman, and his mentor, Georgia Douglas Johnson, all of whom won an honorable mention. Cuney himself would win honorable mentions the following year, in the third *Opportunity* contest, for "A Traditional Marching Song" and "De Jail Blues Song."[13]

In his letters to the prizewinners, Charles Johnson promised, in addition to the prize money, publication in the magazine as well as "in some other medium that will bring [you] to the attention of the public."[14] The editor did not exaggerate: at the awards dinner Cuney met not only members of the white establishment who would help him professionally, such as Amy Spingarn, but also talented Black writers destined to become longtime friends, including Countee Cullen and Arna Bontemps.[15] When Harcourt Brace, the publishing firm co-founded by Joel Spingarn, tapped the eminent James Weldon Johnson, another of the poetry judges, for a second edition of his *Book of American Negro Poetry* (1931), it included eight of Cuney's poems. Cuney—who, Johnson held, "holds exceptional promise"[16]—appeared with seven other new poets: Countee Cullen, Langston Hughes, Sterling Brown, Helene Johnson, Arna Bontemps, Frank Horne, and Gwendolyn Bennett.

To further his goal, calling attention to "great literature and art" of African Americans, Johnson chose work from three dozen poets; from Cuney he selected "No Images" and seven other poems, mostly concerned with religion, love, and death. He argues, in his preface to the anthology, that "the final measure of the greatness of all peoples is the amount and standard of the literature and art they have produced."[17] Praising Cuney's "great economy of phrase," he maintains that "the best of his poems present clear, direct, and vivid images."[18] A trio of poems from the collection paint especially powerful portraits. "Wake Cry," for example, personifies Death as cruelly oblivious to "the widow moan," as Death's heart is "Made o' stone." "Finis" vivifies the "empty ache" of erstwhile lovers who in recent, happier times "stood tip-toe on earth / To touch our fingers to the sky." And in "Conception" we witness the miracle of Jesus's origination from a virgin, as God says, "Mary, chile, kiss ma han.'"

Back at Lincoln, after the awards banquet, Cuney received something of a hero's welcome. Already well regarded, singing with the Glee Club and having pledged Alpha Phi Alpha, the nation's oldest African American fraternity, he was now even more popular.[19] Langston Hughes had won first prize the previous year for "The Weary Blues." Now, thanks to Cuney and "No Images," Lincoln boasted back-to-back top-prize winners, and the university basked in the favorable press. Additional accolades followed two months later, as newspapers announced that Langston had won first prize and Waring an honorable mention in the Witter Bynner contest for undergraduate excellence in poetry:

> Rose McNeill, Vachel Lindsay and Wittner Bynner, judges for the Poetry Society of America's undergraduate contest, held under the auspices of *Palms*, announce that the Bynner prize of $150 is awarded to Langston Hughes (Lincoln university) for five poems and that honorable mention is given . . . [to] Waring Cuney, Lincoln university.[20]

Write-ups about the esteemed Lincoln poets, announcing their various prizes, appeared in magazines and newspapers across the country.[21]

Despite his success, Cuney departed Lincoln in 1926 prior to receiving his baccalaureate. Precisely why he left the school is unclear, although, without the patronage enjoyed by Hughes, he may have had financial difficulties. He may also have been still unsettled by the relatively recent death of his father, during his senior year in high school. We do know that he had left Howard to focus on his writing; now he intended to concentrate on music, with an eye to becoming a professional singer. After a respite in Washington, he moved to Boston to study at the New England Conservatory of Music. The move to Boston was probably encouraged by his father's cousin, Maud Cuney Hare, who had graduated from the conservatory and who had since carved out a career for herself as a concert pianist and accompanist. Initially, he lived with Maud and her husband at their Sheridan Street home in Jamaica Plain and worked at a hotel in downtown Boston. "It's rather exclusive," he remarked to a friend, "so much so that the people don't tip too much."[22] However, a benefit of Boston, he opined to Hughes in an October letter, was that "Up here you don't have to put up with segregation and you know that's alright with me."[23]

At the conservatory, he studied with the noted vocal teacher Madame Mildred Pieretto-Bianco. Born Mildred Turner in Alameda, California, Madame studied voice and piano in Naples and Rome after high school and became an Italian citizen. After divorcing her first husband, she moved to New York City and married an Italian immigrant, Pietro Pieretto-Bianco, in August 1916.[24] Subsequently, she gave concerts across the country and when Waring met her was dividing her teaching between Boston and Rome. With Maud's support, Waring was determined to pursue a career as an opera singer, both for himself and for his brother. "I hold myself responsible for my brother's talent," he explained, and "as soon as I get on my feet I'm going to put him back at the piano. . . . We are twins and no one can accompany me as well as my brother."[25]

Although he left Lincoln to focus on singing, he never viewed music and writing as mutually exclusive. Thus, in addition to his music studies at the conservatory, he also joined the Saturday Evening Quill Club, an organization of aspiring Black Boston writers. Club founder and president Eugene F. Gordon was passionate about writing but was also prickly and iconoclastic. He once wrote a scathing article in *Scribner's Magazine* about the snobbish members of brown Boston's elite "blue-vein society." Like Cuney, Gordon was a Howard man; however, he had graduated, and subsequently served as a second lieutenant on the battlefields of France during World War I. When Cuney met him, he was a successful journalist, a feature writer and later assistant editor at the *Boston Post*. Gordon had grown up in rural Hawkinsville, Georgia, and in New Orleans. After high school he moved to Washington, DC, where he worked as a janitor to finance his studies at Howard University.[26] The two men would certainly have compared their experiences in Washington and at Howard, and Gordon undoubtedly discussed his wartime experiences. One of Gordon's most poignant short stories, critiqued during Quill Club meetings, describes an enemy encounter during World War I.

When Gordon welcomed Cuney, he had already managed to gather a virtual Who's Who among Black Boston's budding artists and intellectuals into his club, including the short story writer Dorothy West and poets Helene Johnson, George Margetson, and Gertrude Parthenia McBrown. The essayist and clubwoman Florida Ruffin Ridley, playwright and actor Ralf Meshack Coleman, and painter Lois Mailou Jones (whose *Breezy Day at Gay Head* President Clinton selected for the White House) were also prominent members of the club. Waring's favorite was apparently Gertrude "Toki" Schalk, editor of Boston's *Sunburst* literary magazine and later society editor of the *Pittsburgh Courier*.[27] In a 1932 *Courier* column, "Smart Talk on Society in Boston," Toki teasingly reports that "Waring Cuney, the poet that-was who has turned into a singer-to-be . . . self-styled the Tenor-Poet . . . never the poet-tenor . . . hied himself home to D.C. for a few weeks. Whether or not he will scuttle back to Rome again for the summer, it is not known at present (neither by the tenor-poet nor others)."[28]

Eugene Gordon managed to publish three numbers of the club's annual, in 1928, 1929, and 1930. The 1928 issue, arguably the most successful, was favorably reviewed by the *Boston Herald*, the *Amsterdam News*, and *Commonweal*, and it was praised by both W. E. B. Du Bois, who deemed it the best of the Black literary journals, and Alice Dunbar Nelson, who appreciated its judicious editing and "seventy-two pages of very excellent material."[29] As he experimented with language and technique, Cuney clearly benefitted from the club's workshops, perhaps most successfully in "Play a Blues for Louise," which appeared in the 1929 publication. The poem tells a story of love gone awry. Louise, heartbroken, leaves town rather than suffer the abuses of an unkind man. Through masterful use of alliteration and the blues form, Cuney transforms a common tale into a tour de force. He would place five poems in the 1928 *Quill* and six in the 1929 issue.

While in Boston, Waring acknowledged his literary precursor by making a pilgrimage to Dayton, Ohio, in 1928 to visit Mrs. Matilda

Dunbar, mother of the late poet.[30] That he would admire the great Paul Laurence Dunbar is fitting, especially given their shared literary, family, and neighborhood connections. Moreover, Cuney grew up in the shadow of Dunbar High School, which was across the street from his school, Armstrong High. While divorcing her first husband in 1901–1902, Maud Cuney moved to Washington, DC, perhaps at the behest of her cousins Wright and Daisy Cuney and her good friends Robert and Mary Church Terrell; they all lived in the city's elegant LeDroit Park community (where Waring would also live), and the Terrells likely introduced her to their next-door neighbors, Paul and Alice Dunbar. In preparation for their March 1898 marriage, Paul, who worked as a page at the Library of Congress, had rented a house at 1934 4th Street NW, while Alice taught school in Brooklyn, New York. "It is a three storey brick with seven rooms," he informed his fiancée, "with pretty alcoves on the upper floors and with all modern improvements. It is just next to Bob Terrell's."[31] Apparently, Paul and Maud, who was two years younger, became fast friends; they made several joint appearances in Washington, as well as in the Midwest. In July 1902, the *Chicago Daily News* announced that "Paul Laurence Dunbar and Maud E. Cuney will be the stars at the annual summer meeting of the . . . St. John's Literary club of Englewood. . . . Mr. Dunbar will recite from his works and Miss Cuney will be the piano soloist."[32] It is tempting to speculate about a possible romance, as Alice left Washington for Baltimore. Paul eventually returned to his mother's home in Dayton. Although Dunbar died prematurely in 1906 at age thirty-three, the year of Waring's birth, Maud would have shared stories of her association with the legendary poet.

Toki Schalk confirmed in her "Society in Boston" column that a particular highlight of Cuney's time at the conservatory was his three trips to Rome, in 1929, 1931, and 1934. On a brisky Thursday morning, September 12, 1929, 23-year-old Waring arrived in New York harbor onboard the ship *Mexique*. He had departed from Le Havre, Normandy, on August 24, after spending three months touring the continent and studying in Madame Pieretto-Bianco's European studio.[33] During his European studies, he joked with Hughes about mastering Italian classics but disavowed any influence on his poetry: "I suppose my dear public is looking for Italian influences in my 'works.' But as I sing Italian classics down-home-like I might as well continue to write as a jigg."[34] Fatigued from the long ship ride, though happy to be back in New York, Cuney hopped a subway to Lenox Avenue and 145th Street. There he booked a room in the chic, three-story Hotel Olga, New York's hotel of choice for African Americans during the '20s and '30s.

Back in Boston, he began planning almost immediately for a second trip to Rome. His work at a local hotel and giving piano lessons to children paid most of the bills but left little for a savings account. However, Langston Hughes wrote in November with fortuitous news. The NAACP board member Amy Spingarn, who had sponsored Hughes at Lincoln University, would help finance Waring's second European trip.[35] Thus, by participating in the patronage system prevalent during the Harlem Renaissance in which wealthy individuals gave money for creative endeavors, he was able to spend summer 1931 in Rome, before returning to the US, via Naples, at the end of September.[36]

The following June, with an eye on a third trip, he applied for a Rosenwald Fellowship. He offered:

> I am a student tenor under the instructorship of Mme. Pieretto-Bianco who conducts studios in Boston during the autumn and winter and in Rome, Italy, during the spring and summer. Recently I learned that altho my expenses for study during the next term which begins on the eighteenth of June have been subscribed for, one of my sponsors, due to financial reverses, will be unable to give me passage to Italy and living expenses there.[37]

Accompanying the application were letters of support from Walter White, the NAACP secretary; Dr. Ernest Just, Cuney's biology professor at Howard University; and Hans Kindler, director of the

National Symphony Orchestra in Washington, DC. But their efforts were to no avail. George Arthur, the Rosenwald Fund's Associate for Negro Welfare, explained: "I regret to advise that this year's meeting of the Fellowship Award Committee of the Fund was held in April. At that meeting the Committee made its decisions concerning grants the Fund would award this year."[38]

Despite the setback, Cuney managed a third trip to Europe in summer 1934. In August, he wrote Hughes and jokingly reported (with a pun on the letter L): "I am throwing out High "l" in regular Italian tenor fashion." On a more serious note, he revealed that he had "almost completed a manuscript of poetry," and he hoped Hughes would "do an introduction to it."[39] While this volume did not come to fruition, Cuney did place a poem in Dorothy West's *Challenge*. At the end of the year, upon receiving "Song of a Song" for her journal, an elated West wrote, "Waring Cuney sent us his poem from Rome . . . his heaven on earth."[40] Waring sailed on the SS *President Monroe* from Naples on December 2, 1934, and arrived back in New York the week before Christmas.[41]

Some claim that while at the conservatory Cuney realized his voice was inadequate; thus, he ceased singing and switched his focus back to writing. However, a more careful reading of his record shows that he continued singing, writing, and composing long after he left Boston. In fact, in 1936, while dividing his time between New York and Washington, he considered enrolling at the Juilliard School. "Maybe if I publish a book of poems," he reasoned, "I can get a scholarship."[42] But 1936 proved particularly difficult for the family. In February, 61-year-old Maud Cuney Hare died of cancer in Boston. In July his aunt Jeanette C. Williamson, with whom his mother had lived her entire life, died at age 61 in Washington. Waring then moved into his parents' home at 503 Florida Avenue, in DC, with his mother, brother, and sister-in-law, probably to help care for his grieving mother. The end of the decade found him back in New York, taking singing lessons alongside the Metropolitan Opera star, John Charles Thomas,[43] and working for the Federal Writers' Project (FWP) in Harlem.

The Federal Writers' Project was established in 1935 as part of President Franklin Roosevelt's antipoverty New Deal program. It provided jobs during the Great Depression for thousands of unemployed writers, including Cuney, Zora Neale Hurston, John Cheever, Saul Bellow, and Dorothy West. Cuney's FWP essays have been ignored, but they constitute a significant part of his oeuvre. He produced fourteen essays, ranging from biographical sketches of Frederick Douglass and Madam C. J. Walker to an account of Marian Anderson's Easter 1939 concert at the Lincoln Memorial. Not unlike Waring, Anderson had begun playing the piano and singing as a child in churches in Philadelphia. She went on to win acclaim across the US and Europe, with a repertoire that ranged from opera to the spirituals. After the segregationist Daughters of the American Revolution refused to allow her to sing in their hall, Secretary of the Interior Harold Ickes invited the famous contralto to perform at the memorial. Cuney provides a captivating, firsthand view of the performance:

> Underneath a sparkling blue sky, 75,000 people of Washington gathered on Easter Sunday to pay homage to a great singer. . . . From the highest government officials of the land to the lowliest government clerk, no matter what their race or creed or color of their skin, they dressed in their Easter Sunday best and gathered at the stately white Abraham Lincoln Memorial. . . . Then Marian Anderson rose to sing. And the great audience rose with her in tribute—"to the proposition that all men are created equal"—members of the Cabinet, senators, Supreme Court justices and plain, ordinary Negro and white Washingtonians.[44]

Along with lauding a personal heroine, Cuney uses the essay to expand on many of the themes that recur in his poetry: protest against racism and Jim Crow segregation, the talent and beauty of Black women, concern for the poor and disenfranchised, and a celebration of Black music, especially spirituals and the blues. Had the Writers' Project not ended three months later, in July 1939, Cuney may well have developed a successful career as a journalist.

Reminiscing about the Harlem Renaissance, Langston Hughes mused, "It was Harlem's Golden Age." He continued, "We had so much fun and liked Harlem so well that we did not think about taking the long subway ride to the Village, where white artists and writers gathered. We let them come uptown to us."[45] Of the throngs of whites who flocked to Harlem, among the best-known, most influential, and most controversial was the novelist, journalist, and photographer Carl Van Vechten. Known for hosting lavish interracial parties and for interacting with young bisexual and homosexual Black men, Van Vechten was in many ways at the center of the Harlem Renaissance.

According to Van Vechten, he first encountered Hughes in November 1924 at the same NAACP benefit hosted by James Weldon Johnson at which Florence Mills performed.[46] There was a large crush of people, but Hughes remembered the prominent New York music critic as "a tall white man with an oddly shambling physique . . . and a jaw from which protruded remarkably ugly teeth."[47] On May 1, 1925, they met again at the famous *Opportunity* dinner where Hughes read some of his poems. This time, Van Vechten was galvanized into action and by May 25, as noted in his journal, he had received a "note from Blanche [Knopf] accepting Langston Hughes's poems."[48] In addition to securing the book contract with Alfred A. Knopf for what would become *The Weary Blues,* Van Vechten presented the poet to Frank Crowninshield, the influential editor of *Vanity Fair* magazine, who would publish his early work and ensure his national recognition. In return, Hughes was a willing companion, introducing Van Vechten to handsome young men like the irrepressible Bruce Nugent and joining him in boozy pub crawls through Harlem's raunchiest night spots.

By August 1925, Van Vechten was writing coyly: "At 6 Langston Hughes comes for dinner. At 9 Richard Bruce Nugent (Riccardo) arrives. The boys stay till midnight."[49] However, despite the undisputed networking opportunities Van Vechten offered to male authors, many, like the poet Sterling Brown and his fellow Washingtonian Waring Cuney, resisted his advances. They declined invitations to his photography sessions, where he took portraits of many now famous Harlemites, and they refused to attend his flamboyantly bisexual soirées. In an interview, Brown remarked,

> I have no relationship to any Harlem Renaissance. When they [the writers and artists of that era] were down there flirting with Carl Van Vechten, I was down south. . . . One of the most conceited things I can say is I am proud that I have never shaken that rascal's hand. . . . He corrupted the Harlem Renaissance and was a terrible influence on them. He was a voyeur. He was looking at these Negroes and they were acting the fools for him. And the foolisher they acted, the more he recorded them.[50]

Cuney and Brown, to their credit, escaped the corrosive effects of patron-artist relations. But when they avoided Van Vechten and his parties, they also hindered their chances for recognition and greater publicity. Hughes, who understood the importance of Van Vechten's public relations machine, was savvier and benefited greatly from his proximity to Van Vechten.

As the decade drew to a close, Cuney would have been justified in experiencing a sense of accomplishment, as every important Renaissance outlet, from Countee Cullen's *Caroling Dusk* to James Weldon Johnson's *Book of American Negro Poetry*, featured his verse. Despite his ubiquitous presence in publications, he always eschewed the "Harlem Renaissance" social scene. His extreme privacy, along with his inability to decide between careers in music or literature, may well have contributed to his omission from early critical assessments of the period. The critic J. Saunders Redding, for example, held that if Waring Cuney were not "so preoccupied with music and could give more time to poetry, he would certainly win wider recognition as a poet of subtle sensibilities."[51] Nevertheless, Cuney's peers, from Langston Hughes and Dorothy West to the renowned Charles

Spurgeon Johnson, recognized his enormous talent and encouraged his work. For his part, Cuney always rejected notions of a divide between music and poetry. He would come to describe himself as a trained singer and his occupation as a writer of lyrics.

Chapter 5

Waring Cuney, Military Poetry, and World War II

The sun makes a three point landing
In the blue eyes of an Irish nurse.

—"Ward Six," July 25, 1945 (previously unpublished)

ON WEDNESDAY MORNING, JULY 29, 1942, THIRTY-SIX-year-old William Waring Cuney enlisted as a private in the US Army at Fort Jay, Governors Island, in New York Harbor. His military photograph shows a handsome young man with squared shoulders, a small moustache, and a thoughtful, serious expression. According to his registration card, he was single, without dependents, and 5 feet 8 inches tall; he weighed 165 pounds, had three years of college, and worked as an office clerk.[1] Two years earlier, on October 16, 1940, his twin brother Norris Wright III, a teacher of printing at Armstrong Technical High School in Washington, DC, had registered for the draft. He listed his mother, Madge Louise Cuney, as next of kin. Apparently because he was married and the caregiver for his widowed mother, Waring's brother Wright III was never called to active duty.[2] However, in answering their country's call to service during World War II, the Cuney brothers followed the precedents of their maternal grandfather Thomas Williamson and their great-uncles, William Waring III and Joseph Cuney, all of whom belonged to the famed United States Colored Troops who fought to end slavery and save the Union. Waring's connection to his grandfather Thomas Williamson, a member of the 88th US Colored Infantry, can be seen in a photograph published in the February 1948 *Negro History Bulletin*, alongside Waring's own photograph. The two men gaze into the camera, regal in their crisp Army uniforms, united in patriotism, with Williamson's Union Victory Cross prominent on his lapel. In fact, Waring's military family connections extend back to the Revolutionary War and the service of his Scots ancestor William Waring.

There are also interesting parallels between paternal great-uncle Joseph Cuney, who joined the 63rd Pennsylvania Volunteers in 1861, and maternal great-uncle William Waring III who, in 1862, accepted an appointment as chaplain of the 102nd Michigan Volunteers. Coincidentally, as teenagers, Joseph and William both attended school in Pittsburgh in preparation for studies at Oberlin College. Although William attended Oberlin, the Civil War derailed Joseph's plans; however, after the war both were able to study at Howard University. Joseph was a member of the class of 1872 and a classmate of novelist Frank J. Webb.[3] William obtained his law degree in 1873 and remained in DC, where he practiced law, pastored the 19th Street Baptist Church, and served for nearly twenty years (1883–1900) on the Howard University Board of Trustees. At his death in 1900, he was buried in Arlington National Cemetery.[4]

Little research has been done on Waring Cuney's Army service during World War II, on his military poetry, or on the effects of his wartime experiences on his mental health. Of his artistic peers, including Langston Hughes, few joined the military or were actively involved in the war effort. Notable exceptions include the poet Samuel W. Allen and the journalist Roi Ottley, both of whom served in Europe; the novelist John Oliver Killens, a veteran of the Pacific theater; and the empresario and entertainer Jimmie Daniels, who served in

England. Yet Cuney came from a long line of military veterans, and his service was thus a foregone conclusion. Despite his pride in the military service of his family and his willingness to serve his country in World War II, there is no doubt that Waring Cuney's service in the Pacific took its toll on his body and mind. As the war dragged on, he must have worried that his youth and promise were dwindling away; in a letter to Langston Hughes, he joked sadly that he "was as grey as Uncle Tom."[5] In June 1945, without mentioning his illness or hospitalization, he explained to Hughes that he doesn't "write much anymore so tell the folks on the Hill [Sugar Hill in Harlem] hello."[6] Around the same time, he composed the poem "Ward Six," about "a sick lonesome soldier / Stretched out on a hospital bed."

Although this was a difficult time for him, he did develop two important relationships. Dr. Stewart G. Wolf, with whom he shared an interest in poetry, was the administrator of the 1,000-bed facility in the Philippines where Cuney was hospitalized.[7] Wolf, a native of Baltimore, belonged to the liberal, enlightened East Coast tradition that stretched back to the New England abolitionists. After graduating from Phillips Academy Andover preparatory school, he enrolled in Yale and then obtained a medical degree from Johns Hopkins. Wolf was particularly interested in neurology, psychosomatic illness, and the role of culture and tradition in disease. His first wartime assignment was doing postgraduate work at Harvard, where he met Walter Cannon, a professor of anthropology who, in 1942, had written a paper on so-called "voodoo death." Cannon was researching the phenomenon of unexplained death due to invisible or psychological stressors, as manifested primarily in Afrocentric cultures; he was also interested in the connection of wartime stress to psychoneurosis.[8] After being posted to the hospital in the Philippines, Wolf apparently utilized Cannon's theories to treat the shell-shocked soldiers. In Waring Cuney, Dr. Wolf would have found a thoughtful and intelligent individual who shared his cultural background and interests in race, psychic phenomena, and the arts. He may have encouraged the young poet to write as part of his therapy; years later, Cuney would autograph a copy of *Puzzles*, his first book of poetry, for Dr. Stewart Wolf.

Another of Cuney's therapeutic encounters at the hospital was with an attractive but unnamed young nurse. In "Ward Six" he borrows an aeronautical image when he writes: "The sun makes a three point landing / In the blue eyes of an Irish nurse." There would have been strict rules at the hospital about fraternization between nurses and patients (as well as between nurses, who were officers, and enlisted personnel, not to mention the complexities of an interracial love affair), so it seems likely that Cuney's relationship with the nurse was more emotional than physical. The poem emphasizes unspoken connections and "confidences" as the nurse's eyes "flash meanings" that reveal her attraction to the soldier. In addition, the poem seems to allude to the psychosomatic theories of Cannon and Wolf in the words: "A long time ago a doctor said: / 'There is as much to the art / Of practicing medicine / As there is to the science.'" The poem concludes with the assertion that the "soft caress" in the nurse's eyes has provided the soldier with "a therapy of faith, and hope."

Long before his service in World War II, Waring Cuney was interested in the dynamic between African Americans and the military. While attending Armstrong Manual Training School in Washington, DC, he and his twin brother Norris Wright III had served with distinction in the Army JROTC (Junior Reserve Officer Training Corps).[9] Begun under the leadership of Civil War hero Major Christian Fleetwood and continuing under Captain Arthur Brooks and Principal G. C. Wilkinson, the Colored Washington High School Cadet Corps, the precursor to the JROTC, was a joint program of the African American Armstrong and Dunbar High Schools. When Dunbar High replaced the famous M Street School in 1917, the Cadets were provided with state-of-the-art facilities, including an armory large enough for several companies and a rifle range. Cuney's enduring interest in the military is not surprising, given that the Dunbar-Armstrong

JROTC is generally credited with the broad participation by young African American Washingtonians in the military.[10]

In April of Waring's senior year, Emmett J. Scott, secretary-treasurer of Howard University, praised the city's JROTC cadets during a commissioning ceremony at Howard. "I have been told," said Scott, "that the men who come from the Washington High School Cadet Corps are those who take first rank in the military organization here at Howard University." Several thousand students from Howard and the "colored" high schools "fringed the campus and witnessed the ceremonies, which included a regimental review."[11] Waring was an active member of the Armstrong-Dunbar JROTC, reflecting his early interest in the Army and presaging the success he would find during WWII. During his senior year he advanced from first sergeant to battalion sergeant major, one of the highest-ranking positions in the unit.[12]

Cuney would have admired Cadet alumni such as gunner John Jordan, a hero of the Battle of Manila, and machinist Joseph Cook, who ran the dynamo on Admiral William T. Sampson's ship during the Spanish–American War. As an aspiring singer he would have been particularly interested in two military musicians, Captain Walter H. Loving, the director of the famous Philippine Band, and his protégé Lieutenant James Reese Europe, who introduced ragtime and jazz to France during World War I and became a world-renowned bandleader and composer.[13]

Cuney retained a lifelong admiration for Brigadier General Charles Young, a West Point graduate. Young was a veteran of the Spanish–American War, a military bandleader, an instructor of Military Science at Wilberforce University, and a close friend of W. E. B. Du Bois. He and Cuney also shared a family connection: at Wilberforce and later in the Army, Young had mentored Waring's second cousin Charles Burroughs, the illegitimate son of Norris Wright Cuney. In 1961, Cuney composed a poem in Young's honor, entitled "The Man Without a Country." The title is a puzzling choice for a poem about such an accomplished military leader; however, as Cuney makes clear, Young advanced his career despite virulent racism. Young had been made a colonel after his success in the Spanish–American War. In 1917, he was fifty-four years old and technically retired. However, he volunteered to serve in World War I where he would undoubtedly have been promoted to general. Unfortunately, the highest level of military command, including President Woodrow Wilson, denied his opportunity. Cuney writes, using quotes around key words: "The United States Army doctors 'examined him'. / They wrote 'unfit for active service'." Undeterred, "Colonel Young rode his horse / From Dayton, Ohio, to the White House, / In order to prove to Woodrow Wilson / That the army doctors were lying." Cuney attributes Wilson's denial to his wife's influence, whom he also blames for the sudden appearance of Jim Crow signs in wartime government offices; he would have known about these signs from his own father who was a lifetime employee of the US Government Printing Office. In the poem, Cuney articulates what Young and his advocates, including W. E. B. Du Bois, had long maintained, which was that the Army simply blocked his career, making him, in effect, a man without a country to serve. Cuney's poem was not in vain, however, given that on November 1, 2021, Charles Young was honorably and posthumously promoted to brigadier general.

Cuney's poem about Young expresses the disillusionment felt by many African Americans who had served honorably in World War I only to return to a country of exclusions and discrimination. For example, Cuney would have known of the treatment of African American veterans in the dreadful Red Summer of 1919, and he would have witnessed the Washington race riots in July 1919. His poem "Defense Factory Blues" features the widow and son of a World War I soldier who died fighting overseas. They receive neither honors nor thanks for their sacrifice. Indeed, as the son quickly learns, racism still reigns:

> Went to the defense factory, trying to find some work to do
> Had the nerve to tell me, "black boy, nothing here for you."

Prior to joining the Army in 1942, Cuney had been working for the Federal Writers' Project (FWP) in New York, run by Harlem native Vincent "Roi" Ottley. Ottley would prove to be an important influence both on Cuney's artistic development and on his decision to join the military. Three months younger than Cuney, Ottley had won a track scholarship to St. Bonaventure University in upstate New York and in 1926 became one of the school's first African American students. In 1928, he transferred to the University of Michigan to study journalism but returned to New York City a year later. From 1931 to 1937 he worked as a columnist and editor for the *Amsterdam News*. He then assumed a supervisory position with the Harlem unit of the FWP; it was in this capacity, leading research on the history of Blacks in New York, that Ottley met Waring Cuney.

As project supervisor, Ottley edited pieces by Cuney and several other literary luminaries, including Claude McKay, Ellen Tarry, Richard Wright, Dorothy West, Ralph Ellison, and journalists Ted Poston and Henry Lee Moon.[14] Cuney's old friend from Washington, Bruce Nugent, also worked on the project.[15] Here, Cuney honed his journalistic skills, conducting interviews and writing vignettes on New York's African American community. His interviewees included John E. Nail, the famous Harlem real estate entrepreneur and patron of the Harlem Renaissance. He also wrote about Frederick Douglass, Adam Clayton Powell's Abyssinian Baptist Church, and African Americans in the Union Army. An interesting essay written in June 1939 describes two Black World War I heroes, infantrymen Dorrance Brooks and Henry Johnson. Johnson, who single-handedly fought off a group of German soldiers, is well-known now and received a belated Medal of Honor from President Barack Obama in 2015, but Cuney was probably the first to celebrate him. Even today, few know about Brooks, who died in combat. However, 10,000 Harlemites attended the dedication of a small park in his honor in 1925.[16] Cuney was well on his way to a successful career in journalism when, in July 1939, federal sponsorship of the Writers' Project ended, leaving him and his colleagues out of work.

Ottley then managed to join the New York WPA Project, the state-funded successor to the FWP, while Cuney was hired as a reception clerk by the upscale Hotel Belleclaire, which still exists at 77th and Broadway. According to their military records, on October 16, 1940, the two men traveled to the Manhattan Selective Service Office and registered for the draft.[17] Ottley was subsequently commissioned as a lieutenant and served primarily as a freelance war correspondent. His journal of his wartime experiences in Europe and North Africa was published posthumously in 2011 as *Roi Ottley's World War II: The Lost Diary of an African American Journalist*. Although Cuney and Ottley both had three years of college, Cuney, like nearly all Blacks, was denied a commission. Tellingly, Cuney's fellow poet Sam Allen was drafted into the Army in 1942 as a private, although his education—first in his class at Fisk University and a law degree from Harvard Law School—clearly qualified him for induction as a commissioned officer.

Despite his disappointment at not receiving an officer's rank, Cuney found success in the military. After completing basic training, Private Cuney was promoted to sergeant toward the end of 1942. Elated, he shared the news with Langston Hughes, and added, "In about a week I'll have six months in Uncle's Army."[18] For initial training, he was assigned to Eglin Field in the Panhandle of Florida, near Fort Walton Beach. Established in 1935, Eglin was part of the US Army Air Corps and was designated the "Proving Ground." As the principal venue, or proving ground, for air warfare experimentation, Eglin was responsible for the testing of aircraft capabilities, aviation tactics and techniques, and air armaments and materials. Cuney worked as a surveyor with the 857th Engineer Aviation Battalion (EAB). These specialized battalions were 800-man units that designed, constructed, maintained, and defended airfields and runways overseas.[19] Military historian Ronald B. Hartzer notes that "of the 157 separate aviation engineer battalions . . . 48 were segregated units designated as 'Colored.'" He adds, "Instead of training in their wartime duties, black units were frequently assigned the more tedious and labor-intensive tasks." "The 857th," for example, "assigned to Eglin Field, Fla., for training was primarily used as labor troops at the installation."[20] Although denied an opportunity to develop their wartime capabilities, their training was finished, as it were, and Cuney's unit prepared to deploy overseas.

The 857th left Florida for the West Coast in February 1943. After arriving at Camp Stoneman in San Francisco, they departed for the South Pacific onboard the USS *Republic*. Cuney would see combat in Asia and the Pacific Islands, primarily in New Guinea and the Philippines, for the next two and a half years before being discharged in December 1945.[21] Many of the precise actions of Cuney's unit are difficult to determine. However, we do know that the 857th, often in poor weather and very difficult living conditions, built airfields, runways, buildings, and roads that facilitated "the Allies' advance toward the Philippines and the Japanese home islands."[22] Lieutenant Karl R. Rittman was one of the white officers who led the Black soldiers of the 857th. Following officers training in Virginia, Rittman joined the 857th in the Pacific. He offered the following firsthand account in 1944, while the unit was stationed in New Guinea: "We work under difficult conditions most of the time. The jungle is often so thick that it's like midnight under the trees, and yet when you cut down some of them the light pours in [and] is literally blinding. . . . Our engineers have performed extraordinary feats in . . . overcoming obstacles of all kinds."[23] In 2005, Major Natalie Pearson shed additional light on the contributions of the engineer aviation battalions:

> The US Army aviation engineer units played a crucial role in the success of General Douglas MacArthur's island hopping campaign in the Southwest Pacific Theater at the tactical, operational, and strategic levels. Allied victory depended on seizing lightly defended enemy territory and neutralizing enemy strongpoints from Australia to the Philippines through the following pattern: conduct air and naval bombardment, land the assault forces, defeat

> any Japanese units in the area, and construct airfields and base facilities. . . . Aviation engineer units rapidly constructed these airbases and provided the necessary facilities for land-based aircraft so that carrier-based aircraft could focus on protecting the navy's fleet.[24]

Despite the difficulties inherent in segregated units, Cuney's letters home were generally upbeat, with few complaints. He routinely asked about various young ladies in Harlem, and he shared amusing anecdotes of military life. The letters reveal a quick wit, an intense interest in poetry, and varying degrees of loneliness and homesickness.

Waring Cuney and Langston Hughes had been steadfast friends since their initial meeting on a Washington, DC, streetcar. When together, their shared interests in music and vernacular African American culture took them to blues bars, rent parties, speakeasies, and vibrant gatherings from Washington to Harlem. Now, with Cuney away, they traded barbs and humorous tales, similar to playing the dozens or "toasting." In one instance, Cuney masks his loneliness with humor:

> Hello Lang,
> I asked you to cuss Zelma and Lucille out for not writing. Then I asked them to cuss you out. Guess I'll wait until the lights go on and do my own cussing.[25]

A letter from home, he realizes—in ways that his friends cannot—does wonders for morale. Carl Van Vechten, older and more knowing, was one friend who understood: he lifted Cuney's spirits by sending him pictures of the gorgeous actress Lena Horne. At the end of 1943, African American nurses arrived in Nadzab, New Guinea, boosting everyone's spirits. "The colored nurses really look nice in their uniforms," an excited Cuney informed Hughes. And he added, with characteristic wit, "I guess I'll have to get sick to get near one. The boys at the club hang around like bees at the honeycomb."[26]

Cuney was right to admire these intrepid young women, whose arrival in the Pacific occurred only after the African American community vigorously protested the discrimination toward Black nurses by the Department of War. The brave Mabel Keaton Staupers, Executive Secretary of the National Association of Colored Graduate Nurses (NACGN), infuriated by such blatant exclusion, led a successful campaign, supported by First Lady Eleanor Roosevelt and Representative Adam Clayton Powell Jr., to admit Black nurses to the Army. By the end of the war, approximately 500 African American nurses held commissions, compared to 59,000 white nurses, with the former accounting for only 8 percent of the Army Nurse Corps.[27] At the time, Cuney could not know that he would indeed be cared for by a pretty young Army nurse or that after the war, a nurse from Wisconsin would play a major role in his life and work.

A few weeks after the nurses arrived in New Guinea, Cuney received what must have been jarring news. His application for a commission as an Army officer had been rejected. Ever a good soldier, he broke the news to Hughes with aplomb, humor, and a reference to the film starring Gary Cooper as an Army sergeant: "Tell the girls they will have to love me with sergeant's stripes as I didn't make the grade at the Candidates' School. Tell them Sgt. York was a sergeant."[28] How, then, did Cuney manage to maintain such equanimity, under the persistent pressures of both bias and war? Evidence suggests that he found relief, in part, by immersing himself in writing. As it had for other war poets, from Siegfried Sassoon to Lorenzo Thomas, poetry helped fulfill his need for emotional expression and proved cathartic. However, even with poetry as an outlet, by the end of the war he had apparently begun to show signs of psychological stress.

It was in Manila in August 1945 that Cuney learned of Japan's surrender, ending World War II. Two months earlier, on June 10, he had written Langston Hughes, sending him "Greetings from the Philippines." In his letter he is cheerful and makes no mention of being ill, although he had been hospitalized since May. He would never confide in Hughes the way he did in his fellow poet and childhood friend Sterling Brown. Perhaps because he knew their penchant for literary gossip, he never mentioned to either Hughes or to Carl Van Vechten that in the summer of 1945, he was hospitalized in Manila for the condition variously known as "battle fatigue," "shell shock," and "psychoneurosis" and now called post-traumatic stress disorder (PTSD). He eventually shared his diagnosis with Sterling Brown, writing in November 1945 from an Army psychiatric facility on Long Island: "At present I am resting from combat fatigue and waiting for my discharge."[29] But throughout his life, Cuney never discussed the illness that resulted in a medical discharge and undoubtedly contributed to his reputation as a recluse in the years after the war.

Cuney's combat unit was inactivated on August 15 with the end of the war, and the soldiers returned to the States.[30] Before permanently changing out of his uniform, Cuney traveled to the 107 West 86th Street office of photographer John D. Schiff and sat for a formal military photograph.[31] Schiff, who had recently escaped Nazi Germany, enjoyed a successful career in New York photographing many of the city's luminaries, including the Harlem Renaissance artists Richmond Barthé and Selma Burke. His image of Sergeant Cuney in full-service dress is striking. The muscular soldier's left sleeve features the 857th Engineer Aviation Battalion patch; his technical sergeant chevrons; five gold bars, each representing six months of service in a combat zone; and a diagonal stripe or hash mark, awarded for three years of honorable service. Above his left pocket are two rows of ribbons, including the Asiatic Pacific Theatre Ribbon with three Bronze Star Medals.

Cuney's mental health after the war would certainly have been exacerbated by the hostile treatment of his fellow soldiers by civilians at home. One does not have to look to the South, where so many of the depredations against Black soldiers had occurred after World War I; on Long Island, just a few miles away from Cuney's home in the Bronx, an Army veteran and his brother were shot in cold blood by a police officer. As usual, Cuney sublimates his anguish in poetry. "Freeport," first published in Reverend Adam Clayton Powell Jr.'s weekly Harlem newspaper, protests the racially motivated shooting:

In the town of Freeport
A soldier and his brother,
New graves in the graveyard
One beside the other.

It was a sorrow and a shame
God what a burying day,
Ashes and dust when they laid
The brothers away.

The biting irony of Blacks fighting and dying overseas to ensure democracy while simultaneously being denied the promises of democracy, at home and abroad, is a recurring theme in Cuney's martial poems.

In the early fifties, Cuney began a long-term relationship with Adeline Norris, a white nurse who worked at Bird S. Coler Hospital on Roosevelt Island. Cuney's friend, the Harlem Renaissance writer Wallace Thurman, had been hospitalized in another hospital on Roosevelt Island (then Welfare Island) when he died in 1934 of tuberculosis. Coler, which opened in 1952, was a chronic care facility that specialized in psychosomatic and other long-term illnesses. Cuney may have sought treatment as an out-patient at Coler, and Adeline Norris could have been one of the nurses who cared for him. However, Cuney was notoriously private about his personal life. Thus, he never discussed his mental health, medical care, or relationship with Adeline Norris, even with close friends Langston Hughes and Arna Bontemps, both of whom lived a few miles away in New York City. He may have felt that, since they had not served, they would be unable to understand his feelings of stress and anxiety.

He does, however, allude clearly to his mental state in his poetry, which explores the dynamic of veterans struggling with PTSD and other psychological issues. His poem "The Neighbors Stood on the Corner" finds an echo years later in Yusef Komunyakaa's "Roll Call," from his collection of Vietnam War verse, *Dien Cai Dau* (Vietnamese for "crazy in the head"). Both poems display what Kali Tal, in *Worlds of Hurt: Reading the Literatures of Trauma*, terms "bearing witness."[32]

She explains that survivors of traumas "constitute themselves as unique communities and bear witness to their traumatic experiences both privately and publicly." The survivors write a "literature of trauma [which] holds at its center the reconstruction and recuperation of the traumatic experience." Tal explains further that "literature of trauma is written from the need to tell and retell the story of the traumatic experience, to make it real both to the victim and to the community."[33]

In Komunyakaa's poem, a veteran recalls a memorial held for five fallen comrades. The roll call began with, "each M-16 / propped upright / between a pair of jungle boots, / a helmet on its barrel / as if it were a man." As was typical, after a name is read, a member of the company responds with "Absent Sir!" The speaker, though now safely back home, reveals that "Only / a few lovers have blurred / the edges of this picture. / Sometimes I can hear them / marching through the house, / closing the distance. All / the lonely beds take me back / to where we saluted those / five pairs of boots / as the sun rose against our faces."[34] His fears, memories of a specific wartime event, have become obsessive, and his lovers cannot help. Recurring war memories also play an important role in Cuney's "The Neighbors Stood on the Corner" and, as with Komunyakaa's "Roll Call," a lover's embrace can provide no lasting relief. We learn from the neighbors that "the night before / A man had turned on the gas." Unnerved and dejected, they converse back and forth, struggling to make sense of the suicide:

"Well, his troubles are over,
His worries are over."

"Me, I'll stay here with troubles,
What's new about worry?"

"He was overseas —
Colored, and in the army —
You know what that did to our boys."

"They say his wife left him —"

Both poems balance expertly drawn pictures with careful attention to sound. However, "The Neighbors Stood on the Corner" is potentially more unsettling, and not entirely because of the traumatic suicide. Absent a description of an actual, detailed war memory, Cuney's reader, like the neighbors, is left to imagine what they "did to our boys."

Cuney's friends, much like the neighbors in his poem, struggled to understand his postwar behavior and his mysterious disappearance from the literary scene. Once gregarious and fun-loving, he now came across as aloof and antisocial. Langston Hughes and Arna Bontemps, for example, frustrated in their efforts to reconnect with him, complained that he refused even to answer phone calls and letters: "My letters to Waring Cuney have NOT been returned, as I expected," commented Bontemps in January 1963, "but they have NOT been answered either."[35] Hughes, apparently naïve or oblivious to the psychological responses to war, replied airily, "Cuney is on a religious kick and won't see sinners."[36] However, Kali Tal helps us to understand that Cuney and other survivors of war, similar to survivors of sexual violence, have "passed through the Hell which for others exists only as metaphor."[37] Although suffering from PTSD, Waring Cuney, the old soldier, continued to "bear witness": his last poem, "Soft Kid," appeared in *The Iowa Review* the year before his death.

Chapter 6

The Later Years

Puzzles and *Storefront Church*

When the lights go on
All over the world again,
Will the light shine on me?

—"When the Lights Go On," January 17, 1943 (previously unpublished)

THROUGHOUT THE THREE LONELY YEARS DURING WHICH Waring Cuney served with the 857th Engineer Aviation Battalion (EAB) in the Pacific, he kept his focus on reestablishing his literary and musical career "when the lights come on," as he often described the end of the war in his letters to friends. His correspondents included Langston Hughes, Carl Van Vechten, NAACP activist Walter White, artist Aaron Douglas, and radical journalist Eugene Gordon. While "helping McArthur [*sic*] in New Guinea," as he drily referred to his military duties, he barraged Hughes with scribbled lyrics of blues songs, poem fragments, and original verses to popular tunes like "Don't Get Around Much Anymore" by Duke Ellington and Bob Russell.[1] Knowing that Hughes, in collaboration with composers W. C. Handy and Elie Siegmeister, was busily writing songs for patriotic rallies and wartime fundraising "pageants" at Madison Square Garden, Cuney probably hoped that Langston would promote the work of a songwriter who was actually serving at the front.[2] In return, he solicited

Hughes's latest poems and arranged for them to be set to music for the entertainment of the troops. Cuney was an active member of both the Orchestra and the Glee Club on base and undoubtedly lent his expressive tenor voice to the performance of Hughes's lyrics.[3] Always generous with praise for others, he never failed to tell Hughes how much the soldiers appreciated hearing his work.

In addition to honing his musical skills in preparation for the return to civilian life, Cuney maintained his literary interests. He eagerly devoured the latest books provided to soldiers in special overseas editions. In 1943 he read *Citizen Tom Paine*, the best-selling historical novel by Howard Fast, who also wrote *Spartacus*; an award-winning biography of George Washington Carver by Rackham Holt, the pseudonym of Margaret Van Vechten Saunders; and *New World A-Coming: Inside Black America* by his old buddy Roi Ottley.[4] Cuney would have recognized much of Ottley's material since the book was a compilation of pieces written when he and Waring had both worked for the New York Federal Writers' Project in 1939.

Cuney also kept up with trusted friends from Washington, DC, including movie star Leigh Whipper, his former neighbor from Florida Avenue. Whipper had appeared in acclaimed films such as *The Ox-Bow Incident* and as Ethiopian emperor Haile Selassie in *Mission to Moscow*. Cuney's aspirations definitely included Hollywood, and he probably hoped that Whipper, a close friend of actors Hattie McDaniel and Clarence Muse, would facilitate his entry to the film business. He knew, for example, that Langston Hughes had written lyrics for producer Sol Lesser, best known for his films featuring child star Jackie Coogan and for the Johnny Weissmuller *Tarzan* series.[5] Although apparently unable to help Cuney professionally, Leigh Whipper did entertain him with all the gossip in Black Hollywood, including tidbits about Lena Horne, with whom Cuney had become infatuated after seeing her in the film *Cabin in the Sky*. Like many soldiers, Cuney solicited pinups of his favorite stars; in a letter to Carl Van Vechten,

Cuney thanked him for the photographs of Horne which he "had passed around as far as they would go."[6]

At the behest of Van Vechten, who was assiduously assembling the James Weldon Johnson Memorial Collection of African American history and culture at Yale University, Cuney sent him a number of handwritten blues and military poems, including "Mississippi Story," "Hollow Log Blues," "No Name Blues," and "When the Lights Go On." He also mailed off a sequence of humorous poems about "Sergeant Dusty," a short, feisty, noncommissioned officer who, trickster-like, uses his wit to defeat bigger, stronger, higher-ranking soldiers. At one point, Sgt. Dusty, who stands an "even four-feet-four / not one half-inch less, not one half-inch more,"[7] takes on Big Mess Sergeant, who promptly insults his mother. Unfazed, "Dusty stood up / 'I don't play the dozens / No sir, not at all! / But so help me / I can make a man / Your size fall.'"[8] Cuney admired Hughes's popular column "Conversations After Midnight" in the *Chicago Defender*. The column featured the urban philosopher Jesse B. Semple and his satirical pronouncements on Harlem life, and Cuney may have intended to develop the Sergeant Dusty sequence along the same lines.

The glamorous photographs of Lena Horne were probably Van Vechten's way of thanking Cuney for the manuscripts, but they also reinforced the latter's exclusion, as a heterosexual male, from the coterie of handsome, talented men that had surrounded Van Vechten for more than twenty years and whose careers he had nurtured and promoted. In addition to Hughes, the group included Harold Jackman, Countee Cullen, Bruce Nugent, Richmond Barthé, Jimmie Daniels, Al Thayer, and Guyanese writer Eric Walrond. As explicitly documented in his "Daybooks," Van Vechten offered professional connections in exchange for companionship. For example, in 1926, at Van Vechten's insistence, Knopf published both Walrond' s book of short stories, *Tropic Death*, and Hughes's first book of poetry, *The Weary Blues*, for which Van Vechten contributed the introduction.[9] Cuney probably met Van Vechten through Hughes around 1926 when the latter was traveling between New York and Washington. Although he certainly fit the profile of the handsome, talented African American men pursued by Van Vechten and would have benefitted from his connections, Cuney, like his friend Sterling Brown, chose to remain outside the charmed circle.

The poet and Howard University professor Sterling Brown was one of Cuney's lifelong friends from Washington, DC, and Cuney certainly knew that Brown distrusted Van Vechten and denied his putative influence on the Harlem Renaissance. In a 1974 interview with *Callaloo* editor Charles Rowell, Brown insisted that "I never had any dealings with those people. . . . I have tremendous distaste for Carl Van Vechten, . . . He was a voyeur. . . . I don't even know what's in the Van Vechten business at Yale. . . . I've never run with any crowd, and I certainly didn't run with that damn Van Vechten kind of foolishness."[10] With his tenured Howard University position, the independent and iconoclastic Brown had the luxury of ignoring a powerful figure like Van Vechten. He had always admired Cuney's work and maintained that the latter's literary career was sidelined by his refusal to join Van Vechten's circle. Unlike Hughes, Cuney was never invited to "read some of his new poems" at Van Vechten's apartment to a glittering audience of artists, critics, rich patrons, and Broadway impresarios. Nor, on the other hand, was he ever obliged to accompany Van Vechten to drag clubs and speakeasies.[11]

Although Brown considered Cuney "[one] of the best writers" of the period, he noted, in a coded description of Van Vechten's milieu, that "Waring Cuney was no Harlemite."[12] For that reason, Brown maintained, Cuney was excluded from Nathan Huggins's book *Harlem Renaissance* (1971) which reified Van Vechten's influence on the movement.[13] Like Brown, Dorothy West was a friend of Waring Cuney and an admirer of his work; in fact, she published his poem "Song of a Song" in her literary magazine *Challenge*. As an eyewitness of the period, West corroborates Brown's claims that Van Vechten fetishized Black bodies. She was only seventeen when she and her cousin Helene

Johnson, both winners of the *Opportunity* literary contest, were taken to Van Vechten's apartment by A'Lelia Walker, the Harlem socialite and philanthropist. Their host had no qualms about fondling and "goosing" the vulnerable young women, despite the protests of their chaperone.[14] West also agreed with Brown that Huggins's account of the Harlem Renaissance was inaccurate and completely unreliable. She told interviewer Genii Guinier in 1978 that although the book was "everybody's Bible . . . I quarreled with everything Huggins said."[15] According to West, the problem was with his sources: Huggins relied on peripheral figures like Louise Patterson when "he should have asked me. I would have told him better than that . . . he didn't know I was in on that."[16]

Despite detractors like West and Brown, Van Vechten was still a powerful influence on African American literature in the nineteen forties. During the war, in his effort to stay connected to the literary scene, Cuney did communicate with him; however, he preserved a polite formality, always addressing his correspondent as "Mr. Van Vechten." He never employed the suggestive nicknames or sexual innuendo that characterized Van Vechten's correspondence with Hughes and others of his circle. In a letter of October 1942, Van Vechten sends Hughes "forty nights of pleasure . . . and days of sin and leisure."[17] Hughes always responded more discreetly, confining his virtual gifts to "pansies and marguerites" and "purple asters and autumn leaves."[18]

Of course, in 1943 Cuney was geographically outside Van Vechten's circle as well, since few of his New York friends, aside from Roi Ottley, were in uniform. In fact, Van Vechten overtly discouraged his acolytes from military service and commiserated with Hughes when it appeared he might be drafted. He was unsuccessful in deterring Jimmie Daniels, the handsome model and café society entertainer who was also a friend of Hughes.[19] Cuney would certainly have been informed by Hughes that Daniels was also serving in an Engineering Aviation Battalion, although his unit, the 847th EAB, was stationed throughout the war in the United Kingdom. Cuney would also have known Daniels was proudly homosexual and may have had him in mind as the model for "Black Doll Blues." Although apparently about an elegant heterosexual man whose "women folk" cry when he is drafted by the Army and killed in Germany, the coded language suggests that Black Doll is gay, and the poem thus recognizes the courage and patriotism of the gay community. Aside from Ottley and Daniels, however, most of Cuney's friends were still partying in New York; while deployed, he vicariously participated in their social and professional lives, writing wistfully to Langston Hughes from Eglin Field in the Florida Panhandle: "I read about the New Year's party. . . . Sorry I was not there."[20]

As Hughes's letters to Cuney demonstrate, his civilian status and his contributions to the war effort had greatly enhanced his professional reputation. Some of his work was pro bono, such as his efforts on behalf of the Negro Victory Committee, a Los Angeles–based organization led by newspaper editor Carlotta Bass that fought discrimination in the defense plants. However, his paid projects included radio scripts, patriotic lyrics, and marketing jingles for war bonds.[21]

As he slogged through the mud on New Guinea, Cuney must have envied Hughes his 1943 summer fellowship at Yaddo, the writers' retreat in Saratoga Springs, New York. There, insulated from the traumatic events of the war, Hughes wrote poems and enjoyed witty dinner parties with Margaret Walker, Carson McCullers, Katherine Anne Porter, and the radical journalist Agnes Smedley. In addition to hosting the writers' colony, Saratoga was a vacation spot for Harlemites in show business; they frequented the racetrack and dined at Spuyten Duyvil, the cozy restaurant owned by Leigh Whipper's estranged wife, the former Cotton Club dancer, Virginia (Be-Be) Wheeler.[22] Hughes also kept up with Harlem gossip as he socialized with the glamorous entertainers Ada "Bricktop" Smith and Blanche Calloway.[23]

That summer, race riots broke out in Harlem. Robert Bandy, a Black soldier, had intervened in the arrest of a woman by a white police officer who then shot and wounded Bandy. When an erroneous rumor circulated that Bandy was dead, two days of property destruction ensued. The disturbance, which Ralph Ellison utilized as the climax of his novel *Invisible Man,* reflected the community's resentment, primarily regarding segregation in the Armed Forces, for which Bandy became an instant symbol, but also on police brutality, wartime shortages, and the dearth of Black-owned businesses in Harlem. Hughes, writing from Saratoga, adopts an oddly irreverent tone, telling Arna Bontemps: "I am sorry I missed the riots. . . . I gather the mob was most uncouth. . . . Lots of Harlem glamour girls up here vacationing say they had their fur coats in 'storage' (née pawn shops). . . . Laundries and pawn shops looted . . . and Sugar Hill is shamed."[24] Mayor Fiorello La Guardia moved quickly to calm the tension: he partnered with the Writers' War Board (a private war propaganda organization, on whose Advisory Council Langston Hughes and Walter White sat) to commission two short plays from Hughes, *In the Service of My Country* and *Private Jim Crow.*[25] The latter dealt with segregation in the military; Hughes, with no personal experience, undoubtedly drew on his letters from Cuney and Jimmie Daniels about their experiences in the Engineering Aviation Battalions which consisted of Black enlisted soldiers and white officers.

Not surprisingly, it rankled Cuney that Hughes, despite being the right age and without dependents, was not in uniform. After passing his physical in October 1942, Hughes was classified 1-A (imminently draftable). However, he had also written an irate letter to his Selective Service Board, protesting segregation in the Armed Forces; in any case, his draft number never came up.[26] At one point, Cuney asks Hughes to inform a mutual friend that "Uncle [Sam] has me"; he then demands pointedly: "What's your story, you are under 45?"[27] To his point, he encloses a satirical poem about Jody, a Harlem "player" who spends his nights at the Sugar Bowl nightclub, flirting with the lonely wives of servicemen. A "Jody," he tells Hughes slyly, is military slang for "a civilian who takes a soldier's girl while the soldier is away."[28]

Since the two would not have been competing for women, Cuney's resentment undoubtedly centered on the fact that Hughes's civilian status was enhancing his career while Cuney languished in the Pacific. Years later, in 1966, Hughes would discover these wartime poems and letters of Cuney's in a box in a closet and send them on to the James Weldon Johnson Collection at Yale.[29]

By the summer of 1945, however, the war was ending, and Cuney was much more optimistic. He knew that the Guggenheim Foundation had announced a special award of $2,500 (approximately $40,000 today) to help artists transition from military to civilian life. An avid reader of the African American press, Cuney probably learned of the competition in the *Pittsburgh Courier*, where the placement of such an announcement signaled a welcome for applicants of color. He promptly wrote to Carl Van Vechten, Langston Hughes, Sterling Brown, and Walter White, outlining his ideas for a project and requesting letters of recommendation. While his application does not survive, it seems likely that his project was an anthology of poems from the Harlem Renaissance that had originally been published in small magazines and newspapers but had never been collected; he proposed a similar project to Langston Hughes a few years later. However, although the African American writer Gwendolyn Brooks did receive a Guggenheim Fellowship in 1946, Cuney's application was not accepted.[30]

In August 1945, the war ended and Cuney's combat unit, the 857th EAB, returned to the States. He had acquitted himself very well, having been promoted to technical sergeant and won three Bronze Stars. However, he was apparently still suffering from the psychological effects of the war because, before receiving his medical discharge, he was transferred to the Army's Mason General Hospital in Brentwood, Long Island. He had informed Hughes of his return immediately, albeit without mentioning his hospitalization, and Hughes passed on the news to Arna Bontemps: "Sgt. Waring Cuney [is] back."[31]

Mason General, which functioned between 1944 and 1946, was the work of New York State Architect William Haugaard, who also designed Attica prison. Upon his arrival in Brentwood, Cuney would have seen a massive brick tower and flanking wings, all with mansard roofs, rather like a forbidding fortress-chateau in the Loire Valley. Shortly before his arrival, Mason General was the subject of a documentary by filmmaker John Huston entitled *Let There Be Light*. The film was intended by the Department of Defense to convince prospective employers that traumatized veterans would transition successfully to civilian life. Nevertheless, despite the film's positive tone and the reassuring vignettes of normalcy depicted among the soldiers, it was deemed too upsetting for public viewing and was not released until 1981. Although sometimes difficult to watch, the film does offer insight into the rigorous program of psychiatric counseling, group sessions, occupational therapy, and athletics that Cuney experienced as he transitioned to civilian life. The G.I. Bill was a big part of the rehabilitation process: the veterans are seen studying college catalogs and listening to academic counselors. For Cuney, who had struggled all through the 1930s to fund his education, this benefit would have been particularly appealing.

Cuney would also have been heartened by Mason General Hospital's policy of racial integration: the film shows soldiers of all ethnicities joking together about the cafeteria food, playing sports, and encouraging one another in group sessions. The vignettes of soldiers interacting with loved ones on the hospital grounds feature both Black and white couples. Even before the war, Cuney was deeply troubled by racism in America. He was particularly incensed that Southern governors like Eugene Talmadge had the power to maintain Jim Crow. His poem "Some Talk for Governor Talmadge," which appeared in the *Pittsburgh Courier* in 1941, complains that Talmadge and his ilk "hold the South / By the throat," and insists: "You and Jim Crow both got to go!" His unpublished poem "When the Lights Go On," written while he was at Eglin Field, expresses his concern that racism will endure after the war. His experiences at Mason General may have instilled in him a certain amount of optimism; however, the brutal police murder of the African American veterans and brothers, Charles and Alphonso Ferguson, in Freeport, Long Island, just twenty miles from Brentwood, in February 1946, must have confirmed his worst fears.

Cuney was clearly not as ill as some of the soldiers in the film; in fact, he may have been treated on an outpatient basis, or given furloughs on the weekends. Even before his official release from the hospital in December 1945, Cuney was out and about, socializing with old friends. In November, he attended a housewarming party in elegant Oyster Bay, Long Island, hosted by Dr. William R. R. Granger. Granger, a Dartmouth graduate and prominent Brooklyn physician whose brother Lester Granger was Director of the National Urban League (NUL), had purchased a home near Teddy Roosevelt's family estate, Sagamore Hill. The *New York Amsterdam News* reported that "Sgt. Waring Cuney" enjoyed the party along with an elite group of African American leaders in medicine, law, civil rights, business, politics, and the arts. Guests included Mollie Moon, a Harlem socialite famous for her NUL fundraisers; journalist Ted Poston, who had accompanied Mollie Moon, Dorothy West, and Langston Hughes to Russia in 1932; Judge and Mrs. Hubert Delany, close friends of Eleanor Roosevelt; Mr. and Mrs. Clifford Alexander, whose son became the first Black Secretary of the Army; and Alta Douglas, wife of artist Aaron Douglas. W. H. Ruffin, the grandson of Boston civil rights leader Josephine St. Pierre Ruffin and an old friend of Waring's from Boston, was also present.[32] As the guest list demonstrates, Waring Cuney returned from combat secure in his social position among the highest circles of the East Coast Black elite.

In addition to these connections, Cuney quickly reestablished contacts with his friends in New York's artistic and liberal political circles. One of the first people he visited was Marguerite Cartwright, the beautiful actress and UN-accredited journalist, whom he may have known from Boston. He was still in uniform when they met, and Cartwright probably urged him to be photographed professionally; he presented her with a handsome print of himself in Army dress uniform, and she always kept it in her papers. Cuney also reconnected with Leighla Whipper, the charming and talented daughter of Leigh and Virginia Whipper. Leighla was a journalist and a composer of popular tunes, and she and Waring shared many musical interests; like Maud Cuney Hare, she was interested in "Creole" or Afrocentric music and had published songs in the Caribbean tradition. Along with Cuney and Hughes, she received royalties from the American Society of Composers, Authors and Publishers (ASCAP). She also wrote the society column for Congressman Adam Clayton Powell Jr.'s weekly newspaper *The People's Voice*. According to her column, Cuney attended a cocktail party hosted by Langston Hughes, where he mingled with the glamorous composer and entertainer Nora Holt, the Spanish teacher and Harlem salon hostess Dorothy Peterson, the novelist Ralph Ellison, and the artist Zell Ingram.[33]

Cuney also reconnected with actress and activist Fredi Washington, another reporter for *The People's Voice* and the stunning sister-in-law of Adam Clayton Powell Jr. Fredi Washington and Leigh Whipper were founding members of the Negro Actors Guild (NAG), the union for African American thespians; Washington was also, along with Langston Hughes and the late Rose McClendon, a proponent of a Black theater, such as the short-lived, radical Suitcase Theatre on 125th Street that Hughes had initiated in 1938 after his return from the Spanish Civil War.[34] The first theatre-in-the-round in New York, located in the International Workers Order, presented satirical skits and musical settings for Hughes's poetry. Waring had lent his tenor voice and acting skills to several productions, along with Fredi Washington, Dorothy Peterson, Alta Douglas, Robert Earl Jones, and Gwendolyn Bennett. In fact, as Hughes told Dorothy Peterson, he wrote a one-act "blues opera" called "De Organizer" specifically for Cuney.[35] Although it must have reassured Cuney to be embraced so readily by his old friends, he may also have felt rather lost in the postwar world.

Shortly after his return to New York Cuney learned, probably from his mother, Madge Louise Williamson Cuney, that Carter G.

Woodson, the editor of *Negro History Bulletin*, was researching the Cuney and Waring families. Woodson had been urged to create the *Bulletin*, an illustrated newsletter for teachers of African American history and culture, by the eminent educator, Mary McCloud Bethune, and he often featured articles on prominent families. He published the journal out of his townhouse at 1538 9th Street NW, just a few blocks from Madge's home at 503 Florida Avenue. Madge Cuney herself was an avid genealogist with an entire wall in her home dedicated to family photographs and memorabilia,[36] and she and Woodson would have belonged to the same Washington, DC, social circles. "The Waring Family" was published in February, followed by "The Cuney Family" in March. While Woodson surely drew on Maud Cuney Hare's 1913 biography of her father for the information on Philip Cuny and Adeline Stuart, he also included more recent details and photographs that could only have come from Madge Cuney. She certainly provided the photos of herself and her two sons for the Waring article (Waring Cuney is wearing his official Army uniform). And she probably contributed to the Cuney article the photos of her husband's father Nelson, her husband, his uncle Joseph, and his cousins Maud Cuney Hare, Lloyd Garrison Cuney, and Charles Sumner Cuney. The two articles, remarkable examples of genealogical research before the existence of digitized public records and Ancestry.com, must have helped to ground Waring Cuney within a strong family framework as he sought to establish himself after the war. In the following years, his Texas roots and his illustrious Texas forebears inspired his poetry; however, as he read Woodson's detailed description of his great-grandmother Adeline Stuart, he could not have known that her name was a harbinger of another Adeline who would eventually enter his life.

Meanwhile, Cuney was considering his postwar career options. Given his talents, and assuming a lessening of the resistance to the success of African Americans in the arts that had hitherto dogged his efforts, he could have contributed in the arenas of theater, film, music, poetry, and journalism. Like his cousin Maud Cuney Hare, Cuney was an excellent writer. Under the supervision of Roi Ottley in 1939, he had contributed to the Federal Writers' Project with profiles and interviews of such African American luminaries as civil rights leader Frederick Douglass; real estate mogul John Nail; entrepreneur Madam C. J. Walker; and World War I hero Henry Johnson. Fredi Washington and Leighla Whipper may have encouraged him to write for *The People's Voice*; although no articles exist under his byline, the newspaper did publish "Freeport," his poem about the police murder of the Ferguson brothers on Long Island.

He eventually decided on a career in music. He was still receiving royalties for the blues album on which he had collaborated with guitarist Josh White and for which Richard Wright had written the line notes. He now sought out composers of popular tunes for which he might contribute the words. When asked, he gave his occupation as "writer of song lyrics."[37] Before the war he had hoped to study voice at the Juilliard School of Music and had unsuccessfully sought a scholarship there. Now he utilized the G.I. Bill and enrolled in the Music Department at Columbia University, which was known for its opera program.[38] At least, he claimed to be enrolled at Columbia; however, the programs of the opera productions from 1946 to 1952 do not mention his name.

On a sunny April day in 1947, Leighla Whipper saw Waring getting a shoeshine on Seventh Avenue; he happily reported that he had found a perfect apartment in the Bronx.[39] Before the war, he had lived in Harlem, near St. Nicholas Avenue and the Victorian townhouses of affluent Sugar Hill. Now, however, perhaps because Harlem's energy was too intense for his fragile mental state, he moved three miles away, across the East River, to 1122 Tinton Avenue. Today, 1122 has been replaced by condominiums, but similar apartment houses remain on the avenue. Constructed around 1915, the five-story brick buildings, adorned only with utilitarian fire escapes, feature small but light-filled rooms and hardwood floors. From Tinton Avenue, the entire city is easily accessible via public transportation; a thirty-minute subway ride would have brought Cuney to either 125th Street in Harlem or to his classes at Columbia University in Morningside Heights. Nearby, the bustling Italian neighborhood of Arthur Avenue with its open-air market, vegetable pushcarts, and tiny shops selling pasta, cheese, and olive oil would have reminded him of his happy days in Rome. His Bronx neighbors hailed from Eastern Europe, the Caribbean, and Latin America; unlike homogeneous neighborhoods like Black Harlem or the white Upper East Side, the Bronx was extremely diverse: a liminal zone in which he could preserve his privacy and anonymity, it was also a vibrant urban environment that stimulated his creativity. Cuney would remain at 1122 Tinton Avenue until his death in 1976.

After moving to Tinton Avenue, he seems to have finally given up the idea of a musical career; instead, he would devote the rest of his life to his poetry. His friendship with Langston Hughes had cooled as the latter's literary star continued to rise; nevertheless, the two remained cordial. In February 1948, Cuney sent a sheaf of poems to Hughes and Arna Bontemps for their comprehensive anthology entitled *The Poetry of the Negro.*[40] Hughes had asked for a biographical sketch but in September, not having received it, he visited Cuney at Tinton Avenue where he pitched his latest idea: a series of photo-essays for *Ebony* magazine on "the colored poets around Harlem."[41] It is unclear how serious Hughes was about the project since, in a note to Arna Bontemps, he waggishly proposed photos of himself bathing in his newly tiled shower; Waring "in his cups"; and seventy-year-old William Stanley Braithwaite gingerly descending the steps of his apartment on Sugar Hill.[42] However, perhaps at the advice of *Ebony* editors, Hughes subsequently eliminated Cuney and the elderly Braithwaite in favor of younger poets such as Robert Hayden, Margaret Walker, and Melvin Tolson, "new voices which were not yet chirping" during the Harlem Renaissance.[43] The magazine ultimately rejected the idea, but one wonders if the omission of Cuney's poetry meant that Hughes felt he had not kept up with the literary scene.

Nevertheless, Hughes continued to promote Cuney's work. In 1950, as guest editor of the journal *Voices*, he included Cuney's poems in a "Negro Poets Issue" along with those of Robert Hayden, Gwendolyn Brooks, and Georgia Douglas Johnson.[44] In 1952, Hughes forwarded a request from Eva Hesse, a German editor and translator who wished to reprint "No Images." The following year, he informed Cuney that his work was included in a Czech anthology of African American poetry. However, Hughes could not resist a sly dig at his friend's expense, noting to Bontemps that the Czech anthology included "Waring's one immortal and ubiquitous 'No Images.'"[45]

Despite Hughes's intimation that Cuney was a one-poem writer, the latter produced work steadily throughout the postwar years with an eye on publication. His subjects included both urban vignettes of his Bronx neighborhood and reflections on his parents, his grandparents, and his Texas background. In 1949, he mailed a group of poems to Yale University which he dedicated to Mrs. James Weldon Johnson. A few years later, he sent a typescript of several poems to his friend, the United Nations journalist Marguerite Cartwright, who had probably encouraged him to publish a book.[46] The poems he sent Cartwright included "The Ledge," inspired by his multicultural Tinton Avenue neighborhood. The poem, which describes the custom in Puerto Rican bars for a penniless drinker to toss his very last coins onto a ledge above the bar in a show of pride or bravado, was one that he would eliminate from his first book of poems; thus, the only extant version is the one sent to Cartwright. Around this time, he penned several poems about the Galveston heavyweight champion, Jack Johnson, one of which seems to allude to his great-uncle Norris Wright Cuney's abuse at the hands of the Lily-White faction of the Texas Republican Party. Waring was aware that in 1959, Robert C. Cotner, a professor at the University of Texas at Austin, had published a biography of Texas governor James Stephen Hogg, in which he included a photograph and a political cartoon of Norris Wright Cuney.[47]

Like Langston Hughes, Cuney was a member of the Poetry Society of America and would often travel downtown to the National Arts Club, the elegant brownstone in Gramercy Park where the group met. The Poetry Society had always encouraged African American writers and had given awards to Countee Cullen, Langston Hughes, and Gwendolyn Brooks. Cuney would have recalled that members Vachel Lindsay and Witter Bynner had awarded his work an honorable mention in the 1926 Witter Bynner Undergraduate Poetry Awards, while Langston Hughes had won first prize. Now, in the club's cozy, paneled rooms, Cuney found a warm reception among the membership, which included Elizabeth Bishop, Marianne Moore, James Merrill, and Wallace Stevens.

In 1953, Cuney's alma mater Lincoln University suggested that he and Langston Hughes produce a reprint of their earlier booklet of poems, "Four Lincoln University Poets," in honor of the school's centennial. Friends from the Poetry Society, with whom Cuney had shared both the original Lincoln booklet and the Hughes-Bontemps anthology *The Poetry of the Negro*, encouraged him to consider a more ambitious project because it "would be unique in both academic and literary circles."[48] In fact, as Cuney reported to Hughes, Gustav Davidson, the secretary of the Poetry Society and the owner of Fine Editions Press, had offered to publish the volume. Hughes agreed to collaborate with Cuney and classmate Bruce M. Wright on an expanded volume of poetry with an original cover illustration by Cuney's friend Romare Bearden, another Lincoln alumnus ('33) who was winning acclaim as an artist in Harlem.[49] Hughes deployed his networking skills and secured funding for the volume; however, once he had the money in hand, Cuney seems to have lost interest in the project. He ignored Hughes's urgent requests, including letters, phone calls, and a telegram, for a meeting to finalize plans.[50] Through the years, Cuney would repeat this pattern in which a period of elation and enthusiasm would be followed by a complete silence and disappearance; the behavior may well have been related to mental health issues and his wartime PTSD.

After the 1954 publication of the *Centennial Anthology of Lincoln University Poets,* which appeared without Bearden's artwork, Cuney proposed an even more ambitious project to Hughes: an anthology of Harlem Renaissance poets that would include the uncollected poems of Arna Bontemps, Countee Cullen, Sterling Brown, Anita Scott Coleman, Georgia Douglas Johnson, and Claude McKay. Once again, Romare Bearden would be asked to illustrate the volume with woodcuts of selected poems. Perhaps still annoyed by Cuney's disappearing act, Hughes replied cautiously that Jean Toomer and James Weldon Johnson should be included. However, he soon distanced himself from the project, advising Cuney that woodcuts by Bearden would be expensive for publishers and that anthologies were difficult to sell, although he did so very successfully through the years. It seems possible that this prospectus was the same one Cuney had submitted unsuccessfully to the Guggenheim Foundation in 1945. In any case, there was apparently no more interest in the Harlem Renaissance in 1954 than there had been in 1945; it would not be until the nineteen seventies that interest in the period once again emerged. As always, Hughes was far more prescient than Cuney about the literary marketplace.

Despite the rejection of his anthology, 1954 was an auspicious year for Cuney. He began corresponding with Paul Breman, a young Dutch writer and editor who would eventually publish his two books of poetry. In May, Breman had written letters to both Hughes and Cuney. His letter to the former was rather prickly: he had read *The Poetry of the Negro* and was disappointed that Hughes had included only a token poem by an African writer. Ever the diplomat, Hughes handled the criticism smoothly: "Langston replied with . . . a large parcel of books" and invited Breman to visit his studio in Harlem where, after browsing in Langston's library, he proposed that the two men should "go downstairs and eat some good old pig feet and sauerkraut with cornbread."[51] Needless to say, Breman was charmed.

Breman's letter to Cuney was more cordial and requested permission to publish thirteen of his poems in the Dutch journal *Minerva.*

By June 1954, the three were all friends; Cuney mailed off copies of his poems and noted: "Langston sends regards. I talked to him yesterday on the phone."[52] In 1958, perhaps encouraged by his friend Marguerite Cartwright, as well as his mother and his brother, whom he often visited in Washington, DC, Cuney proposed that Breman publish a book of his poetry.

Cuney's commitment to the project can be seen in Breman's comment that, while preparing the volume that would become *Puzzles*, he "received a succession of envelopes from Waring, sometimes three or four in a week, each containing three to six typed and signed poems. In the end I had about 400 different poems."[53] Some of the poems, such as "No Images," date from 1926, while others are inspired by Cuney's Texas background and by the urban diversity of Tinton Avenue. The poignant "The Neighbors Stood on the Corner" both particularizes Tinton Avenue and universalizes the theme of postwar trauma, as experienced by Cuney himself and by so many returning veterans.

In 1960, *Puzzles* was published in Utrecht, the Netherlands, in an elegant limited edition of 175 copies with eight two-color woodcuts by Dutch sculptor Ru van Rossem (1924–2007). In his glowing introduction, Breman lauds Cuney's craftsmanship and his ruthless editing "toward greater simplicity . . . greater impact . . . [a] rigid economy of expression."[54] He notes the poet's abrupt decision to eliminate "The Ledge" because he wasn't completely sure of the details of the barroom custom described in the poem. Perhaps in recognition of some of the family-inspired poems, Cuney dedicated the book to his mother, Madge Louise Cuney. He also inscribed a copy for his old friend from the hospital in the Philippines, Dr. Stewart Wolf. The book never received wide distribution: Arna Bontemps only heard of it through the literary grapevine and questioned Hughes about the circumstances of its publication. Arthur Spingarn, however, did his best to publicize it, describing it in his February 1962 *Crisis* magazine column as the work of a "brilliant poet."[55] As Hughes reported to

Cuney, Spingarn had seen the volume displayed in London and found it "very beautiful."[56]

Although Cuney's musical career had not kept pace with his literary success, he maintained a deep interest in music, dance, and theater. Along with Hughes, he patronized Minton's Playhouse on West 118th Street where the new "be-bop" jazz was being developed by Dizzy Gillespie, Thelonius Monk, and Charlie Parker. Inspired by the music, Cuney began to experiment with be-bop rhythms and would immortalize Parker's music in a poem that was eventually mounted in a wall mosaic in the Netherlands.

Cuney never held a regular job after the war, but he was apparently able to support himself on his military pension, his ASCAP royalties, and a modest family legacy. In 1957, the blues album on which Cuney and Josh White had collaborated in 1940 was reissued and well received, so there was probably some remuneration from that source.[57] This income would not have sufficed for a family, however, and Cuney seems to have resigned himself to the fact that he would never marry or have children. Between his colleagues in the Poetry Society, his correspondence with Breman, his friendships with several beautiful, accomplished women, and his nights in the theater and in Harlem jazz clubs, he had arranged his bachelor existence.

In 1955, however, Waring Cuney's personal life took a very dramatic turn. He met the vivacious and loquacious Adeline Norris (1913–2008), a petite, brown-eyed nurse from Wisconsin whose first name, prophetically, was the same as that of his great-grandmother, Adeline Stuart. Waring—reserved, diffident, and probably suffering from periodic bouts of depression—was clearly attracted to Adeline's sunny and outgoing personality. Norris's nephew, Roger Anderson, recalls that Adeline was an "eccentric" and original woman who designed and crafted her own Christmas cards and "loved the arts"; even later in life, her letters to family members were "full of theater events, books she's read, and festivals she had attended."[58] Another relative described her as a "widely travelled . . . active and intellectual woman involved in cultural and civic affairs."[59] A lover of film, music, dance, literature, and theater, Adeline took full advantage of New York's offerings. She was also a member of the New York Theosophical Society, an organization that opposes prejudice and racism in favor of a universal brotherhood of man, a rational study of science and literature, and a liberal and pantheistic philosophy. During these years, Waring too was on a spiritual quest and often visited the small storefront houses of worship that proliferated throughout the city. The two may well have met at a meeting of the Theosophists, at a theater or dance performance, or at a Harlem jazz concert.

Adeline Norris had actually arrived in New York with her RN degree in 1938; she had graduated from Methodist Hospital School of Nursing in Madison, Wisconsin, but "wanted to expand my nursing experience and seek a change in my life."[60] She answered an advertisement for a job at Metropolitan Hospital on what was then Welfare Island, and later became Roosevelt Island, in the East River. When the hospital relocated to East Harlem in 1955, she transferred to Coler Hospital, a state-of-the art medical facility that was also located on Roosevelt Island. From 1938 to 1952, she lived in the Nurses' Residence and probably worked in the hospital's well-known psychiatric ward. She herself apparently felt no reluctance to seek counseling: in "Girl from Oklahoma," Waring marvels that a woman who has "beauty, brains, and bucks" still "Talks to a psychiatrist / Three hours a week, / Because she is lonely." Certainly, her romantic life was a disappointment before she met Waring, and she suffered through various "not too satisfying relationships."[61]

Adeline Norris's colorful family history forms an interesting counterpart to Waring's own forebears. Her pioneering Norwegian grandparents immigrated to Juneau County, Wisconsin, where they took up farming and where her mother, Laila Lee, was born in 1886. Adeline probably inherited her intrepid spirit from Laila. She was known in the family as "an ambitious girl" who, since the age of fourteen, had made her own money by "working out" as a servant for other families.[62]

For years Laila kept company with a young farmer of whom her family approved, but in 1910, perhaps at a dance, she met an itinerant gambler and grifter named Will Norris. Norris, who "could turn his hand at most anything, but was mainly a confidence man," was undoubtedly attracted to Laila's robust bankbook; they married suddenly, and he whisked her away from her family to a remote homestead near the North Dakota line in Terry, Montana. Six months before Adeline's birth in 1913, Norris absconded with Laila's savings and abandoned her in the "shack [on] the homestead" in which she was legally required to remain until the government contract expired.[63] Fortunately, Laila was joined by her young brother Henry and her cousin Inga, who helped to deliver Adeline under the most primitive of conditions. Eventually, Laila and Adeline returned to Wisconsin, where Laila helped her own mother on the family farm until the latter's death in 1951.

In 1952, Adeline invited her mother to join her in New York, and they found an apartment on Manhattan's Upper East Side. While Adeline pursued her bachelor and master of nursing at New York University, Laila read all of her textbooks and nursing journals, amassing so much knowledge that "she should have graduated too." Adeline always claimed that Laila's arrival in New York was fortuitous, recalling that "[good] things began to happen to me after [Laila] arrived. Above all, I met Waring."[64]

Judging from Waring's poetry, theirs was truly a love match. He often honored her with tender little compositions such as "I Tell My Baby," in which he admits "her name is Adeline." His reflections "Figure Eight" and "A Flower" celebrate Adeline's quiet beauty and her glossy brown hair, which she wore in a rather old-fashioned bun at the nape of her neck. Another poem, "Guitar Music," although not explicitly about Adeline, alludes to their harmonious relationship and the fact that "It takes two hearts / To make guitar music." At first, Adeline flew back to Wisconsin periodically to visit her family; after one such airport departure, Waring wrote a sort of proposal in "A

Man and a Woman": "Somehow two people know / When they meet again / They will never say good-bye again." However, like any couple, they occasionally disagreed; she may have objected to her description in his poems. For example, in "Girl from Oklahoma," Waring teasingly identifies Adeline as a woman whose advantages include "beauty, brains, and bucks" (discreetly unstated is her fourth advantage: race privilege), but who still sees a psychiatrist to discuss her "problems." In the poem "Sorry," he humorously complains they "can't get along" because of her constant chatter. "You talk me to death," he writes, "I'm too young to die." Waring also seems to have gotten on famously with Laila Lee, whom he clearly admired and to whom he dedicated a poem. In "Laila," written on the occasion of her death in 1974, he celebrates her vivacious and youthful spirit as he imagines her a young girl welcoming her first beau. Although the couple remained "engaged" from 1955 until Waring's death in 1976, and although Adeline's obituary described him as her "pre-deceased fiancé," the two never married or lived together.[65]

Theirs was certainly an unusual dynamic. As a psychiatric nurse familiar with both medication and counseling therapies, Adeline would have been well qualified to manage Waring's depressed and despairing moods. In fact, she seems to have run interference between Waring and the world. She apparently handled all his literary and business correspondence from her own apartment; at one point Cuney instructs Breman to correspond through Adeline but not to put his name on letters, as she will "know" which letters belong to him.

Starting in 1961, just after the publication of *Puzzles* and during the period when Waring was writing his most romantic poems to Adeline, he became a complete recluse. He ignored letters and phone calls from Langston Hughes, Arna Bontemps, and the Dutch anthologist Rosey Pool. Bontemps wanted to include his work in a new anthology, *American Negro Poetry,* along with poems by Gwendolyn Bennett and Helene Johnson, but claimed he was impossible to locate. Since he never left Tinton Avenue, one wonders how hard Bontemps really tried, especially since Rosey Pool apparently found him at home.

She reported to Hughes and Bontemps, possibly on Waring's ironic instructions, that he had found religion and "won't see sinners."[66] This may or may not have been literally true, although Breman also mentioned that Cuney went through a "born again" phase at this time.[67] It is worth noting that from 1961 until his death in 1976, Waring remained in close contact with Paul Breman, sometimes mailing three or four selections of poems a week. Perhaps he had become disenchanted with Hughes, Bontemps, and other members of the Harlem literary scene and now felt that they did not have his professional interests at heart, as Paul Breman evidently did. He may have felt possessive about his publishing arrangements with Breman and feared that the more gregarious and professionally skilled Hughes could usurp him in the former's eyes. Another possibility is that, given his lifelong commitment to African American culture and identity, Cuney was self-conscious about his interracial relationship with Adeline and wanted to protect their privacy from what would certainly have been gleeful Harlem literary gossip. He certainly succeeded in keeping the relationship quiet, since it was never even alluded to by any of his Harlem acquaintances.

Between 1962 and 1973, Cuney maintained his steady relationship with Adeline and worked assiduously on his last book of poetry, *Storefront Church*. During this period, he returned definitively to his family's Texas roots. In 1965, his brother, Norris Wright III, was contacted by Virginia Hinze, a young graduate student in history at Rice University. Hinze was writing her master's thesis on Waring's great-uncle, Norris Wright Cuney, and she apparently sought and received valuable information. In her acknowledgements, she thanks "N. Wright Cuney of Washington, DC," for his "help and interest." In order to assist Hinze, Norris Wright III would likely have consulted his brother and his mother. It was probably Madge Williamson who shared with Hinze the article by Carter Woodson on the Cuney family. Waring himself may have suggested that Hinze obtain the book *Norris Wright Cuney: A Tribune of the Black People* (1913) by

Maud Cuney Hare. Waring, who had lived with his cousin Maud in Boston, would no doubt have heard many stories about her adored father. Certainly, Hinze's research inspired Waring to reflect on the family's Texas past.

It is unlikely, in the days before digitized and readily available theses and dissertations, that either Waring or Norris Wright III ever saw Hinze's completed project. Had they done so, they would have been appalled at the fact that, given the reliable sources that described Norris Wright Cuney and his mother, the family matriarch Adeline Stuart, in the most glowing and positive terms, Hinze had chosen to undermine them with inaccurate information and racially stereotyped descriptions.

In the late sixties, Waring was busy compiling the poems for his last book, *Storefront Church*, which were inspired by his family's Galveston experiences and by his paternal grandmother, Laura Glover Cuney.[68] A deeply religious woman, she had perished in the 1900 Galveston Hurricane, along with her mother-in-law Adeline Stuart and her son Richard. One of Waring's poems, "Three in a Row," undoubtedly references that tragic event in the description of a family that abruptly loses members from three generations. The heavyweight boxing champion Jack Johnson also inspired several poems, including "Little Arthur (Johnson's Galveston nickname, by which the Cuneys would have known him) and "My Lord, What a Morning." Paul Breman published *Storefront Church* in a limited edition in London in 1973. Unfortunately, the following year, Breman's printing business went bankrupt, and it is unlikely that Waring even received royalties for his book.

As soon as *Storefront Church* was complete, Waring began planning a third volume of "Ragtime, Blues, Ballads, and Gospels" which would have a definite Texas flavor and which he intended to dedicate to his father.[69] As he composed the poems for this book, Waring discussed his family with Breman, who had expressed interest in the political career of Great-uncle Norris Wright Cuney; in one letter, Waring cited a book by Robert Cotner, a professor at the University of Texas, in which Norris Wright Cuney is mentioned.[70] He certainly discussed his Texas family stories with Adeline Norris. According to her nephew, Norris was passionately involved in her own family history and would probably have been equally engaged and curious about Waring's forebears. Waring undoubtedly told her about Maud Cuney Hare's accomplishments, and Adeline may well have identified with such a strong, determined woman artist. Adeline would also have learned about Sunnyside, the family plantation on the Brazos River, the name of which Maud Cuney Hare borrowed, many years later, for her own cottage on the Massachusetts shore. Although Maud never wrote about her own tragic family history, Waring knew all the details, and probably shared them with his life partner. After reading Maud's book about her parents and grandparents, Adeline would also have known about the unconventional, thirty-year relationship between Philip Cuny and Adeline Stuart, and may have noted the ways in which it mirrored her own relationship with the couple's great-grandson.

Waring Cuney continued writing poetry until the end of his life. In the spring of 1975, he published his last poem, "Soft Kid," in *The Iowa Review*. Its deceptively simple, elegiac tone seems to allude to his quiet, unassuming personality and to presage his own passing. Did he recognize himself in the "Soft Kid" who "bought a hotdog" but "needed a steak"? Was it he who "Fell asleep with the Blues — / He forgot to wake"? The following year, on June 30, 1976, Waring Cuney died; the cause of death was cancer, and he was seventy years old. Adeline, who had lost her beloved mother two years earlier, was devastated. She arranged with Waring's brother and sister-in-law, Laura Amelia Cuney, that Waring be buried in the family plot in Hyattsville, Maryland. Although he left no children, his legacy is a body of poetry that celebrates a remarkable African American family.

Technical Sergeant Waring Cuney in his military uniform, 1945. (Photographer John D. Schiff. Courtesy of Marguerite Cartwright Papers, Amistad Research Center, New Orleans, LA.)

MADGE L. CUNEY

NORRIS WRIGHT CUNEY; II

Waring Cuney's parents, Norris Wright Cuney II and Madge Louise Cuney. (C. G. Woodson, "The Cuney Family," *Negro History Bulletin* 11, no. 6 (March 1948): 124 and 11, no. 5 (February 1948): 103.)

Waring Cuney's sister-in-law, Laura Amelia Cuney. (Courtesy of Susan Salus.)

Maud Cuney Hare at her piano. (*The Crisis* 7, no. 5 (March 1914), 216.)

Maud's brother, Lloyd Garrison Cuney. (Photographer C. M. Bell. Courtesy of Library of Congress Prints and Photographs Division, Washington, DC.)

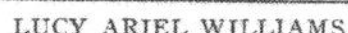
LUCY ARIEL WILLIAMS

WARING CUNEY

F. H. WILSON

ARNA BONTEMPS

Our Prize Winners a

LUCY ARIEL WILLIAMS (Awarded one-half of first and second prizes for poem *Northboun'*)—Has achieved an enviable reputation at both Talladega and Fisk for her versatility. She is quite well known as a modiste, poet and a very talented pianist. She has been heard over the radio from Nashville several times this year, each time giving pleasing performances. Her interest in poetry is innate, as her father is an excellent writer of prose and verse.

WARING CUNEY—Whose pseudonym "Ford Kramer" was awarded one-half of first and second prizes for poem *No Images*—Born May 6, 1906, at Washington, D. C.; a graduate of Armstrong High School; at present a student at Lincoln University, Pa.

MILES MARK FISHER—Awarded second prize for essay *Modernism and the Negro Church.*

HALL JOHNSON—Awarded third prize for musical composition *Way Up in Heaven.*

F. H. WILSON—Awarded first prize for play *Sugar Cain*—Born in New York, has spent 12 years in vaudeville as organizer and baritone singer in "The Carolina Comedy Four"; as lead at the Bramhall Playhouse in Butler Davenport's "Justice"; created Joe in Eugene O'Neill's "All God's Chillun Got Wings"; supported both Paul Robeson and Charles Gilpin in "The Emperor Jones"; played the name part in O'Neill's "The Dreamy Kid," and others. Has written sixteen one-act playlets and four three-act plays; has produced eleven of the playlets and one play. Was three years writing "Sugar Cain."

ARNA BONTEMPS (Awarded Alexander Pushkin poetry prize for *Golgotha Is a Mountain*)—As my name indicates, I was born in Louisiana (Alexandria). That was in 1902, and in about three years my parents carried me to California, where I lived until September, 1924. Attended public and private grammar schools in Los Angeles and Glendale; high school at San Fernando; college at University of California (Southern Branch), and Pacific Union College where I received the degree of B.A. in 1923 (with honors—as they say of all students who pass without difficulty). For one season I earned my salt, ice cream, etc., singing with a male quartet, then came to New York where ever since I have taught in the small private school, Harlem Academy. I can think of nothing remarkable to point to—that is, nothing that would do to tell, still I think that I have had a most interesting and unusual life.

ANITA SCOTT COLEMAN—Awarded second prize for personal experience sketch *The Dark Horse*—Place of birth, Guaymas, Mexico; attended school in Silver City; an ex-school teacher; am married; live on a ranch; engaged in raising children and chickens.

WARREN A. McDONALD—Awarded third prize for play *Blood*—As yet I have not accomplished enough to furnish material for even a brief sketch. I am one of those people who do not have any good excuse or reason for scribbling—but who insist upon doing it.

ARTHUR HUFF FAUSET (Awarded first prize for short story *Symphonesque* and first prize for essay *Segregation*)—A Philadelphian, but by accident born in Flemington, N. J. This accident and my failure to make Phi Beta Kappa are my only two great regrets in life.

Achievements—I feel that I have not achieved anything up to the present, and least of all in literature where I have always hoped to make my greatest contribution. "Symphonesque" marked the first milestone in

MILES MARK FISHER

HALL JOHNSON

ANITA SCOTT COLEMAN

WARREN McDONALD

Opportunity prize winners, June 1926. (*Opportunity* 4, no. 42 (June 1926), 188.)

Waring Cuney in his Tinton Avenue apartment in the Bronx.
(*Black World* (March 1973), 18.)

Adeline Norris, Waring Cuney's lifelong partner. (Courtesy of Roger Anderson.)

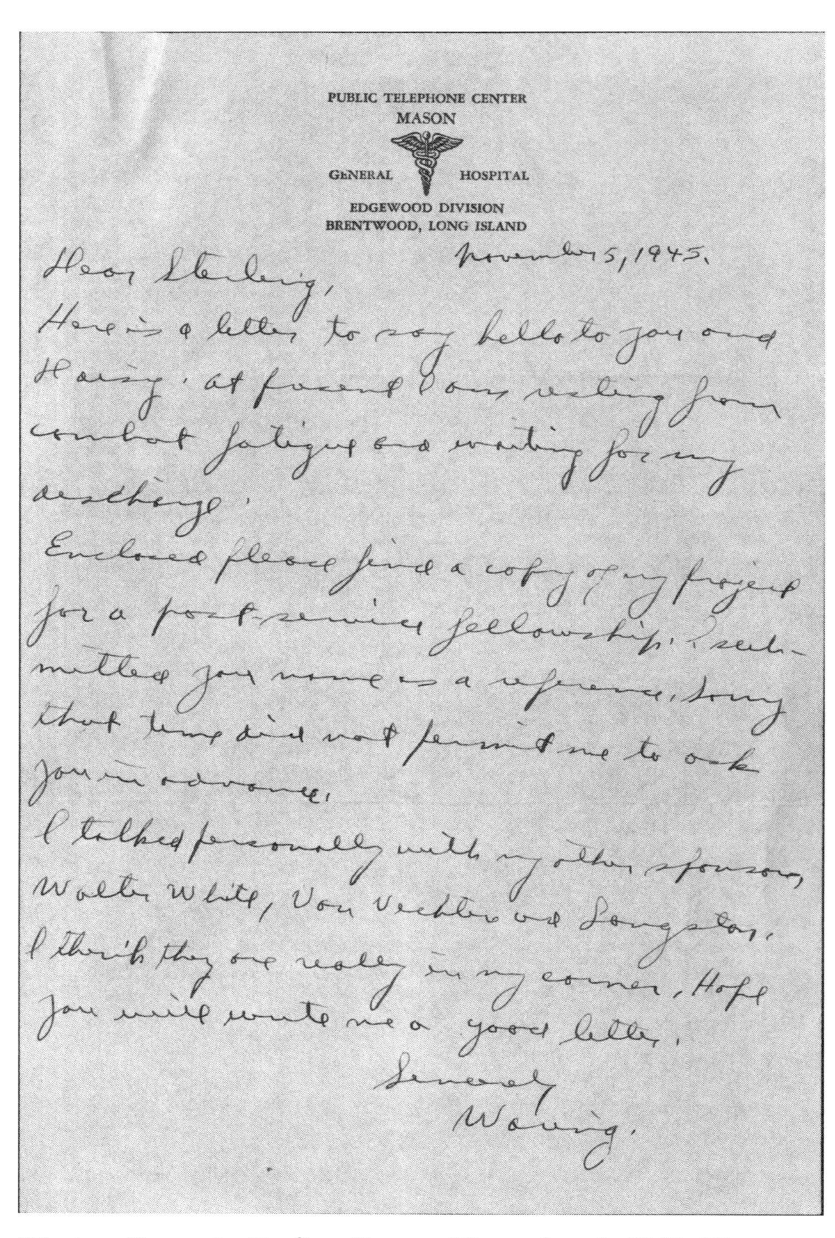

PUBLIC TELEPHONE CENTER
MASON
GENERAL HOSPITAL
EDGEWOOD DIVISION
BRENTWOOD, LONG ISLAND

November 5, 1945.

Dear Sterling,

Here is a letter to say hello to you and Daisy. At present I am resting from combat fatigue and waiting for my discharge.

Enclosed please find a copy of my project for a post-service fellowship. I submitted your name as a reference. Sorry that time did not permit me to ask you in advance.

I talked personally with my other sponsors, Walter White, Van Vechten and Langston. I think they are really in my corner. Hope you will write me a good letter.

Sincerely
Waring.

Waring Cuney to Sterling Brown, November 5, 1945. (Courtesy of Chapin Library, Williams College.)

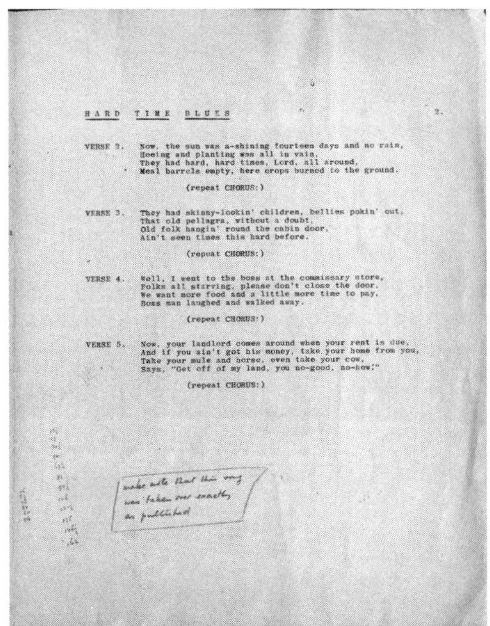

HARD TIME BLUES 2.

VERSE 2. Now, the sun was a-shining fourteen days and no rain,
Hoeing and planting was all in vain.
They had hard, hard times, Lord, all around,
Meal barrels empty, here crops burned to the ground.

(repeat CHORUS:)

VERSE 3. They had skinny-lookin' children, bellies pokin' out,
That old pellagra, without a doubt,
Old folk hangin' round the cabin door,
Ain't seen times this hard before.

(repeat CHORUS:)

VERSE 4. Well, I went to the boss at the commissary store,
Folks all starving, please don't close the door.
We want more food and a little more time to pay,
Boss man laughed and walked away.

(repeat CHORUS:)

VERSE 5. Now, your landlord comes around when your rent is due,
And if you ain't got his money, take your home from you,
Take your mule and horse, even take your cow,
Says, "Get off of my land, you no-good, no-how!"

(repeat CHORUS:)

“Hard Time Blues” score. (Courtesy of Chapin Library, Williams College.)

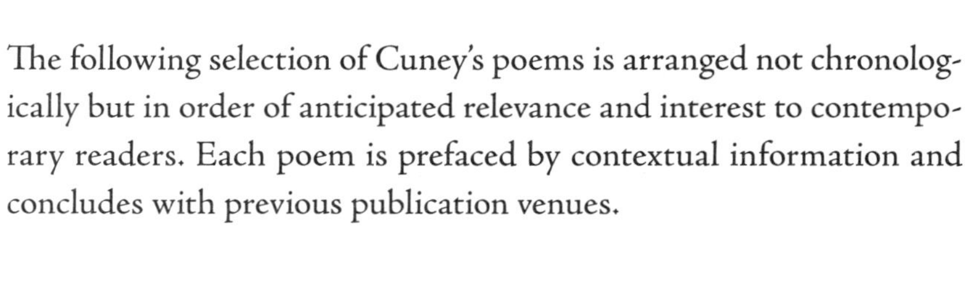

The following selection of Cuney's poems is arranged not chronologically but in order of anticipated relevance and interest to contemporary readers. Each poem is prefaced by contextual information and concludes with previous publication venues.

PART II

100 Selected Poems

After a chance meeting on a Washington, DC, streetcar in 1925, Langston Hughes and Waring Cuney became lifelong friends. Hughes facilitated the publication of Cuney's first poem, "No Images," in the journal Opportunity.

No Images

She does not know
Her beauty,
She thinks her brown body
Has no glory.

If she could dance
Naked
Under palm trees,
And see her image in the river
She would know.

But there are no palm trees
On the street,
And dish water gives back no images.

[*Opportunity* (June 1926): 180 (awarded one-half of first and second poetry prizes); *The Book of American Negro Poetry* (1931), 285–86; *Storefront Church* (1973), 7.]

This poem, about a racially motivated shooting by police of two African American brothers (one a veteran of World War II) was first published in Rev. Adam Clayton Powell Jr.'s weekly Harlem newspaper. Freeport is a town on Long Island, New York.

Freeport*

It was a sorrow and a shame
It rained that day,
Ashes and dust when they laid
The brothers away.

It was a sorrow and a shame
They buried the dead,
A bullet in the heart
A bullet in the head.

In the town of Freeport
Lined against a wall,
Dropped by a cop
Jim Crow caused it all.

In the town of Freeport
A soldier and his brother,
New graves in the graveyard
One beside the other.

It was a sorrow and a shame
God what a burying day,

* http://longisland.news12.com/story/34742843/freeport-police-shooting-sparked-outrage-in-the-1940s.

Ashes and dust when they laid
The brothers away.

[*The People's Voice* (June 1, 1946): 20.]

Upon joining the US Army during World War II, Waring Cuney was assigned to the 857th Engineer Aviation Battalion at Eglin Field, Florida. He composed the following two poems while stationed at Eglin.

When the Lights Go On

When the lights go on
All over the world again,
Will the light shine on me?
Will the lights go on in Georgia, Texas — Tennessee?
When the boys come home
After the War —
Will things be bad like before?
Will colored use the back door,
When the lights go on
All over the world again?
Or, will America turn back
To that simple, yet, great plan
Of Equality, for everyone?
When the lights go on
All over the world again,
In places far away —
Let's make sure the lights
Go on, here, in the U.S.A.

[January 17, 1943, previously unpublished.]

Big Talk

Ruby Jackson
Said to the Lord,
I'm tired
Of this ironing board.
Only one thing
I want to know,
All this talk
On the radio,
Freedom
In every country
Freedom
On every sea
Does that mean me?

[January 17, 1943, previously unpublished.]

This early poem, about death and prayer, was first published in Wallace Thurman's avant-garde journal Fire!!

The Death Bed

All the time they were praying
He watched the shadow of a tree
Flicker on the wall.

There is no need of prayer,
He said,
No need at all.

The kin-folk thought it strange
That he should ask them from his dying bed.
But they left all in a row
And it seemed to ease him
To see them go.

There were some who kept on praying
In a room across the hall
And some who listened to the breeze
That made the shadows waver
On the wall.

He tried his nerve
On a song he knew
And made an empty note
That might have come,
From a bird's harsh throat.

And all the time it worried him
That they were in there praying
And all the time he wondered
What it was they could be saying.

[*Fire!!* 1, no. 1 (November 1926): 19; *Caroling Dusk* (1927), 208–9.]

This poem may have been influenced by the passing of Cuney's father in 1923, at age fifty-one.

Wake Cry

He was a good man.
All men have to die.

O Death,
Did you ever
Fall on your knees
In tears an' cry?

He was a good man,
Hear the widow moan.

O Death,
Do you weep —
Or is your heart
Made o' stone?

[*The Book of American Negro Poetry* (1931), 285.]

This poem addressing prayer and the African American community was included in the anthology Cuney co-edited with Langston Hughes and Bruce McMarion Wright.

Prayer

When I was a boy
The old-folks used to say,
If you never
Prayed for your enemy,
You never learned to pray.

[*Centennial Anthology: Lincoln University Poets* (1954), 16–17.]

A poem on Frederick Douglass's grandson.

A Prayer on a Violin

Major Charles Douglass
The son of Frederick Douglass,
Had two sons, Haley and Joe.
Haley taught in the nation's capital
At Dunbar High School.
Joe was a concert violinist,
A teacher of violin.
He composed a prayer on the violin.
With a stroke of the bow
Joe Douglass played words like,
"Oh Lord" "Have Mercy" "Hallelujah"
"Poor Sinner" "Thy Kingdom" "Amen"
It sounded like a preacher praying.
No doubt about it,
He played a prayer on a violin.

[March 28, 1961, previously unpublished.]

The boxer Jack Johnson, the subject of this poem, was a neighbor of the Cuney family in Galveston, Texas.

My Lord, What a Morning

Oh, my Lord
What a morning,
Oh, my Lord,
What a feeling,
When Jack Johnson
Turned Jim Jeffries'
Snow-white face
Up to the ceiling.
Yes, my Lord,
Fighting is wrong,
But what an uppercut.
Oh, my Lord,
What a morning,
Oh, my Lord
What a feeling,
When Jack Johnson
Turned Jim Jeffries'
Lily-white face
Up to the ceiling.
Oh, my Lord
Take care of Jack.
Keep him, Lord
As you made him,
Big, and strong, and black.

[*Beyond the Blues* (1962), 81–82.]

Another poem on Jack Johnson.

Little Arthur

Lyndon B. Johnson says,
There has been a *Johnson*
In public office in Texas,
For one hundred years back.
As for me when I talk Texas
My hero is "Little Arthur"
Champion of the square circle.
My hero is prize-fighter, *Jack*.

[January 22, 1961, previously unpublished.]

This poem appears in mosaic on a building in Leiden, the Netherlands, as part of the city's public poetry project. That placement speaks to Cuney's international reputation.

Charles Parker, 1920–1955

Listen,
This here
Is what
Charlie
Did
To the Blues.
Listen,
That there
Is what
Charlie
Did
To the Blues.
This here,
bid-dle-dee-dee
bid-dle-dee-dee
bopsheep
have you any cool?
bahdada
one horn full.
Charlie
Filled the Blues
With
Curly-cues.
That's what
Charlie
Did

To the Blues.
Play
That again
Drop
A nickel in,
Charlie's
Dead,
Charlie's
Gone,
But
John Burkes
Carried on.
Drop
A nickel in,
Give
The platter
A spin,
Let's listen
To what
Charlie
Did
To the Blues.

[*Beyond the Blues* (1962), 83–84.]

This poem, published in the Modernist magazine Palms, *in an issue edited by Countee Cullen, was later set to music by the Italian composer Giacomo Manzoni.*

Grave

When I am in my grave
And none are there
Save those who like myself
Must sleep,
I shall wake at times
To weep.

I shall wake at times
To weep,
For I need have no fears
There
That someone see
My tears.

I need have no fears.

[*Palms* 4, no. 1 (October 1926): 12.]

Sterling Brown encouraged Cuney to send this poem to the Boston-born folklorist Benjamin A. Botkin for his anthology, Folk-Say. *Botkin also included poems by Brown, Langston Hughes, and Lewis Alexander.*

Chain Gang Chant

How long, how long,
Oh, tell me how long?

I call ma mother,
But she don't answer me.
No, Lawd.

I call ma brother,
But he don't answer me.
No, Lawd.

I call ma Jesus,
But He don't answer me.
No Lawd.

How long, how long,
Oh, tell me how long?

[*Folk-Say: A Regional Miscellany* (University of Oklahoma Press, 1930), 280.]

When Waring Cuney moved to Boston to study singing at the New England Conservatory of Music, he joined Eugene Gordon's literary group, the Saturday Evening Quill Club, where he met Dorothy West and Helene Johnson. The Quill Club published three annuals, to which Cuney contributed several poems.

Play a Blues for Louise

O jazz band,
Play a blues for Louise tonight —
Play a moanin' sobbin' song
For a good gal
Whose man done her wrong.
O play a blues for Louise tonight.

She packed her trunk
An' left dis town —
Said she was Chicago boun'.
Play a heart-broken song
For a po' heart-broken gal.
Play a blues for her.

De ole wheels turn
An' regret runs through her mind
About a man who was unkind.
O play a song of pain
For a heart-sick gal
On a fast, fast train.

O play a blues for Louise tonight.

[*The Saturday Evening Quill* (April 1929): 31.]

Jazz Band

Wild exotic music fills the air,
A jazz band plays a loud free prayer.

Beat your drum, drummer boy!
Beat in the slow dawn of day.
This is an hour of joy,
When restless weary souls pray!
Mad symphonic rhythm fills the air,
Ten jazz men bow their heads in prayer.

[*The Saturday Evening Quill* (April 1929): 31.]

Nude Walker

I walk nude along a lonely path
And oh, the burn of winds upon my body!
Love was a garment I wore
Before the hands of Fate
Cruelly stripped me naked.

Now without the warmth
Of a woman's love,
I walk nude along my path.

Oh, the burn of winds upon my body!
Oh, the cry of winds in my lorn heart!

[*The Saturday Evening Quill* (April 1929): 31.]

Burial of the Young Love

Weep not,
You who love her.

Place your flowers
Above her
And go your way.
Only I shall stay.

After you have gone
With grief in your hearts,
I will remove the flowers
You laid above her.
Yes, I who love her.

Do not weep,
Friends and lovers.

(Oh, the scent of flowers in the air!
Oh, the beauty of her body there!)

Gently now lay your flowers down.
When the last mourner has gone
And I have torn
Each flower;
When the last mourner has gone
And I have tossed
Broken stems and flower heads
To the winds . . . ah! . . .
I will gather withered leaves there.

Friends and lovers,
Do not weep.

Gently lay your flowers down . . .
Gently, now, lay your flowers down.

[*The Saturday Evening Quill* (April 1929): 75; *The Book of American Negro Poetry* (1931), 285–86.]

This poem, also drawn from Cuney's time in Boston, may suggest how difficult it was for him to gain traction for his music career.

Boston

Take a heavy-coat to Boston
Boston is not a light-coat town.

Take a heavy-coat to Boston
Boston is not a light-coat town.

The wind on the Boston Common
Lifts you up, and turns you around.

[July 29, 1973, previously unpublished.]

In their correspondence, Waring Cuney and Langston Hughes discussed the title of this poem. Although it was composed before her passing, readers believed it alluded to the sudden death of the beloved Broadway star, Florence Mills.

On with the Dirge

Play, O jazz band!
The dance-girl is dead.
(If any one asks for her
Tell him softly
That she has gone) . . .
O play, jazz band!
Play a gay dirge,
For a dead dance-girl.

[*The Saturday Evening Quill* (April 1929): 31.]

In this poem, Cuney draws on Arthurian legend probably to commemorate the life of his cousin and mentor, Maud Estelle Cuney Hare (1874–1936).

Elaine

LANCELOT,
  If you could see the garden now,
The death like beauty
Of our happy place,
You would know that if you come,
I shall greet you
With love upon my face.
Flowers and shrubs and trees
Have grown so still
Before love's ghost. . . !
Oh, Lancelot,
I shall not be a bitter host.

[*Opportunity* (April 1935): 120.]

In the early forties, Waring Cuney collaborated with the protest singer Josh White on a record album. Cuney wrote all the songs. Shortly after writing "Uncle Sam Says," Cuney enlisted in the US Army.

Uncle Sam Says

Well, airplanes flyin' 'cross the land and sea
Everybody flyin' but a Negro like me
Uncle Sam says, "Your place is on the ground
When I fly my airplanes, don't want no Negro 'round"

The same thing for the Navy when ships goes to sea
All they got is a mess boy's job for me
Uncle Sam says, "Keep on your apron, son
You know I ain't gonna let you shoot my big Navy gun"

Got my long gov'ment letters, my time to go
When I got to the Army, found the same old Jim Crow
Uncle Sam says, "Two camps for black and white"
But when trouble starts, we'll all be in that same big fight

If you ask me, I think democracy is fine
I mean democracy without the color line
Uncle Sam says, "We'll live the American Way"
Let's get together and kill Jim Crow today

[*Southern Exposure* (Keynote Recordings, 1941); *Cavalcade* 1, no. 4 (October 1941).]

This poem honors the service of Black soldiers in the Civil War and the Spanish–American War.

Past Events

General Lee had it made
Until the North
Enlisted Colored Soldiers.
Theodore Roosevelt
Did not have it made
On San Juan Hill.
The brave hard-fighting
Negro Tenth Cavalry,
Came to the rescue
Of the Rough Riders.

[March 9, 1961, previously unpublished.]

This poem pays homage to Brigadier General Charles Young (1864–1922), the third African American graduate of West Point and a leader of the famed Buffalo Soldiers of the US 10th Calvary.

The Man Without a Country

Charles Young was a regular army man
When the Battleship Maine
Was blown up by Spanish mines
Laid in Havana Harbor.
President McKinley asked Congress
To declare war on Spain.
The Negro Tenth Cavalry was shipped out.
Charles Young, one of its Lieutenants,
Went to Ohio with the rank of Major
To organize the Ninth Ohio Volunteers.
Admiral Dewey sank the Spanish fleet
In Manilla Harbor making victory certain.
The Negro Tenth and Roosevelt's Rough Riders
Made the victory certain on land,
In the fighting at El Caney and San Juan Hill.
By the time of World War One
Major Charles Young was now Colonel Young.
The United States Army doctors "examined him."
They wrote "unfit for active service."
Colonel Young rode his horse
From Dayton, Ohio, to the White House,
In order to prove to Woodrow Wilson
That the army doctors were lying.
America won World War One without Colonel Young.
If Wilson talked it over with Mrs. Wilson,
I know Colonel Young did not have a chance.

Mrs. Woodrow Wilson had a hobby
While she was First Lady of the land.
She put up some of the prettiest
Little old Jim Crow signs you all ever saw
In those big old government buildings,
That they have all over Washington D.C.
It was just an old southern custom.

[March 30, 1961, previously unpublished.]

In this poem, Cuney acknowledges the African American soldiers who served in World War I.

Defense Factory Blues

Went to the defense factory, trying to find some work to do
Had the nerve to tell me, "black boy, nothing here for you"
My father died, died fighting 'cross the sea
Mama said his dying never helped her or me
I'll tell you brother, well it sure don't make no sense
When a Negro can't work in the national defense

I'll tell you one thing, that boss man ain't my friend
If he was he'd give me some Democracy to defend
In the land of the free, called the home, home of the brave
All I want is liberty, that's what I crave

[*Southern Exposure* (Keynote Recordings, 1941).]

Another poem acknowledging the contributions of African American soldiers.

Black Doll Blues

Black Doll stood on the corner and he was dressed always so neat,
Black Doll stood on the corner and he was dressed always so neat,
The High-Yellows and Pink-Toes said now don't that black man look sweet.

The Army took him and they sent him to Germany to fight,
The Army took him and they sent him to Germany to fight,
He was killed by machine gun bullets in a forest one night.

When the news reached back home now the women folk all of them cried,
When the news reached back home now the women folk all of them cried,
Black Doll gave his life for his country that is how Black Doll died.

[December 2, 1960, previously unpublished.]

Additional poems drawn from Cuney's time in the US Army during World War II.

Sergeant Dusty

He was little and low, he liked to strutt,
the boys called him Sergeant Dusty Butt.

They gave him that name because at Retreat,
he was spic and span all except his seat.

Being built low and close down to the ground,
it was not his fault that dirt flew around.

Sergeant Dusty stood even four-feet-four,
not one-half inch less, not one-half inch more.

So small as a baby his Ma would cry,
but he had a natural shooting eye.

He was proud of the medals on his chest,
a box in his locker held all the rest.

One day he was standing at Mess Hall One,
when the Major walked up and said, "Ten-shun!"

Dusty clicked his heels and pulled in his knees,
stuck out his chest, saluted to a freeze.

Major looked at Dusty neat as a pin,
Dusty wore a smile, Major wore a grin.

Major said, "Sergeant, will you tell me this,
when you go shooting do you ever miss?"

The Sergeant said, "Put my gun in my hand,
I'm a natural not a superman —"

"I can hit any target that you set,
or, I will eat my gun, also my hat."

The target was set at one mile away,
the bull's eye was like a pin's head they say.

But Sergeant Dusty must have won his bet,
because his gun and hat ain't been et yet.

[January 17, 1943, revised January 6, 1960, previously unpublished.]

They Mighty Near Fit

Big Mess Sergeant and Dusty had it out today.
The boys pulled little Dusty away.
It started when Dusty said,
"Not enough salt in this bread.
Furthermore, I don't like this meat.
If you was a civilian cook
You'd walk the street."

Mess Sergeant got hot as his stove.
"Don't worry about me
Walking the street.
My cooking is good enough
For your ma to eat."

Dusty stood up.
"I don't play the dozens,
No, sir, not at all!
But so help me,
I can make a man
Your size fall."

[September 14, 1943, previously unpublished.]

Dusty and Lucky Agree

Lucky and Dusty
Were really a pair,
Always fussing
Getting nowhere,
Argued more than
A man and wife
Never saw two boys like
Dusty and Lucky
In all my life.

If Dusty said
"Grass is green"
Lucky would answer
"Not all I've seen,
If it's news to you
The grass in Kentucky is blue."

One day
Dusty told Lucky
"Sure two and two
Make four, but
It don't have to be,
In mathematics,
A minus one
Might make it three."

So it was —
And so it went,
Nothing they like better
Than an argument.
Might be

How to plow a field,
Might be
Signals, on a railroad track,
Or, Father Divine's philosophy —
Or, why some white folks
Just hate the black.
Could be anything
Politics,
Religion,
Art,
Or science —
Stalin's Dictatorship
Or little ghandi's
Passive Defiance.

What one called
The truth,
The other called
A lie,
What one states
As a fact,
The other would deny,
Sometimes it lasted
Way into the night,
Each swearing he was right.

One night
Lucky was laying
Across the bed
Peaceful-like
Like a happy thought
Was in his head.
He looked at Dusty

This is what he said

"Boy, when the war
Is over,
One thing I gotta do,
I don't mind telling you
Gonna buy a ticket,
And dress up fine,
Konk my hair,
Give my shoes a shine,
Yeah man!
When the war is over,
I hope it ain't long
Marian Anderson's
Gonna sing me a song
I heard her once
On the radio,
Her singing, it got me so."

Dusty said, "Lucky,
You and me,
We got a date.
Her singing is mighty fine
Truly great.
I heard her myself
On the air
She lifted me, man
I don't know where."

Well, I started laughing,
I couldn't stop —
Lucky said, "Boy you need
A doctor, or a cop."

I said, "Soldier, I know
I'm acting queer,
But you, and Dusty, and me
We been buddies for a year,
And it's funny to me,
First time I ever heard
You all agree."

[January 17, 1943, previously unpublished.]

In a famous Cuney family episode, Waring's great-aunt Adelina, wife of Norris Wright Cuney, tricked a train conductor who was attempting to relegate her to the Jim Crow car by climbing through the train window and calmly presenting her ticket when he came through the whites-only car.

Jim Crow Train

Can't you hear that train whistle blow?
Can't you hear that train whistle blow?
Can't you hear that train whistle blow?
Lord, I wish that train wasn't Jim Crow

Stop the train so I can ride this train
Stop Jim Crow so I can ride this train
Stop Jim Crow so I can ride this train
Black and White folks ridin' side by side

Now hear that train whistle blow
Can't you hear that train whistle blow?
Can't you hear that train whistle blow?
O Lord, this train is Jim Crow

[*Southern Exposure* (Keynote Recordings, 1941).]

Eugene Talmadge was governor of Georgia from 1933 to 1937 and 1941 to 1943.

Some Talk for Governor Talmadge

Listen, Governor,
In case you don't know,
Jim Crow has got to go!
Maybe you don't understand,
Jim Crow never did belong
In our great land,
Not in the original plan.
We fought England
So we could be free
To build a Democracy.
So let me tell you now,
Negroes crossed the Delaware
And froze at Valley Forge,
Negroes helped Washington
Beat King George.
Why don't you take a look
In a history book?
Listen, Governor,
Folks like me, well —
We believe in Liberty.
We like the Constitution,
And the Bill of Rights, too.
What's more, we are tired
Of Governors like you,
Who can't find anything to do
But spread race hatred
Across the land,

Instead of trying to make us all
One American band.
Listen, Governor,
We are getting wise
To all you Poll-Tax guys.
We know you hold the South
By the throat,
We know you take away
The right to vote
From all poor people,
White and black.
We know how you stab Democracy
In the back, with lying speeches.
We know you are all
A bunch of leeches,
Taking it easy in high places,
Forgetting the people —
Hungry, with upturned faces.
Listen, Governor,
In case you don't know,
You and Jim Crow both got to go!

[*The Pittsburgh Courier*, September 20, 1941, 6.]

After moving to Boston, Cuney noted the absence of Jim Crow segregation and remarked to Langston Hughes, ". . . and you know that's all right with me." This poem, critical of the Jim Crow South, was published in his final collection.

Carry Me Back

Carry me back to old Virginia.
        Magnolia blossoms fill the air.
Carry me back to old Virginia:
        the only way you'll get me there.

[*Storefront Church* (1973), 11.]

One poem on the Civil War and another on civil rights.

One Hundred Years Later

Grant told the Rebels
To keep their horses,
Now in Washington
They are the bosses.

[February 28, 1961, previously unpublished.]

Golf in Georgia

They did not tell the President
They feared that it might spoil his game
But the brave young Georgia students
Walked the picket line just the same.

[February 28, 1961, previously unpublished.]

This poem was probably written in the late thirties when Cuney worked for the New York office of the Works Progress Administration (WPA).

Bad Housing Blues

I woke up this morning, rainwater in my bed
I woke up this morning, rainwater in my bed
You know, my roof was leaking, Lord, leaking on my head

Now there ain't no reason I should live this way
Now there ain't no reason I should live this way
I done lost my job, can't even get on the WPA

Lord, I wonder when I'll hear good news
Lord, I wonder when I'll hear good news
Right now I'm gonna tell you how I got them bad housing blues

I'm goin' to the capitol, goin' to the White House lawn
Well, I'm going to the capitol, goin' to the White House lawn
Better wipe out these slums, been this way since I was born

[*Southern Exposure* (Keynote Recordings, 1941).]

A blues poem, exploring the life of an African American woman.

T.B. Blues

When I went to the hospital, Lord, Lord, Lord,
When I went to the hospital, Lord, Lord, Lord,
I went to see Beulah in the danger ward.

I said to her Beulah is this really you
I said to her Beulah is this really you
Beulah said, yes I think that my check is due.

Well I thought how she used to sing and dance,
Well I thought how she used to sing and dance,
I could see that she ain't got a chance.

She worked in a hard laundry all day,
She worked in a hard laundry all day,
The Boss said you can't work here and cough that way.

I guess T.B. stands for Tough Breaks, Lord, Lord, Lord,
I guess T.B. stands for Tough Breaks, Lord, Lord, Lord,
Say Tough Breaks put her in the danger ward.

[December 27, 1960, previously unpublished.]

Two blues poems exploring the lives of African Americans.

Hard Time Blues

Went down home 'bout a year ago
things so bad, Lord, my heart was sore.
Folks had nothing was a sin and shame
every-body said hard time was the blame.
        Great-God-a-mighty folks feeling bad
        lost every thing they ever had.

Sun was shining fourteen days and no rain
hoeing and planting was all in vain.
Hard times, Lord, all around
meal barrels empty crops burnt to the ground.
        Great-God-a-mighty folks feeling bad
        lost every thing they ever had.

Skinny looking children bellies poking out
that old pellagra without a doubt.
Old folks hanging 'round the cabin door
ain't seen times this hard before.
        Great-God-a-mighty folks feeling bad
        lost every thing they ever had.

I went to the Boss at the Commissary store
folks all starving please don't close your door
want more food a little more time to pay
Boss Man laughed and walked away.
        Great-God-a-mighty folks feeling bad
        lost every thing they ever had.

Landlord coming 'round when the rent is due
you ain't got the money take your home from you
take your mule and horse even take your cow
get offa my land you ain't no good no how.
        Great-God-a-mighty folks feeling bad
        lost every thing they ever had.

[*Southern Exposure* (Keynote Recordings, 1941); *Storefront Church* (1973), 14.]

Mistreatin' Blues

Woke up last night wanted to wring my hands an' scream
Woke up last night wanted to wring my hands an' scream
You said you loved me in my midnight dream

Honey Babe way I treated you I know was wrong
Honey Babe way I treated you it was wrong
I didn't know I loved you 'till you was gone

When you see me keep your head held high
When you see me keep your head held high
I don't blame you Babe when you pass me by

There's just one thing I wish and I really do
There's just one thing I hope an' I really do
Hope the Mistreatin' Blues never fall on you

[November 26, 1942, previously unpublished.]

This poem challenges traditional views of the Great Depression.

Nineteen-Twenty-Nine

Some folks hollered hard times
in nineteen-twenty-nine.
In nineteen-twenty-eight
say I was way behind.

Some folks hollered hard times
because hard times were new.
Hard times is all I ever had,
why should I lie to you?

Some folks hollered hard times.
What is it all about?
Things were bad for me when
those hard times started out.

[*Storefront Church* (1973), 12.]

Another poem exploring poverty in America.

Saturday Night Talk

Sometimes I wonder,
I really do,
about the kids
and you.

Sometimes I wonder,
the way things are,
if I will come out
ahead of Pa.

The one thing
Pa always said:
"Want to own tis land
before I'm dead."

The day he died
I can't forget,
he left a good name
a farm in debt.

Sometimes I wonder,
I really do,
if other folks
wonder, too.

[*Storefront Church* (1973), 16.]

Cuney was an active member of the Southern Negro Youth Congress (SNYC). From April to October 1941, he published regularly in the SNYC's journal, Cavalcade: The March of Southern Negro Youth.

Organize Blues

Tell you one thing
Will make you mad . . .
When the company store
Says your credit's bad.

Going to the meeting
Hear what I say . . .
Poor folks got to
Organize the blues away.

[*Cavalcade* 1, no. 1 (April 1941): 4.]

Waring Cuney sent this poem to Langston Hughes in a 1929 letter from Italy.

American Negro Labor

My head is bloody and bowed before the constant blows of Nordic
prejudice.
My heart holds hate three centuries of cruel offenses have
bred into it.
In my soul fires from lynched bodies smolder and refuse to go out.
My senses have dulled from much beating but think not that I sleep.

[Rome, Italy, August 22, 1929, previously unpublished.]

Waring Cuney, then a US Army sergeant, sent the following two poems to Langston Hughes from New Guinea. Henry's Sugar Bowl Nightclub, notes Cuney, was located at West 135th Street and 7th Avenue in Harlem.

I Got a Date at the Sugar Bowl

I got a date
I can't wait,
Bless her heart,
Save my soul,
I got a date at the Sugar Bowl.

I got a date
I can't wait,
New Guinea or the North Pole,
I got a date at the Sugar Bowl.

Malted milk
Rye on toast
She'll be my guest
I'll be her host at the Sugar Bowl.

Juke Box'll play
It's a secret what we'll say at the Sugar Bowl.

I'll catch on when the lights go on —
Dig me Jody
Dig me Jack
Soldier boy is coming back to the Sugar Bowl.

I got a date
I can't wait,
She'll be sweet when we meet at the Sugar Bowl.

Whether it's hot
Whether it's cold
We'll be groovy at the Sugar Bowl.

Hitler will be dead and gone when those lights go on at the Sugar Bowl.

[July 4, 1943, previously unpublished.]

Turkey Breast

Turkey was a guy
With no shame,
Called a spade a spade,
Things by their name.

He'd cuss anybody
Anywhere.
He was that way
Didn't care.

He worked at Joe's
SHOE SHINE STAND,
No. 1 chair,
Fastest man.

Talk about
Shining a shoe —
That's one thing
He could do.

Big time boys
Who've been around
Say Turkey's the best
In any town.

He hobo'd North
A year ago.
If you asked him
Was he coming back,
He'd answer, "Hell, no!"

He was a good boy,
Always polite.
I never heard of Turkey
Having a fight.

And his cussing
Was mostly to himself.
But he put all other cussers
On the shelf.

Turkey had names
I can't repeat,
And his style was
Fine-finished sweet.

When he cussed
The boss left the place.
Turkey's mouth
Was a disgrace.

One day Rev. Jones
Stopped at the stand.
Turkey said, "'Morning, Rev,"
As he spied the rally can.

The Reverend said,
"Don't turn me down.
We needs some coal
Till spring rolls round."

Turkey said, "Here's two-bits.
Lemme speak my mind.
How come you can't be
Like Father Divine?

Begging nickels and dimes
Don't make sense
With Father serving dinner
For fifteen cents."

The Reverend said, "A shepherd
Does what the Lawd tells him to."
Turkey said, "The Lawd
Don't think much of you."

The Reverend said, "Run
Your own business, son.
Me and the Lawd will run mine."
I didn't want to hear no more
So I started for the door
Cause I knew Turkey would get out of line.

I was on the curb,
Never heard what Turkey said.
I only saw Reverend Jones
Turn and bow his head.

I felt sorry as he passed
With the rally can.
He's not a jive preacher,
But a real Christian man.

But when it comes to cussing,
If you want the best,
You got to hand it
To Turkey Breast.

[August 1943, previously unpublished.]

Countee Cullen selected the following poems for his renowned Harlem Renaissance anthology, Caroling Dusk.

Dust

Dust,
Through which
Proud blood
Once flowed.

Dust,

Where a civilization
Flourished.

Dust,
The Valley of the Nile,
Dust,

You proud ones, proud of the skill
With which you play this game—Civilization;
Do not forget that it is a very old game.
Men used to play it on the banks
Of the Tigris and the Euphrates
When the world was a wilderness.

There is a circle around China
Where once a wall stood.
Carthage is a heap of ashes.
And Rome knew the pomp and glory
You know now.

The Coliseum tells a story
The Woolworth Building may repeat.

Dust,
Pharaohs and their armies sleep there.

Dust,
Shall it stir again?

Will Pharaohs rise and rule
And their armies march once more?

Civilization continually shifts
Upon the places of the earth.

[*Caroling Dusk* (1927), 210–11.]

A Triviality

Not to dance with her
Was such a trivial thing

There were girls more fair than she, —

To-day
Ten girls dressed in white.
Each had a white rose wreath.

They made a dead man's arch
And ten strong men
Carried a body through.

Not to dance with her
Was such a trivial thing.

[*Caroling Dusk* (1927), 209; *Opportunity* (November 1927): 325.]

The Radical

Men never know
What they are doing.
They always make a muddle
Of their affairs,
They always tie their affairs
Into a knot
They cannot untie.
Then I come in
Uninvited.

They do not ask me in;
I am the radical,
The bomb thrower,
I untie the knot
That they have made,
And they never thank me.

[*Caroling Dusk* (1927), 212–13.]

The composer Albert Hague met Cuney in New York City and put "Telephone Book" to music.

Telephone Book

A phone-book full of names don't mean a thing
If the one you love don't answer when you ring.

A phone-book full of names is nothing at all
Unless the one you love answers when you call.

What good is a phone-book, names from A to Z
If my fine baby won't talk to me?

A phone-book full of names don't mean a thing
If the one you love don't answer when you ring.

[Circa 1952, previously unpublished.]

In this poem, Cuney uses repetition and humor to communicate an old truth, perhaps about death or psychological health.

Old Saying

It is an old saying,
Said with a wry smile,
Said with the wink of an eye,
Said with a shrug of the shoulders,
"They all go when the wagon comes."

A church deacon has an affair
With a young choir singer,
Who is two years older
Than his younger daughter,
Who is a high-school sophomore.
His daughter and the girl
Are members of the same choir.

A married woman
With all the things
That money can buy,
Goes off the beam
Over a man without a cent,
A man that is not worth the cent
That he is without.

A clever divorce lawyer
Thought he could have his cake
And also eat his cake.
When he finds out that his wife
Has been playing the same game,

He begins to lose cases,
He stumbles down booze-alley.

It is an old saying,
Said with a shrug of the shoulders,
Said with a wink of the eye,
Said with a wry smile,

"They all go when the wagon comes."

[*Puzzles* (1960), 16–17.]

The following three lyrics appeared as "A Group of Poems" in the NAACP's Crisis *magazine. The first poem presents an ironic image of upper-class life, probably in Harlem in the 1920s.*

Café Chantant

Night after night
They make the rounds,
Men in full dress clothes
Ladies in evening gowns,
Gay laughing souls
Who come to chat and dine,
Because they know
Sadness will go
After a glass of wine.

[*The Crisis* 42, no. 2 (February 1935): 61.]

Your Singing

If I am sad when you come to sing,
It seems foolish to weep
For any thing.
If I am gay when you bring your song,
I know my heart will break
Before long.

[*The Crisis* 42, no. 2 (February 1935): 61.]

This poem explores belated male and female awareness.

Promise

Some day, weary of winds and waves
Sick of the sea's clear skies,
I shall come home to the heart break
In your tearless eyes, some day.

[*The Crisis* 42, no. 2 (February 1935): 61.]

Cuney was raised in Washington, DC's affluent LeDroit Park neighborhood. This poem was likely inspired by bleak conditions he witnessed several blocks away, in the alleys and side streets off Washington's Seventh Street.

Side Street

Here where cupboards are empty
And walls are bare
And children go hungry
With no clothes to wear —
Life has a greedy heart too
Broken to care.

[*The Crisis* (May 1937): 157.]

About this poem, Dorothy West wrote in her journal Challenge, *"Waring Cuney sent us his poem from Rome. . . . Poetry making is his second love. Singing is his first. And Rome is his heaven on earth."*

Song of a Song

Your song
Will be a rhapsody
For desperate folk.

A symphony
For the working class —

A voice,
For the silence of men
Who inch their way to bread
Night after night.

Your song
Will be the ugliness
Of starvation,
Dedicated to a deserted farm.

[*Challenge* (May 1935): 43.]

Here, Cuney celebrates two of his enduring interests: gospel music and the blues.

Let Me Tell You Blues Singers Something

Let me tell you blues singers something,
one thing maybe that you do not know.
Let me tell you blues singers something,
one thing maybe that you do not know.
The songs of the Lord will take you down any
kind of lonely old road you may have to go.

[*Storefront Church* (1973), 15.]

This is the final poem in Cuney's book of verse, Puzzles*. The third section of* Puzzles *bears the same title as this concluding poem. Drawing from the blues, the poem's closing stanza "worries the line."*

Guitar Music

It takes two hearts
To make guitar music.

First,
The heart of the guitar-maker,
A workman at his bench —
A saw, a plane, a chisel,
Sandpaper, varnish.

Second,
The heart of the guitar-player.
The singing heart
Of a singer of songs.

Two hearts,
To make guitar music.

[*Puzzles* (1960), 79.]

This poem, a celebration of bluesmen Charles Luckeyeth "Luckey" Roberts and Ferdinand "Jelly Roll" Morton, imparts lessons about money. Cuney would have witnessed both performers during their visits to Washington, DC.

Jelly Roll and Lucky

When
Ferdinand Morton
plays
Twelfth Street Rag
it
tells you
soup
can't carry
in a
paper bag.

When
Luckeyeth Roberts
plays
Railroad Blues
it
tells you
dimes
and nickels
add up
ones and twos.

[*Storefront Church* (1973), 9.]

James Weldon Johnson selected the next two poems for his landmark anthology, The Book of American Negro Poetry.

Finis

Now that our love has drifted
To a quiet close,
Leaving the empty ache
That always follows when beauty goes;
Now that you and I,
Who stood tip-toe on earth
To touch our fingers to the sky,
Have turned away
To allow our little love to die —
Go, dear, seek again the magic touch.
But if you are wise,
As I shall be wise,
You will not again
Love over much.

[*The Book of American Negro Poetry* (1931), 287.]

Threnody

Only quiet death
Brings relief
From the wearisome
Interchange
Of hope and grief.
O body
(Credulous heart
And dream-torn head),
What will wisdom be
Or folly —
When you lie dead?
Life-beaten body
Bruised and sore —
Neither hunger nor satiety
Are known beyond death's door.

[*The Book of American Negro Poetry* (1931), 283–84.]

Waring Cuney dedicated the following poems "For Mrs. James Weldon Johnson."

I Thought of My True Love

I was at the station,
The train went by,
I thought of my True Love,
I wanted to cry.

I was on the front porch,
The sun went down,
I thought of my True Love
In a far away town.

I was in my room
Alone that night,
I thought of my True Love
Gone forever from my sight.

[May 2, 1949, previously unpublished.]

Four Little Pictures

Four little pictures
Cost only a dime,
You gave them to me
All four were mine.

I tore them up
I cursed you out,
Thought I'd be happy
With you not about.

I want those pictures
Really, honey, I do.
What's more, honey —
I want you.

[May 2, 1949, previously unpublished.]

Why Call Her Name?

Thinking about a woman
Many miles away,
If I went to see her
Wonder what she'd say.

Last time I saw her
At her front door,
She told me to my face
"Can't use you no more."

Last time I saw her
I felt like crying,
I said, "You got a home
Long as I got mine."

Thinking about a woman
Why call her name?
When true love dies
It's a sorry shame.

[May 2, 1949, previously unpublished.]

Tell Irene Hello

If you go to Birmingham
Tell Irene hello,
She was a good girl
I hated to see her go.

She was a good girl,
Mean as can be,
But I tell the world
She was good to me.

She gave me quarters
Dimes were hard to find,
If Irene had a dollar
Fifty cents was mine.

If you go to Birmingham
Stop past her door,
Tell her I love her
Nothing's right no more.

[May 2, 1949, previously unpublished.]

Nan

When Nan was fourteen
Her drunken ma
Gave a party,
Poured the gin,
Told her to drink hearty.

When she was eighteen
Bless her soul,
Nan wore a red garter
For passion,
A yellow garter for gold.

[May 2, 1949, previously unpublished.]

Three in a Row

Death
Struck the Johnson family
Three times in a row.
Grand-ma, Pa, and baby Joe.
That's no way for folks to go.

[May 2, 1949, previously unpublished.]

Lonesome Yellow Girl

The lonesome yellow girl
Cried last night.
She cried the night before —

"When I see the doctor
I won't cry no more."

The lonesome yellow girl
Is happy to-night.
She is happy and gay —

It's her secret how soon
She'll be laid away.

[May 2, 1949, previously unpublished.]

From 1947 until his death in 1976, Waring Cuney lived on Tinton Avenue in the Bronx. In the 1950s, he sent the following six poems to his friend Dr. Marguerite Cartwright, an educator, journalist, and United Nations reporter, originally from Boston, Massachusetts.

September Sun on Tinton Avenue

The Mothers

The mothers
Push the carriages
The way the sun goes
Half way up the street
Then across to the other side.

The chocolate-fudge babies
Kick tiny feet
And fall asleep
To dream
Soft September sun dreams.

Young Girl

The young girl
With books in her arms,
Talks to the mothers
Who are minding their babies.

This young girl
In a Jersey sweater,
This next June's graduate,
Plays with the babies
As she talks to the mothers.

[Circa 1952, previously unpublished.]

The Ledge

In the Puerto Rican bars
In the Bronx,
Up over the bottles
Of whiskey, rum, wine, and gin,
There is a wooden ledge
Lined with frosted glass.
From the other side of the bar
You can see coins,
Nickels, pennies, dimes, and quarters,
Lying on the frosted glass.
A drinker goes broke
And throws his last coin
Up on the ledge.
It is a custom.

[Circa 1952, previously unpublished.]

Tenants

The old frame building
On Prospect Avenue,
Sandwiched in between
A flower shop
And a perfume factory,
Has a strange combination
Of tenants.

On the first floor
There is a sign that reads —

> "Happy Pilgrims Baptist Church
> Services, Sunday 11:00 A.M.
> Rev. Hartwell Johnson, Pastor."

Three gypsy women
Live on the second floor,
A gypsy grandmother
With her two daughters,
And their children.

[Circa 1952, previously unpublished.]

April Funeral

They buried Mr. Keyes
In Washington last April,
Tall, dark, square-shouldered,
Friendly Mr. Keyes.

He was our teacher
In machine-shop,
At Armstrong High School
A long time ago,
The kind of teacher kids like.

It was a big funeral they say.
More cars than most funerals
With police escort,
To the Arlington Cemetery.

Mr. Keyes joined the Navy
When he was a young man.
He learned his trade and sailed
To many strange places,
Before he became a school-teacher.

That is why they buried him
In the National Cemetery
In Arlington, Virginia,
With a military escort:

The Marines stood at attention,
A Navy Chaplain read from the Bible,
Young soldiers folded the American flag
Into the shape of a heart,
And presented it to his widow.

[Circa 1957, previously unpublished.]

Rain Sounds

People on the top floor
Know something about rain
That the other tenants don't know.
They know the sound of rain on the roof.
They learn to welcome or curse the rain
By rain-sounds on the roof.
People on the top floor
Know when it first starts to rain.
They don't have to look
Out of their window.

[Circa 1952, previously unpublished.]

Sunrise for Six People

East River at 19th Street
Scenario for Ballet
(For Ruth)

To a man who works
The night-shift
In a factory,
Busy with tools
And the hum of lathes,
The grey creeping dawn
Brings relief from weariness.

To a street-walker
Who picked up nine men,
And came home drunk
To fall asleep
With her clothes on,
The sun is a gentle caress
On a tired face.

For the night-counter man
And the day-counter man
In a greasy-spoon restaurant,
Sun is a time for saying hello.
The night-counter man
Takes off his apron
To have a cup of coffee,
The day-counter man
Puts on his apron
To have a cup of coffee.
They say hello, and so-long,
Over a cup of coffee
At sunrise.

For a private detective
Shadowing a married man,
Out for a spree
With his girl-friend,
Dawn outside a hotel-lobby
Is an excuse for a tired oath,
An exclamation,
How long are they going to stay
In that room anyhow?

What is sunlight
On new-fallen snow,
To a nurse
Who stands at the window
Of the charity ward,
A nurse who all night long
Watched the fever
Leave the brain and body
Of a patient booked to go?

To a tired charwoman
Changing clothes,
In the locker room
Of a down-town office-building,
Tears are forgotten sorrows.
Sunrise and tears
Are a whisper,
What will he say
When he knows we have a child,
After fourteen years of waiting?

[Circa 1952, previously unpublished.]

Religion figured prominently in Cuney's verse throughout his career. "I Think I See Him There" is from the 1920s; James Weldon Johnson selected the next poem for his anthology, The Book of American Negro Poetry (1931); *the last five poems appeared four decades later in Cuney's final collection,* Storefront Church.

I Think I See Him There

I think I see Him there
With a stern dream on his face

I see Him there —

Wishing they would hurry
The last nail in place.

And I wonder, had I been there,
Would I have doubted too

Or would the dream have told me,
What this man speaks is true.

[*Caroling Dusk* (1927), 210.]

Troubled Jesus

Ma Jesus
Was a troubled man,
Wid lots o' sorrow
In His breast.
Oh, he was weary
When they laid Him
In the tomb to rest.
Po', good Jesus.

[*The Book of American Negro Poetry* (1931), 284; *Golden Slippers* (1941), 59.]

My Jesus

Conception

Jesus' mother never had no man.
God came to her one day and said:
Mary, child, kiss my hand.

Crucifixion

Oh my, oh yes, up on the cross
with a wound in His side,
oh my, oh yes, up on the cross —
that is how Jesus died.

Resurrection

Way before the break of day
angels rolled the rock away.
So early in the morning,
so early in the morning,
way before the break of day.
Angels rolled the rock away.

[*Storefront Church* (1973), 6.]

Darkness Hides His Throne

My God is so high,
you cannot get over Him.

My God is so low,
you cannot get under Him.

My God is so wide,
you cannot get around Him.

He cannot be measured,
He cannot be known.

Darkness covers His pavilion
darkness hides His throne.

[*Storefront Church* (1973), 3.]

Roll, Jordan, roll

Will the river be chilly,
will the river be cold,
will the river freeze my soul?

Roll, Jordan, roll

Oh brother,
when my face is a looking-glass
some morning —

Oh sister,
when my room is a public hall
some evening —

Roll, Jordan, roll

Oh sister,
will you bow down your head for me
some morning?

Oh brother,
will you say a last prayer for me
some evening?

Will the river freeze my soul?

Will the river be chilly,
will the river be cold,
will the river freeze my soul?

[*Storefront Church* (1973), 4.]

Storefront Church

Brothers and sisters,
by way of the love of the Lord —
we sang a song this evening
about the blind man
who stood on the road and cried
"Lord, show me the way to go home."

Brothers and sisters,
by way of the love of the Lord —
I want to say this evening:
unless we accept the love of the Lord
unless we accept Jesus Christ
to heal our sins
to guide us in this wicked world —
we are like the blind man
who stood on the road crying
"Lord, show me the way to go home."

Brothers and sisters,
by way of the love of the Lord —
thank God, the Father!
Praise Jesus, the Son!

[*Storefront Church* (1973), 17.]

Prayer for a Visitor

Lord —
this white man
here this evening —
may he be blessed by Thee.

Lord —
this white man
in our midst tonight —
may he see the light.

Lord —
this white man
here in our church —
if he is a policeman
come to listen about
the sit-ins, and the sit-downs,
the meetings, and the picket lines —
Lord,
You tell him
that we have just begun.

Lord —
this white man
here this evening —
if he is a detective
come to find out
what we are about,
what our next move will be —
Lord, You tell him
that we do not know.

Pharaoh
rules so hard in the land
that God let Pharaoh feel
the strength of God's hand.

Lord —
this white man
here this evening —
may he be blessed by Thee.

Amen.

[*Storefront Church* (1973) 19.]

The following two poems, published in Puzzles *in 1960, may have been inspired by Adeline Norris, a nurse from the Midwest, whom Cuney met and fell in love with in New York City.*

Girl from Oklahoma

I know a girl from Oklahoma.
She has a pretty face,
And a fine figure.
She has brains,
And money in the bank.
This girl from Oklahoma
Has the three B's,
Beauty, brains, and bucks.
She has what nine out of ten men
Are looking for.

This girl I know from Oklahoma
Talks to a psychiatrist
Three hours a week,
Because she is lonely.

[*Puzzles* (1960), 15.]

Sunset Thoughts

The best laughter of all
Is the laughter of two lovers.

The best talk of all
Is the talk of two lovers.

The deepest peace is the silence
Between two lovers.

[*Puzzles* (1960), 63.]

Additional poems celebrating Cuney's longtime partner, Adeline Norris.

Well Now

Well now she walked me into her parlor
Well now she placed my skimmer on the stand,
Well now she told her ma in Norwegian —
"I am in love with this dark handsome man."

Well now here comes my sweet Adeline
Well now I can tell you just how I know,
Well now the answer is very simple —
"Each day she is prettier than before."

[December 23, 1960, previously unpublished.]

I Tell My Baby

I told my Baby
A week ago,
I love her more
Than she can know.

I told my Baby
The other day,
Promise never
To go away.

I tell my Baby
Most all the time,
How much I love her —
Her name is Adeline.

[January 1, 1960, previously unpublished.]

A Man and A Woman

A man and a woman at an airport
Know they will
Never say good-bye again.
The parting is hurried,
Quick, with unsaid words,
Flowers, a touch of a kiss.
Somehow two people know
When they meet again
They will never say good-bye again.

[Previously unpublished.]

Sorry

We can't get along
I will tell you why,
You talk me to death
I'm too young to die.

[February 11, 1960, previously unpublished.]

Cuney penned this poem in tribute to Adeline Norris's mother, Laila Lee Norris, on her death.

Laila

Laila is a pretty girl
Her smile will make your heart sing,
I will be her first caller
When she has callers in the spring.

Laila is a pretty girl
She has never been from home,
I told her that I love her —
I want her for my very own.

[May 12, 1974, previously unpublished.]

Although Cuney never married, his brother and sister-in-law met in their teens and were reportedly inseparable. They were likely the model for the following poem.

Couples

There are no statistics
On these couples.
You see them, now and then,
Although you can't tell them
From other couples, by looking.
One in ten thousand?
One couple out of
Maybe a million couples?
Who knows?
There are no statistics.
It is a way with two people —
A woman and her man.
People who know them say,
They are as close as the hands
Of a clock at midnight,
They are like white on rice.

[*Puzzles* (1960), 51.]

This poem, about a veteran who succumbs to PTSD, may allude to Cuney's own struggles with mental health issues during and after World War II.

The Neighbors Stood on the Corner

The neighbors
Stood on the corner
In front of the building,
Where the night before
A man had turned on the gas.

'Well, his troubles are over,
His worries are over.'

'Me, I'll stay here with troubles,
What's new about worry?'

'He was overseas —
Colored, and in the army —
You know what that did to our boys.'

'They say his wife left him —'
Two little girls were busy with chalk
Marking up the pavement,
In front of the building
Where the night before
A man had turned on the gas.

Another little girl
Who was bouncing a rubber ball
Bumped into a pregnant woman
On the way home from the night shift.

'Excuse me, lady,'
The little girl said,
'We are going to play a game,
Excuse me.'

[*Puzzles* (1960), 39–41.]

Cuney wrote "Ward Six" and "Two Words" while hospitalized in the Philippines toward the end of World War II. He was being treated for battle fatigue, now called PTSD.

Ward Six

The sun makes a three point landing
In the blue eyes of an Irish nurse.

The eyes of an Irish nurse
Say things, flash meanings, speak confidences
To a sick lonesome soldier,
Stretched out on a hospital bed.

A long time ago a doctor said:
"There is as much to the art
Of practicing medicine
As there is to the science."
Maybe so, I do not know.

I do know the soft caress
In the eyes of an Irish nurse
Is a therapy of faith, and hope.

[July 25, 1945, previously unpublished.]

Two Words

Lovers always use the word, "forever."
Lovers always use the word, "always."
Two words: Whisper them, O Lovers,
Whisper them between kisses.
Swear by them in the park at night,
Or, on the top of a bus.
Drop a nickel into the telephone.
It is a good nickel's worth
When a guy asks a girl—"always?"
When a girl answers back—"Forever."

[July 25, 1945, previously unpublished.]

One of several poems that captures Cuney's abiding interest in children and the elderly.

Old Workman

The old man sits on a bench in the sun,
A feeble frame of his youthful self.

How many years has it been —
A nine-pound sledge-hammer,
Made a rainbow around his shoulders?
Now the strength has gone from his hands.
A once powerful steel-driving man
Sits on a bench in the morning sun,
A shadow of the days of his youth.
He teases the children as they go to school.
As the children come and go he tells them,
John Henry said, "Don't cry until I cry."
The children ask, "Who was John Henry?"
The old man answers, "He was a steel-driving man."
The children ask, "What is a steel-driving man?"
Why did he say, "Don't cry until I cry?"
The old man says, "Run along, you'll be late for school."

[*Puzzles* (1960), 44–45.]

In September 1928, Waring Cuney acknowledged his literary precursor by making a pilgrimage to Dayton, Ohio, to visit Mrs. Matilda Dunbar, mother of the late poet.

A Big Book of Poetry

I bought a big book of poetry
For a little girl who is eight years old.
The book is full of pretty pictures.
I knew a poem that is not in the book,
So I taught it to the little girl.
She calls it a good-morning poem.
It goes like this —

> "An angel robed in spotless white
> Bent down to kiss the sleeping Night,
> Night woke to Blush, the Sprite was gone —
> Men saw the Blush and called it, Dawn."

The name of the poem is *Dawn.*
It was written by Paul Dunbar,
A poet who was born in Dayton, Ohio,
Who died in 1906.

[February 12, 1961, previously unpublished.]

A New Book

Van Wyck Brooks
Has written a new book,
The Life of William Dean Howells.
It tells the reader how well
Mark Twain could imitate
A poor crippled Colored Uncle.
As the book reviewers say,
You can see the relationship
Howells, the man of letters,
Has to Rutherford B. Hayes,
The man in the White House.
The friendship between Howells
And Paul Laurence Dunbar
For some reason is omitted.
The book is eloquent.

[March 2, 1961, previously unpublished.]

Cuney long admired his sister Washingtonian, the poet Georgia Douglas Johnson, whose Saturday night literary salon he frequented.

Skies Less Grey

Georgia Douglas Johnson
Wrote a poem
In which she asked
For skies less grey,
Neither joy, nor happiness,
Neither love, nor peace,
Only skies less grey.
I wonder how many people
Have felt that way.

[January 16, 1960, previously unpublished.]

During their undergraduate years in Boston, W. E. B. Du Bois dated Waring's cousin, Maud Cuney, the concert pianist.

Interview

This is not verbatim.
This is not word for word,
At the time this is what I heard.
Two government men called
On W. E. B. Du Bois
In down-town New York,
At the N. A. A. C. P. office.
One government man said,
"Dr. Du Bois, we realize
That you are a busy man."
Du Bois answered them,
"Gentlemen, I am a busy man."
The other government man said,
"What is the purpose
Of the N. A. A. C. P. ?"
Du Bois answered them,
"My purpose and the purpose
Of the N. A. A. C. P. is
The enforcement of the Constitution
Of the United States of America."
The old man is ninety years old now.

[March 27, 1961, previously unpublished.]

Set in the Esplanade Park on Boston's Charles River, this poem reflects Cuney's sense of urban geography and his fascination with rivers.

October Winds

It was a long time ago.
We watched a red sunset
Over the Esplanade.
A crazy runaway moon
Came racing across the sky.
With your hand in mine
We listened to the river,
The splashing of the water,
October winds swept our faces —
I made up a nickname for you.
It was a long time ago.

[*Puzzles* (1960), 69.]

Another poem in which Cuney celebrates urban geography, the blues, and the Mississippi River.

Beale Street

Did you know
That Beale Street
In Memphis,
Has a grave yard
At one end,
A river,
At the other?

No wonder
They say the blues
Began on Beale Street.
You could pick
A guitar,
You could make
A song about that:

Walkin' down
Beale Street
Sad an' low,
Nobody cares
If I stay or go.
Walkin' any which way down
Beale Street,
What do I see?
Nothin' but a
Grave yard,
Or a river,
In front of me.

[*Puzzles* (1960), 77.]

Set in Chicago, this poem celebrates urban geography, the blues, and the Great Lakes.

Down-home Boy

I'm a down-home boy
trying to get ahead.
It seems like I go
backwards instead.

Been in Chicago
over a year.
Had nothing down home,
not much here.

A measly job,
a greedy boss —
that's how come
I left Waycross.

Those Great Lake winds
blow all around:
I'm a light-coat man
in a heavy-coat town.

[*Storefront Church* (1973), 10.]

Born in rural South Carolina in 1908, the entertaining, dignified Beasley Daniels, the subject of this poem, was an acquaintance of Cuney's during their youth in Washington, DC. The Washington poet Sterling A. Brown also published a poem based on Daniels, "Sporting Beasley."

I Dreamed I Saw Lord Daniels

I dreamed I saw Lord Daniels
Standing at 12th and G —
He twirled a satellite
In his big black hand
Where his cane used to be,
He wore a space suit
In place of his cut-a-way.
He looked up and down
He looked all around,
Then he said,
   Hey! Hey!
   Hey! Hey!
Every time he saw an ofay
He hollered,
   Scat!
And the chalks ran
This way and that
They prayed,
They got on their knees
Crying,
   O *Mister* Daniels
   Please
   Don't let that ball
   Fall.
Daniels said,

    Damn you all.
Eisenhower came running
With a golf stick
In his hand,
But Daniels told him,
    I'm not your fan.
I said,
    Hello, Brother Daniels,
    Bless my soul!
Lord Daniels smiled at me,
Then he said:
    These barbarians —
    Every-thing is under control!
I dreamed I saw Lord Daniels
Standing at 12th and G —
Then I woke up
While he was talking to me.

P.S. The late lamented Mr. Daniels was the subject of a poem during his lifetime by Sterling Brown.

[*Negro History Bulletin* 21, no. 7 (April 1958): 158.]

Cuney was a passionate aficionado of the blues; this poem refers to the rumors that Bessie Smith died because a white hospital refused to admit her after a traffic accident.

Bessie Smith

Oh, Tennessee road,
late at night —
where do you die
if your face ain't white?

[*Storefront Church* (1973), 18.]

This was Cuney's last poem, published the year before his death.

Soft Kid

Soft kid bought a hot dog
He needed a steak,
Went to bed with the chills
Too tired to shake.

Soft kid bought a hot dog
He needed a break,
Fell asleep with the Blues —
He forgot to wake.

[*The Iowa Review* 6, no. 2 (Spring 1975): 5.]

Appendix

Cuney and Waring Family Trees

POET WILLIAM WARING CUNEY (1906–1976) WAS THE child of Norris Wright Cuney II (1871–1923) and Madge Louise Williamson Cuney (1877–1967). Madge's mother was Maria Louisa Waring Williamson (1843–1886). Both the Cuneys and the Warings made significant contributions to American politics, arts, civil rights, education, and the military. In the book we discuss seven generations of these accomplished African American families. In order to assist the reader in keeping track of so many individuals and relationships, we have compiled genealogical charts for Waring Cuney's paternal and maternal forebears. The first is the descendant chart for Hester Neale Stuart (1800–1900), the matriarch of the Cuney family. The second chart illustrates the forebears of Waring Cuney's mother, Madge Williamson Cuney, beginning with Captain William Waring (1750–1815), a Scottish officer in the Revolutionary War and Arrica Vessels (1764–1825), a former bondswoman and his life partner.

Descendant Chart for
Hester Neale Stuart

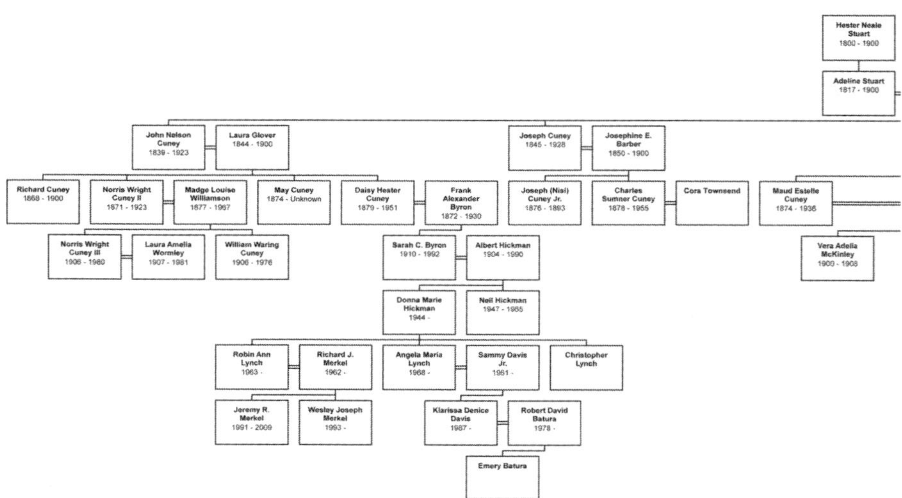

Descendant Chart for
William Waring

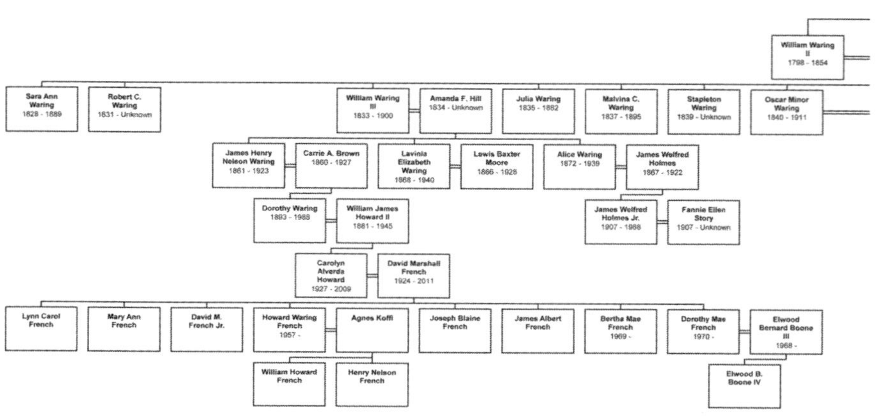

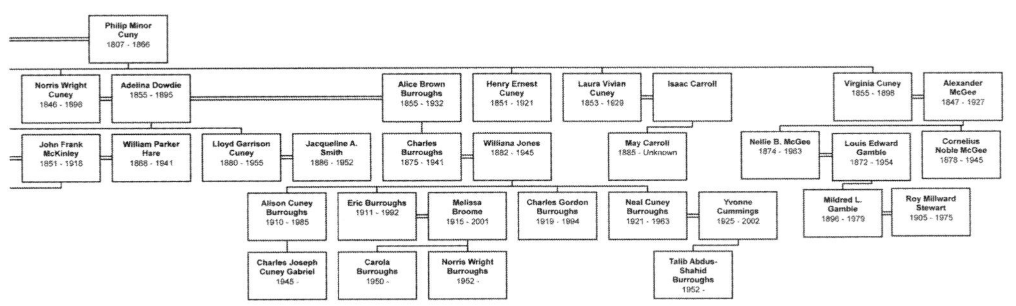
Philip Minor Cuny 1807 - 1866
Norris Wright Cuney 1846 - 1898
Adelina Dowdie 1855 - 1895
Alice Brown Burroughs 1855 - 1932
Henry Ernest Cuney 1851 - 1921
Laura Vivian Cuney 1853 - 1929
Isaac Carroll
Virginia Cuney 1855 - 1898
Alexander McGee 1847 - 1927
John Frank McKinley 1851 - 1918
William Parker Hare 1868 - 1941
Lloyd Garrison Cuney 1880 - 1955
Jacqueline A. Smith 1886 - 1952
Charles Burroughs 1875 - 1941
Williana Jones 1882 - 1945
May Carroll 1885 - Unknown
Nellie B. McGee 1874 - 1963
Louis Edward Gamble 1872 - 1954
Cornelius Noble McGee 1878 - 1945
Alison Cuney Burroughs 1910 - 1985
Eric Burroughs 1911 - 1992
Melissa Broome 1915 - 2001
Charles Gordon Burroughs 1919 - 1994
Neal Cuney Burroughs 1921 - 1963
Yvonne Cummings 1925 - 2002
Mildred L. Gamble 1896 - 1979
Roy Millward Stewart 1905 - 1975
Charles Joseph Cuney Gabriel 1945 -
Carola Burroughs 1950 -
Norris Wright Burroughs 1952 -
Talib Abdus-Shahid Burroughs 1952 -

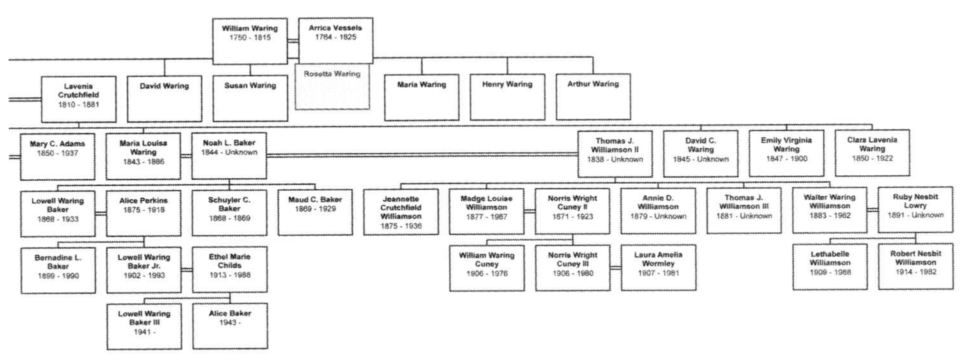
William Waring 1750 - 1815
Arrica Vessels 1764 - 1825
Lavenia Crutchfield 1810 - 1881
David Waring
Susan Waring
Rosetta Waring
Maria Waring
Henry Waring
Arthur Waring
Mary C. Adams 1850 - 1937
Maria Louisa Waring 1843 - 1886
Noah L. Baker 1844 - Unknown
Thomas J. Williamson II 1838 - Unknown
David C. Waring 1845 - Unknown
Emily Virginia Waring 1847 - 1900
Clara Lavenia Waring 1850 - 1922
Lowell Waring Baker 1868 - 1933
Alice Perkins 1875 - 1918
Schuyler C. Baker 1868 - 1869
Maud C. Baker 1869 - 1929
Jeannette Crutchfield Williamson 1875 - 1936
Madge Louise Williamson 1877 - 1967
Norris Wright Cuney II 1871 - 1923
Annie D. Williamson 1879 - Unknown
Thomas J. Williamson III 1881 - Unknown
Walter Waring Williamson 1883 - 1962
Ruby Nesbit Lowry 1891 - Unknown
Bernadine L. Baker 1899 - 1990
Lowell Waring Baker Jr. 1902 - 1993
Ethel Marie Childs 1913 - 1988
William Waring Cuney 1906 - 1976
Norris Wright Cuney III 1906 - 1980
Laura Amelia Wormley 1907 - 1981
Lethabelle Williamson 1909 - 1988
Robert Nesbit Williamson 1914 - 1982
Lowell Waring Baker III 1941 -
Alice Baker 1943 -

Notes

Introduction

1. Arthur B. Spingarn, "Books by Negro Authors in 1961," *The Crisis* 69, no. 2 (February 1962), 85, https://books.google.com/books?id=m-lsEAAAAMBAJ&pg=PA67&source=gbs_toc&cad=2#v=onepage&q&f=false; Arthur P. Davis, J. Saunders Redding, and Joyce Ann Joyce, eds, *The New Cavalcade: African American Writing from 1760 to the Present* (Washington, DC: Howard University Press, 1991), 583.
2. The account of the convention was originally published in the *Austin Daily State Journal,* July 5 and 7, 1873. The reference to Cuney is on p. 148 of an article titled "Platforms of Political Parties in Texas" by Ernest W. Winkler, published in the *Bulletin of the University of Texas,* no. 53 (September 20, 1916), https://omeka.coloredconventions.org/files/original/dcaefd1ccdb5354af55f9acaf1e7e5db.pdf.
3. Virginia Neal Hinze, "Norris Wright Cuney" (MA thesis, Rice University, 1965), 6.
4. Sofia Betancourt, "Between Dishwater and the River: Toward an Ecowomanist Methodology," *Worldviews* 20, no. 1 (2016): 64.
5. Ibid., 72.
6. David Levering Lewis, *When Harlem Was in Vogue* (New York: Penguin, 1997), 249.
7. Sterling Brown, quoted in Lorenzo Thomas, "Authenticity and Elevation: Sterling Brown's Theory of the Blues," *African American Review* 31, no. 3 (Autumn 1997), 414.
8. Ronald Primeau, "Frank Horne and the Second-Echelon Poets of the Harlem Renaissance," in *The Harlem Renaissance Remembered,* ed. Arna Bontemps (New York: Dodd, Mead & Co., 1972), 248.

Chapter 1

1. Geoffrey C. Ward, *Unforgivable Blackness: The Rise and Fall of Jack Johnson* (New York: Vintage, 2006), 33.
2. Ellen Beasley, *The Alleys and Back Buildings of Galveston* (College Station:

Texas A&M University Press, 1996), 43.
3. Ward, *Unforgivable Blackness*, 6.
4. Maud Cuney Hare, *Norris Wright Cuney: A Tribune of the Black People* (New York: The Crisis Publishing Company, 1913), 64; "Nelson Cuney," "Joseph Cuney," "Wright Cuney," "Henry Johnson," 1880 US Federal Census, Galveston, Texas, Ancestry.com.
5. Ward, *Unforgivable Blackness*, 8.
6. See chapter 6 of this book, note 36.
7. "It has been suggested that in lieu of the 'Island City' Galveston should be called the 'Oleander City.'" *Galveston Daily News*, January 14, 1874, 4.
8. "Austin, Texas, April 10.—We have been down at Galveston for a week, had fine weather about 75 degrees to 80 degrees every day. At Oleander city we had strawberries, new potatoes, green peas every day. It is one of the cleanest cities, Broadway being 150 feet wide." *Oshkosh* (WI) *Daily Northwestern*, April 15, 1876, 2.
9. Carter G. Woodson, "The Cuney Family," *Negro History Bulletin* 11, no. 6 (March 1948): 123.
10. Telephone interview with Robert (Bob) Powell, May 8, 2020.
11. G. M. G. Stafford, "Some Prominent Rapides Names of Long Ago," *Alexandria Daily Town Talk*, July 18, 1928, 12.
12. Douglas Hales, *A Southern Family in White and Black: The Cuneys of Texas* (College Station: Texas A&M University Press, 2003), 4.
13. According to Maud Cuney Hare, who was apparently in touch with them in 1912, two of her white great-aunts, then in their eighties, were still living on the family property. Cuney Hare, *Norris Wright Cuney*, 2.
14. Hales, *A Southern Family in White and Black*, 4.
15. "All U.S., College Student Lists, 1763–1924 results for Philip Minor Cuny," https://www.ancestry.com/search/collections/2207/?name=Philip+Minor_Cuny&name_x=1_1&residence=1826.
16. Unpublished letters of Philip Minor Cuny to Adaline Spurlock, 1852–1864; all letters courtesy of Cuny descendant Robert (Bob) Powell.
17. Unpublished letter from Philip Cuny to Adaline Spurlock Cuny, April 21, 1860.
18. Cuney Hare, *Norris Wright Cuney*, 2; and telephone interview with Bob Powell, May 10, 2020.
19. Hales, *A Southern Family in White and Black*, 6.
20. Cuney Hare, *Norris Wright Cuney*, 4.
21. Ibid., 1.

22. Ibid., 7.
23. Ibid., 2; and Hales, *A Southern Family in White and Black,* 4n4.
24. "Adeline Stuart in the New Orleans, Louisiana, U.S. Slave Manifests, 1807–1860," National Archives, Washington, DC, Microfilm Serial: M1895, Microfilm Roll: 7, Ancestry.com.
25. Calvin Schermerhorn, "Capitalism's Captives: The Maritime United States Slave Trade, 1807–1850," *Journal of Social History* 47, no. 4 (Summer 2014): 905–6.
26. Joshua D. Rothman, *The Ledger and the Chain: How Domestic Slave Traders Shaped America* (New York: Basic Books, 2021), 162.
27. Ibid., 3.
28. Ibid., 203.
29. "Slavery in the District of Columbia," *The Liberator* 2, no. 6, February 11, 1832, 22, http://fair-use.org/the-liberator/1832/02/11/the-liberator-02-06.pdf, February 11, 1832.
30. Rothman, *The Ledger and the Chain,* 203.
31. Ibid., 206.
32. Schermerhorn, "Capitalism's Captives," 907.
33. Rothman, *The Ledger and the Chain,* 163.
34. Ibid., 150.
35. Ibid.
36. Ibid., 151.
37. Cuney Hare, *Norris Wright Cuney,* 2.
38. Hales, *A Southern Family in White and Black,* 5.
39. Ibid, 6.
40. Letter from José Justo Liendo, January 15, 1830, https://texashistory.unt.edu/ark:/67531/metapth217398/.
41. Hinze, "Norris Wright Cuney," 3. José Justo Liendo, then residing in Nacogdoches, Texas, had originally purchased the eleven-league property from the Mexican government; he sold the remainder of the tract to Leonard Groce, who established a cotton plantation and built the still-extant Liendo Plantation home.
42. Sankofa Slavery Data Collection for Sunnyside Plantation, http://sites.rootsweb.com/~afamerpl/plantations_usa/TX/sunnyside.html.
43. Hales, *A Southern Family in White and Black,* 6.
44. Hinze, "Norris Wright Cuney," 7.
45. Ibid., 3.
46. Letter to Adaline Spurlock, June 18, 1852.

47. Eusibia Lutz, "LIENDO: The Biography of a House," *Southwest Review* 16, no. 2 (January 1931), 194.
48. Letter to Adaline Spurlock, June 18, 1852.
49. Cuney Hare, *Norris Wright Cuney*, 4.
50. Ibid.
51. Ibid.
52. Ibid.
53. Julia Beazley, "Liendo Plantation," Texas State Historical Association *Handbook of Texas*, https://www.tshaonline.org/handbook/entries/liendo-plantation.
54. Lutz, "LIENDO," 193.
55. Cuney Hare, *Norris Wright Cuney*, 3.
56. Hinze, "Norris Wright Cuney," 5.
57. Hales, *A Southern Family in White and Black*, 6.
58. Ibid., 8.
59. Ralph A. Wooster, "Wealthy Texans, 1860," *Southwestern Historical Quarterly* 71, no. 2 (October 1967), 166.
60. Hales, *A Southern Family in White and Black*, 10.
61. Ibid., 7.
62. Ibid.
63. Hinze, "Norris Wright Cuney," 4: Andrew F. Muir, "The Free Negro in Galveston County, Texas," *Negro History Bulletin* 22, no. 3 (December 1953): 69.
64. Letter from Philip Cuny to Adaline Spurlock Cuny, September 6, 1860.
65. "Philip Minor Cuny," Roster ID 1287, entered VMI September 7, 1859, dismissed January 28, 1860, for neglect of duties, Virginia Military Institute Archives Digital Collection, https://www.vmi.edu/archives/genealogy-biography-alumni/find-your-vmi-ancestor-/.
66. Woodson, "The Cuney Family," 123.
67. Cuney Hare, *Norris Wright Cuney*, 6.
68. Ibid., 4–5.
69. Ibid., 5.
70. Ibid., 5–6.
71. "Adeline Cuney," 1870 and 1880 US Federal Census, Houston, Texas, and 1900 US Federal Census, Galveston, Texas, Ancestry.com.
72. Letter from Philip Cuny to Adaline Spurlock Cuny, April 29, 1861.
73. Woodson, "The Cuney Family," 123.
74. Cuney Hare, *Norris Wright Cuney*, 6.

75. Merline Pitre, "George Thompson Ruby (1841–1882)," Texas State Historical Association *Handbook of Texas*, https://www.tshaonline.org/handbook/entries/ruby-george-thompson; Hinze, "Norris Wright Cuney," 12. Ruby, described with questionable objectivity as a "mulatto carpetbagger" in Hinze's unpublished 1962 master's thesis for Rice University, was born in New York in 1841 to Reuben and Rachel Humphrey Ruby, both free. The family relocated to Portland, Maine, when George was ten; he graduated from Portland High School and then moved to Boston where he became a journalist with the abolitionist press. He became the first Black senator for the Texas 12th District.
76. Frank Lincoln Mather, *Who's Who of the Colored Race*, vol. 1 (Chicago, IL: Kessinger Publishing, 1915), 583; Cuney Hare, *Norris Wright Cuney*, 10; "Josephine E. Barber," U.S. Passport Application, September 12, 1871, Washington, DC; "Jos Cuney," "Henry Cuney," "Virginia Cuney," 1870 US Federal Census, Washington, DC, Ancestry.com.
77. Izola Ethel Fedford Collins, *Island of Color: Where Juneteenth Started* (Bloomington, IN: AuthorHouse, 2004), 38–39.
78. Cuney Hare, *Norris Wright Cuney*, 8; Hales, *A Southern Family in White and Black*, 40.
79. Hinze, "Norris Wright Cuney," 12.
80. Ibid., 12; Cuney Hare, *Norris Wright Cuney*, 12.
81. Hales, *A Southern Family in White and Black*, 40.
82. Cuney Hare, *Norris Wright Cuney*, 39.
83. James M. Smallwood, "Early 'Freedom Schools': Black Self-Help and Education in Reconstruction Texas, A Case Study," *Negro History Bulletin* 41, no. 1 (January/February 1978): 790.
84. Ralph Albert Scull, *The Scull Papers*, 1931, 13, MS85-0003, Rosenberg Library, Galveston, Texas.
85. Barnes Papers, Diary, March 14, 1868.
86. Scull, *The Scull Papers*, 77.
87. Ibid.
88. Cuney Hare, *Norris Wright Cuney*, 93.
89. Ibid., 303.
90. Collins, *Island of Color*, 178.
91. Scull, *The Scull Papers*, 19.
92. Alwyn Barr, *Black Texans: A History of African Americans in Texas, 1528-1995* (Norman: University of Oklahoma Press, 1995), 22.
93. That building was destroyed in the Hurricane of 1900. The

present imposing brick edifice was erected in 1916 and is still a vibrant congregation.

94. Collins, *Island of Color*, 143.
95. Ibid., 6.
96. Ibid., 170.
97. Scull, *The Scull Papers*, 23.
98. Collins, *Island of Color*, 169.
99. Ward, *Unforgivable Blackness*, 5; Jack Johnson, *My Life in the Ring & Out* (New York: Dover, 2018), 33.
100. Johnson, *My Life in the Ring & Out*, 70.
101. Ibid., 33.
102. Muir, "The Free Negro in Galveston County, Texas," 68.
103. Collins, *Island of Color*, 4.
104. Cuney Hare, *Norris Wright Cuney*, 8.
105. Ibid., 9.
106. Ibid., 80.
107. Ibid., 45.
108. Ibid., 4.
109. Ibid., 15, 79.
110. Hales, *A Southern Family in White and Black*, 13.
111. Ibid., 8.
112. Ibid., 21.
113. "Cuney, Master Politician for Generation in Washington and New York, Passes Away," *Houston Informer*, February 26, 1921, 1.
114. Woodson, "The Cuney Family," 124; "Henry E. Cuney," Atlanta, Georgia, U.S. Penitentiary Prisoner Index, 1880–1922, Ancestry.com.
115. Cuney Hare, *Norris Wright Cuney*, 220.
116. Du Bois published the book through his *Crisis* publishing company in 1913.
117. Cuney Hare, *Norris Wright Cuney*, 19.
118. Hinze, "Norris Wright Cuney," 138.
119. Hales, *A Southern Family in White and Black*, 62.
120. Cuney Hare, *Norris Wright Cuney*, iii.
121. Ibid., 222.
122. Ward, *Unforgivable Blackness*, 37.
123. Ibid., 31.
124. Bernard Bell, "Contemporary African-American Poetry as Folk Art," *Black World*, March 1973, 77–78.

125. Joe Holley, "Norris Wright Cuney Never Stopped Fighting," *Houston Chronicle*, June 14, 2020, https://www.houstonchronicle.com/news/columnists/native-texan/article/Norris-Wright-Cuney-never-stopped-fighting-15338633.php.
126. Waring Cuney to Langston Hughes, January 14, 1944, Box 49, Folder 923, Langston Hughes Papers, Beinecke Rare Book and Manuscript Library, Yale University.

Chapter 2

1. "Armstrong High Holds Graduation," *Evening Star* (Washington, DC), June 20, 1923, 16. The name of the school was changed to Armstrong Technical High School in 1925.
2. Galveston City Directory, 1891–1892.
3. "Catalog of the Officers and Students of Howard University, 1870–1871," *Howard University Catalogs*, 46, https://dh.howard.edu/hucatalogs/74.
4. Izola Ethel Fedford Collins, *Island of Color: Where Juneteenth Started* (Bloomington, IN: AuthorHouse, 2004), 43.
5. See the Howard University Catalogues 1900–1901, p. 76, 1901–1902, p. 74, and 1902–1903, p. 83, https://www.google.com/books/edition/Catalogue_of_the_Officers_and_Students_o/CZ9GAQAAMAAJ?hl=en&gbpv=1&bsq=cuney. Also see Carter G. Woodson, "The Cuney Family," *Negro History Bulletin* 11, no. 6 (March 1948): 123–24.
6. "A Short History of GPO," https://www.govinfo.gov/app/details/GPO-AShortHistoryofGPO.
7. Ibid.
8. Ibid.
9. Letter from Carolyn Alverda Howard French to Henry Minton Francis, May 12, 1981, H. Minton Francis Papers, Box 3, Folder 9, Moorland-Spingarn Research Center, Manuscript Division, Howard University.
10. "The Graduates," *Evening Star* (Washington, DC), June 18, 1896, 9. Also see "High School Graduates," *Evening Star* (Washington, DC), June 12, 1895, 9.
11. "Thomas Williamson," 1850 US Federal Census, Madison, Tennessee, Ancestry.com.
12. Carter G. Woodson, "The Waring Family," *Negro History Bulletin* 11,

no. 5 (February 1948): 99–100; "Men of the Month: Two Supervising Architects," *The Crisis* 14–15 (May 1917), 32. In spring 1924, Baker's son and the twins' first cousin Lowell W. Baker Jr. (1902–1993) received a BS from the University of Detroit. For his graduation photograph, see *The Crisis* 28, no. 3 (July 1924), 24.

13. Woodson, "The Waring Family," 100; Ancestry.com, US passport application for Walter W. Williamson, October 25, 1916; WWI Draft Registration Card for Walter Waring Williamson, September 12, 1918; WWII Draft Registration Card for Walter Waring Williamson, April 27, 1942; New York Arriving Passengers and Crew List for Walter Williamson, February 27, 1917.
14. *1896: Alumni Catalogue*, Howard University, p. 46, https://dh.howard.edu/cgi/viewcontent.cgi?article=1028&context=hucatalogs.
15. According to the *Columbus City Directory*, Maud's brother Lowell worked as a carpenter and lived at 39 East Spring.
16. Adah Ward Randolph, "Champion Avenue School: A Historical Analysis," paper presented at the Annual Meeting of the American Educational Research Association, Chicago, IL, March 27, 1997, https://files.eric.ed.gov/fulltext/ED411333.pdf," 8–9. Also see Court of Appeals of Ohio, January 1930, "Haddox, Exr. v. Jordan," 214, https://casetext.com/case/haddox-exr-v-jordan.
17. Interestingly, Maria Louisa, Madge's mother, had also given birth to twin sons.
18. Deeds of Trust, *Washington Post*, September 17, 1907, 10.
19. Woodson, "The Waring Family," 100.
20. "John R. Wright and Gertrude V. Clarke, 1 July 1905," Washington, DC, Marriage Index, 1830–1921, Ancestry.com.
21. "John R. Wright," 1920, 1930, and 1940 US Federal Census, Washington, DC, Ancestry.com; "108 Diplomas Won by Dunbar Class," *Evening Star* (Washington, DC), June 17, 1924, 13.
22. "Obituary of John Ralph Wright," *Evening Star* (Washington, DC), September 13, 1941, A-4.
23. "Ralph Clarke Wright and Carolyn Beatrice Evans," August 10, 1935, US Marriage Records, Washington, DC, 1810–1953, Ancestry.com; "Ralph Clarke Wright," World War II Draft Registration Card, Washington, DC, February 16, 1942, Ancestry.com.
24. Ronald M. Johnson, "From Romantic Suburb to Racial Enclave: LeDroit Park, Washington, DC, 1880–1920," *Phylon* 45, no. 4 (1984): 264.

25. Ibid., 265.
26. Ibid., 266.
27. "Obituary for Missouri B. Williams," *Evening Star* (Washington, DC), February 11, 1938, A-10.
28. Mary Church Terrell, *A Colored Woman in a White World* (New York: Prometheus Books, 2005), 150.
29. Ibid.
30. Ibid., 151.
31. Ibid., 280.
32. Quoted in Adele Logan Alexander, *Homelands and Waterways: The American Journey of the Bond Family, 1846–1926* (New York: Vintage Books, 2000), 446.
33. Terrell, *A Colored Woman in a White World*, 280; Alexander, *Homelands and Waterways*, 448.
34. Alexander, *Homelands and Waterways*, 446.
35. "Highland Beach Notes," *The Colored American*, August 29, 1903, 6.
36. Alexander, *Homelands and Waterways*, 446.
37. Ibid., 448.
38. Ibid., 449.
39. "Obituary of Jacqueline Allean Cuney," *Evening Star* (Washington, DC), May 2, 1952, 16; *Washington Post*, May 3, 1952, B-2.
40. "Judge Scott Will Address Dinner for Negro Leaders," *Evening Star* (Washington, DC), March 20, 1952, A-25.
41. "Many School Pleas," *Evening Star* (Washington, DC), April 7, 1935, D-4.
42. Stanley Turkel, "Hotel History: Wormley Hotel," *hospitalitynet*, February 17, 2001.
43. Ibid. Also see *1896: Alumni Catalogue*, Howard University, 23.
44. "G. Smith Wormley Active in Schools," *Sunday Star* (Washington, DC), July 1, 1923, 16.
45. "G. N. Wormley Arrested," *Evening Star* (Washington, DC), June 15, 1909, 12; "Cora Wormley," 1910 US Federal Census, District of Columbia, Ancestry.com.
46. "Garrett Wormley Accused of Violating the Postal Laws," *Evening Star* (Washington, DC), July 13, 1909, 11.
47. "Garrett Wormley," Michigan, US, Divorce Records, 1897–1952, Ancestry.com.
48. "Woman Ends Life," *Washington Times*, December 8, 1912, 4.
49. "Garrett N. Wormley and Emily F. Russell," June 24, 1914, Michigan, US,

Marriage Records, 1867–1952, Ancestry.com.

50. "John Gearit Wormley," World War II Draft Registration Card, Ann Arbor, Michigan, October 16, 1940, Ancestry.com.
51. "Emily R. Wormley," 1920 US Federal Census, Ann Arbor, Ward 4, Washtenaw, Michigan, Ancestry.com. Interestingly, Emily Wormley is also listed as Black in the 1940 US Federal Census, Ann Arbor, Washtenaw, Michigan, Ancestry.com.
52. "Amelia Wormley," 1920 US Federal Census, Philadelphia, Ward 36, Pennsylvania, Ancestry.com.
53. "8th Grade Pupils Advance to District High Schools," *Evening Star* (Washington, DC), June 21, 1922; and *Washington Herald*, June 22, 1922, 6.
54. "Laura Amelia Wormley," 1930 US Federal Census, Washington, DC, USA, Ancestry.com. The 1917 Washington, DC, Directory shows dentist C. Sumner Wormley living at 997 Florida Avenue NW with his widowed mother, Amelia E. Wormley. G. Smith Wormley teaches at the Myrtilla Miner School. Several Wormleys are teachers residing at 547 Florida Avenue NW.
55. Dunbar High School Yearbook for 1926, courtesy of Mrs. Susan Salus.
56. Edgar Allan Toppin, "Scott, Emmett Jay," *American National Biography*, February 2000, http://www.anb.org/articles/09/09-00668.html. Also see Maceo C. Dailey Jr., *Emmett J. Scott: Power Broker of the Tuskegee Machine*, edited by Will Guzmán and David H. Jackson Jr. (Lubbock: Texas Tech University Press, 2023).
57. Maceo Crenshaw Dailey Jr., "The Business Life of Emmett Jay Scott," *Business History Review* 77, no. 4 (Winter 2003): 668.
58. "Scott-Delany Nuptial in Washington," *Pittsburgh Courier*, October 16, 1926, 6.
59. "182 Are Graduated from Dunbar High, Awarded Diplomas Last Night in Amphitheater of Howard University," *Evening Star* (Washington, DC), June 22, 1926.
60. Dunbar High School yearbook for 1926, courtesy of Mrs. Susan Salus.
61. "Armstrong Manual Training," *Evening Star* (Washington, DC), November 19, 1922, 20; "Armstrong Manual Training School," *Evening Star* (Washington, DC), February 18, 1923, 22.
62. "Armstrong High Holds Graduation," *Evening Star* (Washington, DC), June 20, 1923, 16.
63. "Obituary of Norris Wright Cuney," *Evening Star* (Washington, DC),

March 26, 1923, 7.

64. Howard University Catalogue, Register of Students 1925–1926, lists "In Degree Courses" Norris W. Cuney (School of Music 1; Evening Classes) and William W. Cuney (College of Liberal Arts 1); Ernest Just Letter of Recommendation for Waring Cuney, March 15, 1932, NAACP's Walter White Papers. Also see Waring Cuney to Walter White, June 1, 1932, Walter White Papers, file:///C:/Users/vdmtchll/Downloads/Cuney%20 CV%20Walter%20White.pdf.
65. Langston Hughes, *The Big Sea* (New York: Hill and Wang, 1993 [1940]), 219.
66. "Marriage Licenses," *Evening Star* (Washington, DC), December 23, 1933, 7; "Laura Amelia Wormley and Norris Wright Cuney," December 24, 1933, Washington, DC, US Marriage Records, 1810–1953, Ancestry.com.
67. Waring Cuney to Langston Hughes, October 8, 1936, Box 49, Folder 922, Langston Hughes Papers, Beinecke Rare Book and Manuscript Library, Yale University.
68. Emily Bernard, ed., *Remember Me to Harlem: The Letters of Langston Hughes and Carl Van Vechten, 1925–1964* (New York: Knopf, 2001), 22.
69. Ibid.
70. Waring Cuney to Langston Hughes, October 6, 1925, Box 49, Folder 922, Langston Hughes Papers, Beinecke Rare Book and Manuscript Library, Yale University.
71. Faith Berry, *Before and Beyond Harlem: A Biography of Langston Hughes* (New York: Wings Books, 1983), 68–69, 98.
72. Hughes, *The Big Sea*, 203, 206, 208.
73. Ibid., 208–9.
74. Sterling A. Brown, "Sporting Beasley," *The Collected Poems of Sterling A. Brown* (Chicago: TriQuarterly Books, 1983), 109–10.
75. "Arthur Daniels," 1920 US Federal Census, *Concord, Clarendon County, South Carolina*, USA, Ancestry.com; "Beasley Daniels," US WWII Draft Cards Young Men, 1940–1947, Baltimore, Maryland, Ancestry.com.
76. Jean Toomer, *Cane* (New York: Harper & Row, 1969 [1923]), 41.
77. Georgia Douglas Johnson Papers, Box 162-1, Folder 4, Manuscript Division, Moorland-Spingarn Research Center, Howard University.
78. Hughes, *The Big Sea*, 216.

Chapter 3

1. Waring Cuney to Langston Hughes, October 8, 1936, Box 49, Folder 922, Langston Hughes Papers, Beinecke Rare Book and Manuscript Library, Yale University.
2. Susan P. Casteras, "Pre-Raphaelite Challenges to Victorian Canons of Beauty," *Huntington Library Quarterly* 55, no. 1 (1992), 15.
3. Ibid., 32.
4. W. E. B. Du Bois, "Maude Cuney Hare," *Pittsburgh Courier*, April 4, 1936, http://credo.library.umass.edu/view/pageturn/mums312-b218-i007/#page/3/mode/1up.
5. W. E. B. Du Bois, *The Autobiography of W. E. B. Du Bois: A Soliloquy on Viewing My Life from the Last Decade of its First Century* (New York: International Publishers, 1968), 138.
6. Death certificates for Joseph Cuney and Nelson Cuney list Lakeview as place of burial.
7. Ibid.
8. See, for example, "Nelson Cuney," "Joseph Cuney," and "Wright Cuney" in the 1880 US Federal Census, Galveston, Texas, Ancestry.com.
9. Mary Church Terrell, *A Colored Woman in a White World* (New York: Prometheus Books, 2005), 126.
10. "Alexander McGee and Jennie Cuney," *Texas*, US, *Select County Marriage Index, 1837–1965, FHL Film Number: 1008866, Ancestry.com.*
11. "Jennie McGee," 1880 US Federal Census, *Ancestry.com.*
12. Carter G. Woodson, "The Cuney Family," *Negro History Bulletin* 11, no. 6 (March 1948): 124.
13. "Alex H. McGee," 1910 US Federal Census, *Ancestry.com.*
14. "Miss Laura V. Cuney" and "Mrs. Jennie McGee (widow)," U.S. City Directories, 1822–1995, Houston, Texas, City Directory, 1882, 79, 213, Ancestry.com.
15. Karl Jacoby, *The Strange Career of William Ellis: The Texas Slave Who Became a Mexican Millionaire* (New York: W. W. Norton, 2017), 62.
16. Ibid.
17. "Laura V. Carroll" and "May Carroll," 1920 US Federal Census, Chicago Ward 3, Cook County, IL, Ancestry.com.
18. Ibid., 63.
19. Ibid., 61.
20. "Louis E. Gamble and Nellie B. McGee," Pennsylvania, US County

Marriage Records, 1845–1963, Allegheny, 1895–1896, 382, Ancestry.com.

21. "Jennie C. MaGee [*sic*]," Pittsburgh, Pennsylvania, US Deaths, 1870–1905, 511, Ancestry.com. We thank Dr. Robert Sbaschnig, MD, for his help interpreting the death certificate.
22. See Britt Bennett's *The Vanishing Half* (New York: Riverhead, 2020), the story of identical twins, Desiree who lives Black and Stella who disappears into the white world, for a contemporary account of family pain caused by racism and passing.
23. Woodson, "The Cuney Family," 124. See also "May Cuney," 1900 US Federal Census, Ancestry.com.
24. "Byron, Naval Expert. Dead," Associated Press, Washington, DC, February 20, 1930, https://www.wikitree.com/wiki/Byron-717.
25. "St. Edmund's Episcopal Church Archives," Vivian G. Harsh Research Collection of Afro-American History and Literature, Carter G. Woodson Regional Library, Chicago Public Library. See also obituary of "Mrs. Daisy Cuney Byron," *Chicago Tribune*, December 13, 1951, 91, Ancestry.com, https://www.chipublib.org/fa-st-edmunds-episcopal-church-archives-2/.
26. See Amelia Cuney's Last Will and Testament, which at her death in 1981 bequeathed money to her husband's cousin, "Mrs. Sarah Hickman, 10425 South Rhodes Ave., Chicago, Illinois." H. Minton Francis Papers, Box 3, Folder 9, Moorland-Spingarn Research Center, Howard University.
27. Rafia Zafar, *We Wear the Mask: African Americans Write American Literature, 1760–1870* (New York: Columbia University Press, 1997), 165.
28. William Craft and Ellen Craft, *Running a Thousand Miles for Freedom; or, the Escape of William and Ellen Craft from Slavery* (London: William Tweedie, 1860), 68, electronic edition, https://docsouth.unc.edu/neh/craft/craft.html.
29. For more on the Crafts, see Barbara McCaskill, *Love, Liberation, and Escaping Slavery: William and Ellen Craft in Cultural Memory* (Athens: University of Georgia Press, 2015).
30. Roi Ottley, "5 Million U.S. White Negroes," *Ebony*, March 1948.
31. Eugene Gordon, "Massachusetts: Land of the Free and Home of the Brave Colored Man," 1925, reprinted in *These "Colored" United States: African American Essays from the 1920s*, eds. Tom Lutz and Susanna Ashton (New Brunswick, NJ: Rutgers University Press, 1996), 145, 151.
32. Ibid., 151.

33. Coleman and Cuney appeared alongside each other in the *Opportunity* "prize winners" photo gallery of June 1926, p. 188.
34. James Weldon Johnson, *The Autobiography of an Ex-Colored Man*, 1912 (New York: Penguin, 1990), 154.
35. Maud Cuney Hare, *Norris Wright Cuney: A Tribune of the Black People* (New York: The Crisis Publishing Company, 1913), 154.
36. Ibid.
37. Ibid.
38. "Colored High School," *Galveston Daily News*, June 2, 1890, 8.
39. Ibid.
40. Ibid.
41. Woodson, "The Cuney Family," 124.
42. "Joseph Cuney Junior," Massachusetts, US, Death Records, 1841–1915, Ancestry.com.
43. Cuney Hare, *Norris Wright Cuney*, 131.
44. Maud Cuney Hare, *Negro Musicians and Their Music* (New York: G. K. Hall, 1996 [1936]), 209, 213.
45. *Prospectus of the New England Conservatory of Music, 1890*, 55, https://archive.org/details/prospectusofnewe1890newe/page/n79/mode/2up.
46. Willard B. Gatewood, *Aristocrats of Color: The Black Elite, 1880–1920* (Fayetteville: University of Arkansas Press, 1990), 92.
47. Cuney Hare, *Norris Wright Cuney*, 131–32.
48. Ibid, 132.
49. Ibid., 132–33.
50. Ibid, 133.
51. W. E. B. Du Bois, "A Negro Student at Harvard at the End of the Nineteenth Century," in *Blacks at Harvard: A Documentary History of African-American Experience at Harvard and Radcliffe*, ed. Werner Sollors (New York: New York University Press, 1993), 77.
52. Norris Wright Cuney, Large Scrapbook, Fondren Library, Rice University (microfilm), 44.
53. Ibid.
54. Du Bois, "Maud Cuney Hare."
55. Cuney Hare, *Norris Wright Cuney*, 176.
56. Ibid., 177; "Social Notes," *The Woman's Era* 1, no. 6 (September 1894): 11.
57. Michael Barnes, "What's Left of Austin's Lost Blind, Deaf and Orphan School?" *Statesman News Network*, September 25, 2018, https://www.statesman.com/news/20160915/whats-left-of-austins-lost-blind-

deaf-and-orphan-school.

58. Ibid.
59. Cuney Hare, *Norris Wright Cuney*, 177.
60. Michael Corcoran, "Maud Cuney-Hare, A Former Austinite You Need to Know About," MichaelCorcoran.net, March 21, 2016, https://www.michaelcorcoran.net/maude-cuney-hare-a-former-austinite-you-need-to-know-about.
61. "Social Notes," *The Woman's Era* 3, no. 3 (August 1896).
62. Douglas Hales, *A Southern Family in White and Black: The Cuneys of Texas* (College Station: Texas A&M University Press, 2003), 102.
63. Cuney Hare, *Norris Wright Cuney*, 215; Hales, *A Southern Family in White and Black*, 104.
64. Jacoby, *The Strange Career of William Ellis*, 137.
65. Cuney Hare, *Norris Wright Cuney*, 222.
66. "Miss Cuney Weds," *Colored American* 6, no. 27 (October 10, 1898), 5; "Miss Maud Cuney," *Washington Bee* XVII, no. 18 (October 1, 1898), 5.
67. Jacoby, *The Strange Career of William Ellis*, 137.
68. Ibid., 138.
69. "Miss Cuney Weds," *Colored American* 6, no. 27, 5.
70. "Prefers Whites to Own Race: Mrs. McKinley Tells Court of Doctor's Likes and Dislikes," *Chicago Broad Ax*, October 26, 1907, 1.
71. "St. John's Literary," *Chicago Daily News*, July 22, 1902, 9.
72. "Prefers Whites to Own Race," *Chicago Broad Ax*, 1.
73. "Mrs. Maude [*sic*] Cuney McKinley," *Washington Times*, April 24, 1903, 7.
74. Fannie Barrier Williams, "Obituary of Vera McKinley," *New York Age*, September 17, 1908.
75. Terrell, *A Colored Woman in a White World*, 420.
76. "Pretty Summer Wedding," *The Colored American*, August 1, 1903, 5.
77. Waring Cuney to Langston Hughes, October 10, 1926, Box 49, Folder 926, Langston Hughes Papers, Beinecke Rare Book and Manuscript Library, Yale University.
78. Williams, "Obituary of Vera McKinley," September 17, 1908.
79. Du Bois, "Maud Cuney Hare."
80. Ibid.
81. "The Week in Society," *Washington Bee*, January 8, 1910, 5.
82. R. W. Thompson, "The Passing Show in Washington," *The National Forum*, October 15, 1910, 3.
83. Hales, *A Southern Family in White and Black*, 114.

84. Ibid.
85. Tera W. Hunter, "Introduction: Maud Cuney Hare," in *Norris Wright Cuney: A Tribune of the Black People* (New York: G. K. Hall & Co., 1995), xix.
86. "Joint Costume Recital," *Evening Star* (Washington, DC), February 27, 1924, 2.
87. Hunter, "Introduction: Maud Cuney Hare," xix.
88. Ibid.
89. Hales, *A Southern Family in White and Black*, 114.
90. "Drama 'Antar of Araby' Presented by Students," *Boston Globe*, December 15, 1925, 17.
91. J. W. Youngblood, "Brief Items from Nearby Cities and Towns: Boston," *New York Amsterdam News*, May 18, 1927, 14.
92. Letter from Maud Cuney Hare to W. E. B. Du Bois, December 5, 1926, W. E. B. Du Bois Papers (MS 312), Special Collections and University Archives, University of Massachusetts Amherst Libraries, https://credo.library.umass.edu/view/full/mums312-b033-i440.
93. Hales, *A Southern Family in White and Black*, 124.
94. Du Bois, "Maud Cuney Hare," *Pittsburgh Courier*, April 4, 1936: "Maud Cuney was the bravest woman I have ever known. For those born in adversity, fighting fate becomes a habit, rather than a virtue; but when one is born to the purple and is first in mid-life overwhelmed by successive and relentless blows of every kind of cruelty and adversity, then to keep one's chin up, the eye unflinching, and the courage unfaltering, calls for the sort of soul men seldom see." Quoted in Douglas Hales, *A Southern Family in White and Black*, 186.

Chapter 4

1. Langston Hughes, "The Twenties: Harlem and Its Negritude," *African Forum* (Spring 1966). Reprinted in *The Langston Hughes Review* 4, no. 1 (Spring 1985): 30.
2. Eugene Gordon, "The Thirteen Most Important Negroes in the United States," *Richmond* (Virginia) *Planet*, June 28, 1930, 6.
3. Waring Cuney to Langston Hughes, November 21, 1925, Box 49, Folder 922, Langston Hughes Papers, Beinecke Rare Book and Manuscript Library, Yale University.
4. Waring Cuney to Langston Hughes, October 6, 1925, Box 49, Folder 922,

Langston Hughes Papers, Beinecke Rare Book and Manuscript Library, Yale University.

5. Waring Cuney to Langston Hughes, October 10, 1926, Box 49, Folder 926, Langston Hughes Papers, Beinecke Rare Book and Manuscript Library, Yale University.
6. Hughes, "The Twenties: Harlem and Its Negritude," 33. Also see "Germans Publish Poetry Anthology," *New York Amsterdam News*, January 16, 1929, 16.
7. Arnold Rampersad, "Langston Hughes's *Fine Clothes to the Jew*," *Callaloo* 26 (Winter 1986): 144.
8. Jean Toomer, *Cane* (New York: Harper & Row, 1969 [1923]), 71, 91.
9. Arna Bontemps, ed., *The Harlem Renaissance Remembered* (New York: Dodd, Mead, 1972), 59.
10. Luke 23:34, King James Version.
11. See Charles S. Johnson to Dorothy West, May 4, 1926, in Verner D. Mitchell and Cynthia Davis, eds., *Dorothy West: Where the Wild Grape Grows: Selected Writings, 1930–1950* (Amherst: University of Massachusetts Press, 2005), 182.
12. "Editorials," *Opportunity*, June 1926, 174.
13. We have been unable to find a copy of these two poems. After the third contest, Cuney and the other winners from Boston—Eugene Gordon, Dorothy West, and Helene Johnson—were feted at "a semi-formal reception" at which Maud Cuney Hare gave an "impromptu address." J. W. Youngblood, "Brief Items from Nearby Cities and Towns: Boston," *New York Amsterdam News*, May 18, 1927, 14.
14. Charles S. Johnson to Dorothy West, May 4, 1926, in Mitchell and Davis, eds., *Dorothy West*, 182.
15. For an account of the festivities, see Eugene Gordon, "The Awards Dinner," *Opportunity: A Journal of Negro Life* 4, no. 42 (June 1926): 186. He writes that among the four hundred attendees were "Mary White Ovington, Dr. and Mrs. Arthur B. Spingarn, Mrs. Joel [Amy] Spingarn . . . and many other white and Negro persons interested in letters and in the younger Negro writers whom, to mention, would require more space than we have. They included visitors from Boston, Philadelphia, Baltimore, Washington, and even as far west as Columbus, Ohio."
16. James Weldon Johnson, "Waring Cuney," *The Book of American Negro Poetry*, revised edition (New York: Harcourt Brace & Company, 1931), 283.

17. James Weldon Johnson, "Preface to the First Edition," *The Book of American Negro Poetry*, revised edition (New York: Harcourt Brace & Company, 1931), 9.
18. Johnson, "Waring Cuney," 283.
19. "Waring Cuney," *Centennial Anthology: Lincoln University Poets* (New York: The Fine Press), 1954, 68. On Cuney and Alpha Phi Alpha, see *The Sphinx* 12, no. 4 (Fall 1926), and "Washington Youths Visit in Zanesville," *Times Recorder* (Zanesville, Ohio), September 14, 1928, 2.
20. "Bynner Prize Awarded," *Springfield Republican*, August 8, 1926, 51.
21. See, for example, "No Images," *Greensboro Daily News*, June 24, 1926, 8; "Win Contest Prizes for Literature," *Pittsburgh Courier*, May 8, 1926, 1–2; and "Witter Bynner Poetry Awards Announced," *Santa Fe New Mexican*, August 12, 1926.
22. Waring Cuney to Langston Hughes, October 10, 1926, Box 49, Folder 926, Langston Hughes Papers, Beinecke Rare Book and Manuscript Library, Yale University.
23. Waring Cuney to Langston Hughes, October 18, 1927, Box 49, Folder 922, Langston Hughes Papers, Beinecke Rare Book and Manuscript Library, Yale University.
24. "Mildred Turner Pieretto-Bianco," US of America, Petition of Citizenship, US District Court of Mass. at Boston, November 3, 1930, Ancestry.com.
25. Waring Cuney to Langston Hughes, November 3, 1929, Box 49, Folder 922, Langston Hughes Papers, Beinecke Rare Book and Manuscript Library, Yale University.
26. Cynthia Davis and Verner D. Mitchell, "Eugene Gordon, Dorothy West, and the Saturday Evening Quill Club," *CLA Journal* 52, no. 4 (June 2009): 394.
27. Ibid., 399–401. Cuney says to Hughes in a November 3, 1929, letter: "I saw Arna at a Pill Club Meeting. He is writing a novel."
28. Toki Schalk, "Smart Talk on Society in Boston," *Pittsburgh Courier*, June 4, 1932, 8, ellipses Schalk. A few weeks earlier, she reported that "Waring Cuney, the poet who turned singer . . . has returned from a long visit to his family in DC . . . and any day we wouldn't be surprised to hear he's gone back to Rome. He's been twice . . . or is it three times." *Pittsburgh Courier*, April 23, 1932, 8, ellipses Schalk.
29. The quotes appear on the inside front cover of the April 1929 *Saturday Evening Quill*, in a section titled "Excerpts from Comments on the First

Number of *The Saturday Evening Quill.*"

30. "Washington Youths Visit in Zanesville," *Times Recorder* (Zanesville, Ohio), September 14, 1928, 2.
31. Quoted in Eleanor Alexander, *Lyrics of Sunshine and Shadow: The Tragic Courtship and Marriage of Paul Laurence Dunbar and Alice Ruth Moore, A History of Love and Violence Among the African American Elite* (New York: New York University Press, 2001), 118.
32. "St. John's Literary," *Chicago Daily News*, July 22, 1902, 9. Maud considered living permanently in Washington. She worked as a copyist for the Department of the Interior's General Land Office before resigning to accept a position teaching music at Prairie View College, in Prairie View, Texas. See the Washington, DC, newspaper *The Colored American*, October 24, 1903, 9; and "Mrs. Maud C. McKinley," *US, Register of Civil, Military, and Naval Service, 1863–1959*, volume 1, July 1, 1903, 940, Ancestry.com.
33. Waring Cuney, *US, Arriving Passenger and Crew Lists, New York, 1929*, Microfilm Serial: *T715, 1897–1957*, line *17*, p. *58, Ancestry.com.*
34. Waring Cuney to Langston Hughes, August 21, 1929, Box 49, Folder 922, Langston Hughes Papers, Beinecke Rare Book and Manuscript Library, Yale University.
35. Ibid., November 6, 1929.
36. William Cuney, *US, Arriving Passenger and Crew Lists, New York, 1931*, Microfilm Serial: *T715, 1897–1957*, line 24, p. 108, Ancestry.com.
37. Waring Cuney to Walter White, June 1, 1932, Walter White Papers, NAACP Administrative Files, Personal Correspondence.
38. George R. Arthur to Walter White, June 6, 1932, Walter White Papers.
39. Waring Cuney to Langston Hughes, August 14, 1934, Box 49, Folder 922, Langston Hughes Papers, Beinecke Rare Book and Manuscript Library, Yale University.
40. Dorothy West, "Voices," *Challenge* 1, no. 3 (May 1935): 47.
41. William Cuney, *US, Arriving Passenger and Crew Lists, New York, 1934*, Microfilm Serial: *T715, 1897–1957*, line *18*, p. *3*, Ancestry.com.
42. Waring Cuney to Langston Hughes, October 8, 1936, Box 49, Folder 922, Langston Hughes Papers, Beinecke Rare Book and Manuscript Library, Yale University.
43. Waring Cuney to Langston Hughes, November 12, 1940, Box 49, Folder 923, Langston Hughes Papers, Beinecke Rare Book and Manuscript Library, Yale University.

44. Waring Cuney, "Secretary Ickes' Remarks at the Marian Anderson Concert," July 13, 1939, Schomburg Center for Research in Black Culture, Manuscripts, Archives and Rare Books Division, New York Public Library.
45. Langston Hughes, "The Twenties: Harlem and Its Negritude," 30, 34.
46. Bruce Kellner, ed., *Carl Van Vechten, The Splendid Drunken Twenties: Selections from the Daybooks, 1922–1930* (Urbana: University of Illinois Press, 2003), 60.
47. Arnold Rampersad, *The Life of Langston Hughes. Volume I: 1902–1941, I, Too, Sing America* (Oxford: Oxford University Press, 1986), 97.
48. Kellner, *Carl Van Vechten*, 85.
49. Ibid., 93.
50. Quoted in Thomas H. Wirth, *Gay Rebel of the Harlem Renaissance: Selections from the Work of Richard Bruce Nugent* (Durham, NC: Duke University Press, 2002), 22; Genevieve Ekaete, "Sterling Brown: A Living Legend," *New Directions: The Howard University Magazine* 1 (Winter 1974), 9.
51. J. Saunders Redding, "Introduction," *Centennial Anthology: Lincoln University Poets* (New York: The Fine Press, 1954), xvii.

Chapter 5

1. "William W. Cuney," US World War II Army Enlistment Records, 1938–1946, Ancestry.com.
2. "Norris Wright Cuney," US WWII Draft Cards Young Men, 1940–1947, Ancestry.com. Wright III's draft card also indicates that he was unable to bend his left knee, which would have made him ineligible for enlistment.
3. "Catalog of the Officers and Students of Howard University, 1870–1871," *Howard University Catalogs*, 74.
4. "Cpt. William Waring," obituary from *Howard University Journal*, Washington DC, February 1900.
5. Waring Cuney to Langston Hughes, August 1943, Box 49, Folder 923, Langston Hughes Papers, Beinecke Rare Book and Manuscript Library, Yale University.
6. Waring Cuney to Langston Hughes, June 1945, Box 49, Folder 923, Langston Hughes Papers, Beinecke Rare Book and Manuscript Library, Yale University.
7. "Stewart G. Wolf, Jr," *The Oklahoman*, September 26, 2005.

8. Walter B. Cannon, "'Voodoo' Death," *American Anthropologist* 44, no. 2 (1942): 169–81.
9. "Armstrong Manual Training," *Evening Star* (Washington, DC), November 19, 1922, 20.
10. Mary Church Terrell, *A Colored Woman in a White World* (New York: Prometheus Books, 2005), 253, 260; Sandra Fitzpatrick and Maria Goodwin, *The Guide to Black Washington* (New York: Hippocrene Books, 1990), 123.
11. "Scott Gives Praise to Colored Cadets," *Evening Star* (Washington, DC), April 19, 1923, 14.
12. "Armstrong Manual Training," *Evening Star* (Washington, DC).
13. Terrell, *A Colored Woman in a White World*, 264–65.
14. Kathleen A. Hauke, *Ted Poston: Pioneer American Journalist* (Athens: University of Georgia Press, 1998), 70–71.
15. Thomas H. Wirth, *Gay Rebel of the Harlem Renaissance: Selections from the Work of Richard Bruce Nugent* (Durham, NC: Duke University Press, 2002), 32–33.
16. Waring Cuney, "A Sketch of Dorrance Brooks and Henry Johnson," June 7, 1939, Schomburg Center for Research in Black Culture, Manuscripts, Archives and Rare Books Division, The New York Public Library, *The New York Public Library Digital Collections*, 1936–1941.
17. "William W. Cuney" and "Roi Vincint [*sic*] Ottley," US WWII Army Enlistment Records, 1938–1946, Ancestry.com.
18. Waring Cuney to Langston Hughes, February 9, 1943, Box 49, Folder 923, Langston Hughes Papers, Beinecke Rare Book and Manuscript Library, Yale University.
19. Ronald B. Hartzer, "A Look Back at Black Aviation Engineer Units of World War II," February 27, 2013, Air Force News Service, Tyndall Air Force Base, Florida; Karl R. Rittman, "WWII Sketches of the Men from the 857th Engineer Aviation Battalion," http://www.rittmann-art.com/wwii.htm.
20. Hartzer, "A Look Back at Black Aviation Engineer Units of World War II."
21. Karl R. Rittman, "857th Engineer Aviation Battalion Tour of Duty," http://www.rittmann-art.com/857th.htm.
22. Natalie M. Pearson, "Engineer Aviation Units in the Southwest Pacific Theater during World War II" (MA thesis, US Army Command and General Staff College, Fort Leavenworth, Kansas, 2005), 64.

23. Rittman, "WWII Sketches."
24. Pearson, "Engineer Aviation Units in the Southwest Pacific Theater," iii.
25. Waring Cuney to Langston Hughes, May 24, 1944, Box 49, Folder 923, Langston Hughes Papers, Beinecke Rare Book and Manuscript Library, Yale University.
26. Ibid., December 1943.
27. Alicia Henneberry, "The Closed Door of Justice: African American Nurses and the Fight for Naval Service," February 4, 1920, Blog of the Textual Records Division at the National Archives, https://text-message.blogs.archives.gov/2020/02/04/the-closed-door-of-justice-african-american-nurses-and-the-fight-for-naval-service/; Leila McNeill, "The Black Nurse Who Drove Integration of the U.S. Nurse Corps," *JSTOR Daily*, May 9, 2020, https://daily.jstor.org/the-black-nurse-who-drove-integration-of-the-u-s-nurse-corps/.
28. Waring Cuney to Langston Hughes, January 14, 1944, Box 49, Folder 923, Langston Hughes Papers, Beinecke Rare Book and Manuscript Library, Yale University.
29. Waring Cuney to Sterling Brown, November 5, 1945, Cuney Box, Folder 1, Sterling A. Brown Papers, Chapin Library Special Collections, Williams College. For hospital records showing his admission in May 1945 and his medical discharge and retirement in December 1945, see William W. Cuney, National Archives and Records Administration, Hospital Admission Card Files, ca. 1970–ca. 1970, NAI: 570973, Record Group Number: Records of the Office of the Surgeon General (Army), 1775–1994, Record Group Title: 112, Ancestry.com.
30. Rittman, "857th Engineer Aviation Battalion."
31. We thank Lisa C. Moore, reference archivist at the Amistad Research Center, for her help locating TSgt Cuney's military photograph.
32. Kali Tal, *Worlds of Hurt: Reading the Literatures of Trauma* (New York: Cambridge University Press, 1996), 7.
33. Ibid., i, 17, 137.
34. Yusef Komunyakaa, "Roll Call," in *Dien Cai Dau* (Hanover, NH: Wesleyan University Press, 1988), lines 5–9, 13–22.
35. Charles H. Nichols, ed., *Arna Bontemps–Langston Hughes Letters, 1925–1967* (New York: Dodd, Mead & Company, 1980), 451.
36. Ibid., 454.
37. Tal, *Worlds of Hurt*, 37.

Chapter 6

1. Waring Cuney to Langston Hughes, August [?] 1943, Langston Hughes Papers, Box 49, Folder 923, Beinecke Rare Book and Manuscript Library, Yale University.
2. Faith Berry, *Before and Beyond Harlem: A Biography of Langston Hughes* (New York: Wings Books, 1983), 309.
3. Waring Cuney to Langston Hughes, August [?] 1943, Langston Hughes Papers, Box 49, Folder 923, Beinecke Rare Book and Manuscript Library, Yale University.
4. Waring Cuney to Langston Hughes, January 8, 1944, Langston Hughes Papers, Box 49, Folder 923, Beinecke Rare Book and Manuscript Library, Yale University.
5. Langston Hughes to Arna Bontemps, September 10, 1942, in *Arna Bontemps–Langston Hughes Letters, 1925–1967*, ed. Charles H. Nichols (New York: Dodd, Mead & Company, 1980), 112.
6. Waring Cuney to Carl Van Vechten, November 30, 1943, James Weldon Johnson Collection, Box 5, Folder 146, Beinecke Rare Book and Manuscript Library, Yale University.
7. See "Sergeant Dusty," lines 7–8, in this volume.
8. See "They Mighty Near Fit," lines 13–18, in this volume.
9. Bruce Kellner, ed., *Carl Van Vechten, The Splendid Drunken Twenties: Selections from the Daybooks, 1922–1930* (Urbana: University of Illinois Press, 2003), 60, 82.
10. Charles H. Rowell, "'Let Me Be with Ole Jazzbo': An Interview with Sterling A. Brown," in *After Winter: The Life and Art of Sterling Brown*, eds. John Edgar Tidwell and Steven C. Tracy (Oxford: Oxford University Press, 2009), 297–98.
11. Kellner, *The Splendid Drunken Twenties*, 128.
12. Rowell, "'Let Me Be with Ole Jazzbo,'" 302.
13. Ibid.
14. Katrine Dalsgård, "Alive and Well and Living on the Island of Martha's Vineyard: An Interview with Dorothy West, October 29, 1988," *Langston Hughes Review* 12, no. 2 (Fall 1993): 33.
15. Genii Guinier, "Interview with Dorothy West, May 6, 1978," in *The Black Women Oral History Project*, vol. 10, ed. Ruth Edmonds Hill (Westport, CT: Meckler, 1991), 174.
16. Ibid.

17. Emily Bernard, ed., *Remember Me to Harlem: The Letters of Langston Hughes and Carl Van Vechten, 1925–1964* (New York: Knopf, 2001), 213.
18. Ibid., 20, 29.
19. Ibid., 219.
20. Waring Cuney to Langston Hughes, February 9, 1943, Langston Hughes Papers, Box 49, Folder 923, Beinecke Rare Book and Manuscript Library, Yale University.
21. Berry, *Before and Beyond Harlem*, 308–9.
22. Carole Ione, *Pride of Family: Four Generations of American Women of Color* (New York: Harlem Moon, 1991), 10, 41.
23. Langston Hughes to Arna Bontemps, August 19, 1943, in *Arna Bontemps–Langston Hughes Letters*, 137.
24. Langston Hughes to Arna Bontemps, August 5, 1943, in *Arna Bontemps–Langston Hughes Letters*, 135.
25. Bernard, *Remember Me to Harlem*, 224n2.
26. Ibid., 215n1.
27. Waring Cuney to Langston Hughes, February 9, 1943, Langston Hughes Papers, Box 49, Folder 923, Beinecke Rare Book and Manuscript Library, Yale University.
28. Waring Cuney to Langston Hughes, July 4, 1943, Langston Hughes Papers, Box 49, Folder 923, Beinecke Rare Book and Manuscript Library, Yale University.
29. Langston Hughes to Arna Bontemps, October 31, 1966, in *Arna Bontemps–Langston Hughes Letters*, 476.
30. "The Guggenheim Foundation during the Second World War," https://paulingblog.wordpress.com/2020/03/18/the-guggenheim-foundation-during-the-second-world-war/.
31. Langston Hughes to Arna Bontemps, Fall 1945, in *Arna Bontemps–Langston Hughes Letters*, 182.
32. "Grangers' Party Celebrates Dual Family Festival," *New York Amsterdam News*, November 3, 1945, 11.
33. Leighla Whipper, *The People's Voice*, November 16, 1946, 20.
34. Langston Hughes to Dorothy Peterson, August 30, 1938, in *Selected Letters of Langston Hughes*, eds. Arnold Rampersad and David Roessel, 205–6 (New York: Knopf, 2015).
35. Ibid.
36. Lowell Waring Baker III visited his great-aunt Madge Cuney in the summer of 1960 while a 19-year-old intern with the Department of the

Interior. He remembers seeing the "wall of family photos" and enjoying his time with Aunt Madge, a "very dignified" woman who wore her "long gray hair rolled in a huge bun." Telephone interview with L. W. Baker III, June 6, 2022.

37. Waring Cuney to Paul Breman, May 31, 1954, Breman Collection, Box 2, folder 4, Chapin Library Special Collections, Williams College.
38. "Waring Cuney" biographical note in *Lincoln University Poets: Centennial Anthology*, eds. Waring Cuney, Langston Hughes, and Bruce McMarion Wright (New York: The Fine Editions Press, 1954), 68; Waring Cuney to Langston Hughes, October 8, 1936, Langston Hughes Papers, Box 49, Folder 922, Beinecke Rare Book and Manuscript Library, Yale University.
39. *The People's Voice*, April 12, 1947, 18.
40. Waring Cuney to Langston Hughes, February 27, 1948, and Langston Hughes to Waring Cuney, March 1, 1948, Langston Hughes Papers, Box 49, Folder 923, Beinecke Rare Book and Manuscript Library, Yale University.
41. Langston Hughes to Arna Bontemps, September 14, 1948, in *Arna Bontemps–Langston Hughes Letters*, 235.
42. Ibid., October 11, 1948, 237.
43. Arna Bontemps to Langston Hughes, October 17, 1948, in *Arna Bontemps–Langston Hughes Letters*, 239.
44. Reported in the *Washington Post*, May 3, 1952, B2.
45. Langston Hughes to Arna Bontemps, July 13, 1953, in *Arna Bontemps–Langston Hughes Letters*, 311.
46. A Bostonian educated at Boston University and New York University, Dr. Marguerite Dorsey Cartwright (1910–1986) was an educator, journalist, actress, and United Nations reporter. She traveled throughout Africa, Asia, the Caribbean, and the Middle East, and attended the 1945 Institute on Race Relations at Fisk University, the 1951 UN Assembly in Paris, France, and the 1955 Bandung Conference in Indonesia. She wrote for the *Pittsburgh Courier*, the *New York Amsterdam News*, and the *Chicago Sun Times*, taught at Hunter College, Brooklyn College, and the New School, and served as a founder-trustee for the University of Nigeria in Nsukka. At age nineteen, she married the chemist Leonard Carl Cartwright, whom she had met at Boston University.
47. Waring Cuney to Paul Breman, August 22, 1975, Paul Breman Collection, Box 1, Folder 5, Chapin Library Special Collections, Williams College.

48. Waring Cuney to Langston Hughes, August 6, 1953, Langston Hughes Papers, Box 49, Folder 924, Beinecke Rare Book and Manuscript Library, Yale University.
49. Ibid.
50. After the book was published, an apparently exasperated Hughes sent a telegram: "TRIED REACHING YOU BY PHONE ALL WEEK TO REMIND YOU OF LINCOLN BOOK PARTY AT LIBRARY TONITE. PLEASE COME." Langston Hughes to Waring Cuney, May 28, 1954, Langston Hughes Papers, Box 49, Folder 924, Beinecke Rare Book and Manuscript Library, Yale University.
51. Arnold Rampersad, *The Life of Langston Hughes, Volume II: 1941–1967, I Dream a World* (Oxford: Oxford University Press, 2002), 236.
52. Waring Cuney to Paul Breman, June 2, 1954, Breman Collection, Box 2, Folder 4, Chapin Library Special Collections, Williams College.
53. Quoted in Lauri Ramey, ed., *The Heritage Series of Black Poetry, 1962–1975: A Research Compendium* (New York: Routledge, 2008), 161–62, https://archivesspace.williams.edu/repositories/4/archival_objects/250520.
54. Paul Breman, "Introduction," in *Puzzles,* Waring Cuney (Utrecht, The Netherlands: De Roos, 1960), xiv.
55. Arthur B. Spingarn, "Books by Negro Authors in 1961," *The Crisis* (February 1962), 85.
56. Langston Hughes to Waring Cuney, June 10, 1961, Langston Hughes Papers, Box 49, Folder 926, Beinecke Rare Book and Manuscript Library, Yale University.
57. Langston Hughes to Arna Bontemps, January 28, 1957, in *Arna Bontemps–Langston Hughes Letters,* 357.
58. Roger L. Anderson, email to authors, January 10, 2020.
59. Roger L. Anderson, *History of the Lee Family: Descendants and the Ancestry of the Norwegian immigrants, Aslak Halvorson Lee and Liv Tarjeisdatter* (self-published, 1989), 70.
60. Ibid., 69.
61. Ibid.
62. Ibid.
63. Ibid., 70.
64. Ibid., 69.
65. Adeline Norris obituary, December 13, 2008, Madison Media Partners, Inc., Madison.com, https://madison.com/news/local/obituaries/

article_79f5f493-53aa-5723-b39b-92aaf12be512.html.

66. "Waring Cuney is on a religious kick and won't see sinners, Rosey Pool reports," Langston Hughes to Arna Bontemps, March 7, 1963, in *Arna Bontemps–Langston Hughes Letters*, 454.
67. Paul Breman to Lauri Ramey, 2004, Breman Collection, Box 1, Folder 5, Chapin Library Special Collections, Williams College.
68. Cuney compiled a collection of poems in February 1957, *I Couldn't Hear Nobody Pray*, and dedicated it "For My Grandmother Laura Cuney." In the Breman Collection, Box 2, Folder 7.
69. Cuney to Paul Breman, March 11, 1975, Breman Collection, Box 1, Folder 5.
70. Ibid., August 12, 1975.

Selected Bibliography

Alexander, Adele Logan. *Homelands and Waterways: The American Journey of the Bond Family, 1846–1926*. New York: Vintage Books, 2000.

Alexander, Eleanor. *Lyrics of Sunshine and Shadow: The Tragic Courtship and Marriage of Paul Laurence Dunbar and Alice Ruth Moore, A History of Love and Violence Among the African American Elite*. New York: New York University Press, 2001.

Anderson, Roger L. *History of the Lee Family: Descendants and the Ancestry of the Norwegian Immigrants, Aslak Halvorson Lee and Liv Tarjeisdatter*. Self-published, 1989.

"Armstrong High Holds Graduation." *Evening Star* (Washington, DC), June 20, 1923, 16.

"Armstrong Manual Training." *Evening Star* (Washington, DC), November 19, 1922, 20.

Barnes, Michael. "What's Left of Austin's Lost Blind, Deaf and Orphan School?" *Statesman News Network*, September 25, 2018. https://www.statesman.com/news/20160915/whats-left-of-austins-lost-blind-deaf-and-orphan-school.

Barnes, Sarah M. *The Sarah M. Barnes Papers, 1867–1871*. MS93-0011. Rosenberg Library. Galveston, Texas.

Barr, Alwyn. *Black Texans: A History of African Americans in Texas, 1528–1995*. 2nd ed. Norman: University of Oklahoma Press, 1995.

Beasley, Ellen. *The Alleys and Back Buildings of Galveston*. College Station: Texas A&M University Press, 1996.

Bell, Bernard. "Contemporary African-American Poetry as Folk Art." *Black World* (March 1973): 16–26, 74–87.

Bernard, Emily, ed. *Remember Me to Harlem: The Letters of Langston Hughes and Carl Van Vechten, 1925–1964*. New York: Knopf, 2001.

Berry, Faith. *Before and Beyond Harlem: A Biography of Langston Hughes*. New

York: Wings Books, 1983.

Betancourt, Sofia. "Between Dishwater and the River: Toward an Ecowomanist Methodology." *Worldviews* 20, no. 1 (2016): 64–75.

Bontemps, Arna, ed. *The Harlem Renaissance Remembered.* New York: Dodd, Mead, 1972.

Brown, Sterling A. *The Collected Poems of Sterling A. Brown.* Chicago: TriQuarterly Books, 1983.

———. *The Negro in American Fiction.* Reprinted Port Washington, NY: Kennikat Press, 1968 [1937].

Casteras, Susan P. "Pre-Raphaelite Challenges to Victorian Canons of Beauty." *Huntington Library Quarterly* 55, no. 1 (1992): 13–35.

"Catalog of the Officers and Students of Howard University, 1870–1871." *Howard University Catalogs,* 74. https://dh.howard.edu/hucatalogs/74.

"Catalog of the Officers and Students of Howard University, 1923–24." *Howard University Catalogs,* 47. https://dh.howard.edu/hucatalogs/47.

Collins, Izola Ethel Fedford. *Island of Color: Where Juneteenth Started.* Bloomington, IN: AuthorHouse, 2004.

Corcoran, Michael. "Maud Cuney-Hare, A Former Austinite You Need to Know About." MichaelCorcoran.net. March 21, 2016. https://www.michaelcorcoran.net/maude-cuney-hare-a-former-austinite-you-need-to-know-about.

"Cpt. William Waring." Obituary from *Howard University Journal.* Washington, DC, February 1900. https://www.findagrave.com/memorial/49333784/william-waring.

"Cuney, Daisy." https://www.google.com/books/edition/Catalogue_of_the_Officers_and_Students_o/CZ9GAQAAMAAJ?hl=en&gbpv=1&dq=daisy+cuney+byron&pg=PA87&printsec=frontcover.

"Cuney, Master Politician for Generation in Washington and New York, Passes Away." *The Houston Informer,* February 26, 1921, 1.

Cuney Hare, Maud. "Antar, Negro Poet of Arabia." *The Crisis* 28, no. 2 (June 1924), 64–67; *The Crisis* 28, no. 3 (July 1924), 117–19.

———. "Mabed Ibn Ouhab." *The Crisis* 29, no. 6 (April 1925), 258–60.

———, ed. *The Message of the Trees.* Boston: The Cornhill Company, 1918.

———. *Negro Musicians and Their Music.* New York: G. K. Hall, 1996 [1936].

———. *Norris Wright Cuney: A Tribune of the Black People.* New York: The Crisis Publishing Company, 1913.

Cuney, Norris Wright. Small and Large Scrapbooks, Fondren Library, Rice University, (microfilm).

Cuney, Waring. Letters to Langston Hughes, 1925–1961. James Weldon Johnson Memorial Collection, Beinecke Rare Book and Manuscript Library, Yale University, New Haven, Connecticut.

———. *Puzzles*. Utrecht, The Netherlands: De Roos, 1960.

———. "Secretary Ickes' Remarks at the Marian Anderson Concert," 1939. Schomburg Center for Research in Black Culture, Manuscripts, Archives and Rare Books Division, The New York Public Library. *The New York Public Library Digital Collections*. https://digitalcollections.nypl.org/items/00669580-5b2d-0133-dd0d-00505686d14e.

———. "A Sketch of Dorrance Brooks and Henry Johnson," June 7, 1939. Schomburg Center for Research in Black Culture, Manuscripts, Archives and Rare Books Division, New York Public Library. *The New York Public Library Digital Collections*, 1936–1941. https://digitalcollections.nypl.org/items/30917c40-5bce-0133-9a4c00505686a51c.

———. *Storefront Church*. London: Paul Breman, 1973.

Cuney, Waring, Langston Hughes, and Bruce McMarion Wright, eds., *Lincoln University Poets: Centennial Anthology*. New York: Fine Editions Press, 1954.

Dailey, Maceo C., Jr. "The Business Life of Emmett Jay Scott." *The Business Review* 77, no. 4 (Winter 2003): 667–86.

———. *Emmett J. Scott: Power Broker of the Tuskegee Machine*. Edited by Will Guzmán and David H. Jackson Jr. Lubbock: Texas Tech University Press, 2023.

Dalsgård, Katrine. "Alive and Well and Living on the Island of Martha's Vineyard: An Interview with Dorothy West, October 29, 1988." *Langston Hughes Review* 12, no. 2 (Fall 1993): 28–44.

Davis, Cynthia, and Verner D. Mitchell. "Eugene Gordon, Dorothy West, and the Saturday Evening Quill Club." *CLA Journal* 52, no. 4 (June 2009): 393–408.

"Drama 'Antar of Araby' Presented by Students." *Boston Globe*, December 15, 1925, 17.

Du Bois, W. E. B. *The Autobiography of W. E. B. Du Bois: A Soliloquy on Viewing My Life from the Last Decade of its First Century*. New York: International Publishers, 1968 [circa 1961].

———. "Maud Cuney Hare." *Pittsburgh Courier*, April 4, 1936. http://credo.library.umass.edu/view/pageturn/mums312-b218-i007/#page/3/mode/1up.

———. "A Negro Student at Harvard at the End of the Nineteenth Century." In *Blacks at Harvard: A Documentary History of African-American Experience at Harvard and Radcliffe*, edited by Werner Sollors, et al., 69–90. New York:

New York University Press, 1993.

Ekaete, Genevieve. "Sterling Brown: A Living Legend." *New Directions: The Howard University Magazine* 1 (Winter 1974): 9.

Fitzpatrick, Sandra, and Maria Goodwin. *The Guide to Black Washington*. New York: Hippocrene Books, 1990.

Gates, Henry Louis, Jr. *Stony the Road: Reconstruction, White Supremacy, and the Rise of Jim Crow*. New York: Penguin, 2019.

Gatewood, Willard B. *Aristocrats of Color: The Black Elite, 1880–1920*. Fayetteville: University of Arkansas Press, 1990.

Gordon. Eugene. "Massachusetts: Land of the Free and Home of the Brave Colored Man." *The Messenger* 7, no. 6 (June 1925): 219–22, 243. Reprinted in *These "Colored" United States: African American Essays from the 1920s*, edited by Tom Lutz and Susanna Ashton, 145–57. New Brunswick, NJ: Rutgers University Press, 1996.

———. "The Awards Dinner." *Opportunity: A Journal of Negro Life* 4, no. 42 (June 1926): 186.

Government Printing Office. KEEPINGAMERICAINFORMED/pdf/GPO- https://www.govinfo.gov/content/pkg/GPO- https://www.govinfo.gov/content/pkg/GPO-.

Guinier, Genii. "Interview with Dorothy West, May 6, 1978." In *The Black Women Oral History Project*, vol. 10, edited by Ruth Edmonds Hill, 143–223. Westport, CT: Meckler, 1991.

Haddox, Exr. v. Jordan, 36 Ohio App. 209, 173 N.E. 11 (Ohio Ct. App. 1930). https://casetext.com/case/haddox-exr-v-jordan.

Hales, Douglas. *A Southern Family in White and Black: The Cuneys of Texas*. College Station: Texas A&M University Press, 2003.

Hardwick, Susan W. *Mythic Galveston*. Baltimore, MD: Johns Hopkins University Press, 2002.

Hartzer, Ronald B. "A Look Back at Black Aviation Engineer Units of World War II." February 27, 2013. *Air Force News Service*. Tyndall Air Force Base, Florida. https://www.af.mil/News/Article-Display/Article/109658/a-look-back-at-black-aviation-engineer-units-of-world-war-ii/.

Hauke, Kathleen A. *Ted Poston: Pioneer American Journalist*. Athens: University of Georgia Press, 1998.

Heller's Galveston City Directories, 1870–1900.

Hinze, Virginia Neal. "Norris Wright Cuney." MA thesis, Rice University, 1965.

Holley, Joe. "Norris Wright Cuney Never Stopped Fighting." *Houston Chronicle*,

June 14, 2020. https://www.houstonchronicle.com/news/columnists/native-texan/article/Norris-Wright-Cuney-never-stopped-fighting-15338633.php.

Howard University Catalogues, 1899–1906. https://www.google.com/books/edition/Catalogue_of_the_Officers_and_Students_o/CZ9GAQAAMAAJ?hl=en&gbpv=1&bsq=cuney.

Huggins, Nathan Irvin, ed. *Voices from the Harlem Renaissance*. New York: Oxford University Press, 1976, 1995.

Hughes, Langston. *The Big Sea*. New York: Hill and Wang, 1993 [1940].

———. "The Twenties: Harlem and Its Negritude." *African Forum* (Spring 1966). Reprinted in *The Langston Hughes Review* 4, no. 1 (Spring 1985): 29–36.

Hunter, Tera W. "Introduction: Maud Cuney Hare." In *Norris Wright Cuney: A Tribune of the Black People*, xxxi–xxxiv. New York: G. K. Hall & Co., 1995.

Ione, Carole. *Pride of Family: Four Generations of American Women of Color*. New York: Harlem Moon, 1991.

Jacoby, Karl. *The Strange Career of William Ellis: The Texas Slave Who Became a Mexican Millionaire*. New York. W. W. Norton, 2017.

Johnson, Jack. *My Life in the Ring & Out*. New York: Dover, 2018 [1927].

Johnson, James Weldon. "Preface to the First Edition." *The Book of American Negro Poetry*. Revised edition, 9–48. New York: Harcourt Brace & Company, 1931.

———. "Waring Cuney." *The Book of American Negro Poetry*. Revised edition. New York: Harcourt Brace & Company, 1931.

Johnson, Ronald M. "From Romantic Suburb to Racial Enclave: LeDroit Park, Washington, D.C., 1880–1920." *Phylon* 45, no. 4 (1984): 264–70.

"Joint Costume Recital." *Evening Star* (Washington, DC), February 27, 1924, 2.

Kellner, Bruce, ed. *Carl Van Vechten, The Splendid Drunken Twenties: Selections from the Daybooks, 1922–1930*. Urbana: University of Illinois Press, 2003.

Komunyakaa, Yusef. "Roll Call." *Dien Cai Dau*. Hanover, NH: Wesleyan University Press, 1988, 15.

Lewis, David Levering, ed. *The Portable Harlem Renaissance Anthology*. New York: Viking, 1994.

———. *When Harlem Was in Vogue*. 1979. New York: Penguin, 1997.

Lutz, Eusibia. "LIENDO: The Biography of a House." *Southwest Review* 16, no. 2 (January 1931): 190–99.

"Madge L. Williamson." District of Columbia, Compiled Marriage Index, 1830–1931. FHL Film Number 2108270, Book 100, p. 98, Ancestry.com.

Mather, Frank Lincoln. *Who's Who of the Colored Race*. Vol. 1. Chicago:

Kessinger Publishing, 1915.

McCaskill, Barbara. *Love, Liberation, and Escaping Slavery: William and Ellen Craft in Cultural Memory*. Athens: University of Georgia Press, 2015.

McComb, David G. *Galveston: A History*. Austin: University of Texas Press, 1986.

McDowell, Deborah E. "Conversations with Dorothy West." In *The Harlem Renaissance Re-Examined: A Revised and Expanded Edition*, edited by Victor A. Kramer, 265–82. New York: AMS Press, 1987.

"Men of the Month: Two Supervising Architects." *The Crisis* 14–15 (May 1917), 32.

"Miss Cuney Weds." *Colored American* 6, no. 27 (October 10, 1898): 5.

"Miss Maud Cuney." *Washington Bee* XVII, no. 18 (October 1, 1898): 5.

Mitchell, Verner D., and Cynthia Davis, eds. *Dorothy West: Where the Wild Grape Grows: Selected Writings, 1930–1950*. Amherst: University of Massachusetts Press, 2005.

"Mrs. Maude Cuney McKinley." *Washington Times*, April 24, 1903, 7.

Muir, Andrew F. "The Free Negro in Galveston County, Texas." *Negro History Bulletin* 22, no. 3 (December 1953): 68–70.

Nichols, Charles H., ed. *Arna Bontemps–Langston Hughes Letters, 1925–1967*. New York: Dodd, Mead & Company, 1980.

"Norris Wright Cuney." US WWII Draft Cards Young Men, 1940–1947, Ancestry.com.

O'Toole, James. *Passing for White: Race, Religion and the Healy Family, 1820–1920*. Amherst: University of Massachusetts Press, 2003.

Patton, Venetria K., and Maureen Honey, eds. *Double-Take: A Revisionist Harlem Renaissance Anthology*. New Brunswick, NJ: Rutgers University Press, 2001.

Pearson, Natalie M. "Engineer Aviation Units in the Southwest Pacific Theater during World War II." MA thesis, US Army Command and General Staff College, Fort Leavenworth, Kansas, 2005. https://apps.dtic.mil/dtic/tr/fulltext/u2/a439239.pdf.

Pool, Rosey E. *Beyond the Blues*. Lympnes, Kent: Hand & Flower Press, 1962.

Powell, Robert. Letters of Philip Minor Cuny to Adeline Spurlock, 1852–1864. Unpublished.

"Prefers Whites to Own Race: Mrs. McKinley Tells Court of Doctor's Likes and Dislikes." *Chicago Broad Ax*, October 26, 1907, 1.

Primeau, Ronald. "Frank Horne and the Second-Echelon Poets of the Harlem Renaissance." In *The Harlem Renaissance Remembered*, edited by Arna Bontemps, 247–67. New York: Dodd, Mead & Co., 1972.

Prospectus of the New England Conservatory of Music, 1890. https://archive.org/details/prospectusofnewe1890newe/page/n79/mode/2up.

Ramey, Lauri, ed. *The Heritage Series of Black Poetry, 1962–1975: A Research Compendium.* New York: Routledge, 2008.

Rampersad, Arnold. "Langston Hughes's *Fine Clothes to the Jew.*" *Callaloo* 26 (Winter 1986): 144–58. www.jstor.org/stable/2931083. Accessed April 27, 2021.

———. *The Life of Langston Hughes. Volume I: 1902–1941, I, Too, Sing America.* Oxford: Oxford University Press, 1986.

———. *The Life of Langston Hughes. Volume II: 1941–1967, I Dream a World.* Oxford: Oxford University Press, 2002.

Rampersad, Arnold, and David Roessel, eds. *Selected Letters of Langston Hughes.* New York: Knopf, 2015.

Randolph, Adah Ward. "Champion Avenue School: A Historical Analysis." Paper presented at the Annual Meeting of the American Educational Research Association. Chicago, IL, March 27, 1997. https://files.eric.ed.gov/fulltext/ED411333.pdf.

Rittman, Karl R. "857th Engineer Aviation Battalion Tour of Duty." http://www.rittmann-art.com/857th.htm.

———. "WWII Sketches of the Men from the 857th Engineer Aviation Battalion." http://www.rittmann-art.com/wwii.htm.

Rothman, Joshua D. *The Ledger and the Chain: How Domestic Slave Traders Shaped America.* New York: Basic Books, 2021.

Rowell, Charles H. "'Let Me Be with Ole Jazzbo': An Interview with Sterling A. Brown," 1974. *Callaloo* 14, no. 4 (Autumn 1991): 795–815. Reprinted in *After Winter: The Life and Art of Sterling Brown,* edited by John Edgar Tidwell and Steven C. Tracy, 287–310. Oxford: Oxford University Press, 2009.

Sankofa Slavery Data Collection for Sunnyside Plantation. http://sites.rootsweb.com/~afamerpl/plantations_usa/TX/sunnyside.html.

Schermerhorn, Calvin. "Capitalism's Captives: The Maritime United States Slave Trade, 1807–1850. *Journal of Social History* 47, no. 4 (Summer 2014): 897–921.

"Scott Gives Praise to Colored Cadets." *Evening Star* (Washington, DC), April 19, 1923, 14.

Scull, Ralph Albert. *The Scull Papers.* 1931. MS85-0003. Rosenberg Library. Galveston, Texas.

Smallwood, James M. "Early 'Freedom Schools': Black Self-Help and Education in Reconstruction Texas, A Case Study." *Negro History Bulletin* 41, no. 1 (January/February 1978): 790–93.

Smethurst, James Edward. *The New Red Negro: The Literary Left and African American Poetry, 1930–1946*. New York: Oxford University Press, 1999.

Spingarn, Arthur B. "Books by Negro Authors in 1961." *The Crisis* 69, no. 2 (February 1962), 83–89.

"St. John's Literary." *Chicago Daily News*, July 22, 1902, 9.

Stafford, G. M. G. "Some Prominent Rapides Names of Long Ago." *Alexandria Daily Town Talk*, July 18, 1928.

"Stewart G. Wolf, Jr." *The Oklahoman*, September 26, 2005. https://obits.oklahoman.com/obituaries/oklahoman/obituary.aspx?n=stewart-g-wolf&pid=15224952.

Tal, Kali. *Worlds of Hurt: Reading the Literatures of Trauma*. New York: Cambridge University Press, 1996.

Terrell, Mary Church. *A Colored Woman in a White World*. New York: Prometheus Books, 2005 [1940].

———. "History of the High School for Negroes in Washington." *Journal of Negro History* 2, no. 3 (July 1917): 252–66.

Thomas, Lorenzo. "Authenticity and Elevation: Sterling Brown's Theory of the Blues." *African American Review* 31, no. 3 (Autumn 1997): 409–16.

Thompson, R. W. "The Passing Show in Washington." *The National Forum*, October 15, 1910, 3.

Toomer, Jean. *Cane*. New York: Harper & Row, 1969 [1923].

Toppin, Edgar Allan. "Scott, Emmett Jay." *American National Biography*. February 2000. http://www.anb.org/articles/09/09-00668.html.

Turkel, Stanley. "Hotel History: Wormley Hotel." *Hospitalitynet* (February 17, 2001). https://www.hospitalitynet.org/opinion/4103033.html.

Verga, Christopher. *The Ferguson Brothers Lynchings on Long Island: A Civil Rights Catalyst*. Charleston, SC: The History Press, 2022.

Walter White Papers, NAACP Administrative Files, Personal Correspondence, 1932. file:///C:/Users/vdmtchll/Downloads/Cuney%20CV%20Walter%20White.pdf.

Ward, Geoffrey C. *Unforgivable Blackness: The Rise and Fall of Jack Johnson*. New York: Vintage, 2006.

"The Week in Society." *Washington Bee*, January 8, 1910, 5.

West, Dorothy. "Voices." *Challenge* 1, no. 3 (May 1935): 46–47.

Wheeler, Belinda, and Louis J. Parascandola, eds. *Heroine of the Harlem Renaissance and Beyond: Gwendolyn Bennett's Selected Writings*. University Park:

Pennsylvania State University Press, 2018.

"William W. Cuney." US, World War II Army Enlistment Records, 1938–1946, Ancestry.com.

Williams, Fannie Barrier. "Obituary of Vera McKinley." *New York Age*, September 17, 1908.

Wintz, Cary D., ed. *Black Writers Interpret the Harlem Renaissance*. New York: Routledge, 1996, 2020.

Wirth, Thomas H., ed. *Gay Rebel of the Harlem Renaissance: Selections from the Work of Richard Bruce Nugent*. Durham, NC: Duke University Press, 2002.

Woodson, Carter G. "The Cuney Family." *Negro History Bulletin* 11, no. 6 (March 1948): 123–25, 143.

———. "The Waring Family." *Negro History Bulletin* 11, no. 5 (February 1948): 99–107.

Youngblood, J. W. "Brief Items from Nearby Cities and Towns: Boston." *New York Amsterdam News*, May 18, 1927, 14.

Zafar, Rafia. *We Wear the Mask: African Americans Write American Literature, 1760–1870*. New York: Columbia University Press, 1997.

Index

Note: Entries in bold refer to images.